Romantic Sensation

Romantic Sensation

The Queer Lives of Leon A. Belmont 1853–1927

Lizzie Ehrenhalt

MIN
NE
SO
TA

UNIVERSITY OF MINNESOTA PRESS
MINNEAPOLIS | LONDON

A portion of chapter 6 was previously published in "'Curious and Romantic Sensation': Sex, Fraud, and Celebrity in the Leon A. Belmont Case of 1880," *Minnesota History* 67, no. 5 (Spring 2021): 215–25; available at https://mnhs.gitlab.io/archive/minnesotahistory/.

Published by the University of Minnesota Press
111 Third Avenue South, Suite 290
Minneapolis, MN 55401-2520
http://www.upress.umn.edu

ISBN 978-1-5179-1583-4 (hc)
ISBN 978-1-5179-1584-1 (pb)

A Cataloging-in-Publication record for this book is available from the Library of Congress.

Printed in the United States of America on acid-free paper

The University of Minnesota is an equal-opportunity educator and employer.

35 34 33 32 31 30 29 28 27 26 10 9 8 7 6 5 4 3 2 1

The known parts of her history were so queer that folks were "just dying" to learn it all, but, unless some new exploit makes her again the subject of investigation, the public will never know how this young woman, now not over 24, beginning life as a factory girl and apparently without resources, went about the country and never lacked for means, nor why she masqueraded in men's clothes.

—"The Last of the Strange Addie Stanley Case"
Springfield Republican, December 12, 1876

Contents

Author's Preface on Pronouns

People who moved between genders in the 1800s force historians to face the "dilemma of the pronoun," as Ann Heilmann has called it,[1] and Leon A. Belmont is no exception. Having been assigned a female sex at birth in 1853, the subject of this book lived as a woman named Addie Walker and responded to she/her pronouns for more than two decades. Walker also, however, occasionally presented as a man named Ernest Ellwood before claiming the name of Belmont (and the pronouns he/him/his) in 1878. Belmont transitioned to living as a woman, Nova McClure Carr, in 1902, and again used she/her pronouns.

Given this complexity, what are the most respectful and appropriate pronouns to use when talking about Belmont? What about Walker, and Ellwood, and Carr? When choosing pronouns for *Romantic Sensation,* I followed the consensus among scholars who study the lives of gender-variant people in the nineteenth and early twentieth centuries. In general, they rally around two goals: matching the way historical figures thought about themselves (so far as it's known) and reflecting their lived experience.

Writers have achieved these goals through different means. Jen Manion makes a case for using they/them to describe a range of gender-variant people from the late 1800s and early 1900s "whose gender is unknown, irrelevant, or beyond classification" in order "to minimize disruption and avoid a false sense of stability when writing about a person over a long period of time, marked by varied gender expressions."[2] Cameron Awkward-Rich uses they/them to talk about Jack Garland (1869–1936), a contemporary of Belmont.[3] Clare Sears takes a hybrid approach, choosing pronouns that correspond to self-identification when they are known and s/he, his/her when they are not.[4] Rebecca L. Davis, meanwhile, opts for they/them only when it's clear that a person "saw themselves as *both* male and female or *neither* male nor female."[5]

Others (Leslie Feinberg, Lou Sullivan, Jack Halberstam, C. Riley Snorton, Jesse Bayker, Scott Larson, Emily Skidmore, Peter Boag, Rachel Mesch, and Ann Heilmann) have avoided they/them and other pronoun alternatives in favor of she/her and he/him. In *True Sex: The Lives of Trans Men at the Turn of the Twentieth Century,* Skidmore explains that she uses he/him to talk about the people in her book since each one "chose to live as a man for many years prior to his appearance within the public record." Many of them, she adds, kept on living as men even after they were arrested and/or put in jail for it. Skidmore also chooses "to prioritize the names chosen by the historical subjects . . . rather than the names assigned to them at birth as a way of honoring their self-identification."[6] This is the approach that aligns most closely with mine.

Addie Walker's gender identification between her birth in 1853 and her transition to living as Belmont in 1878 is unknown. For much of this period she was a child, so her personal preferences of all kinds are invisible in the historical record. In the early 1870s, she did dress as a man and use the name Ernest Ellwood, and these episodes point to an interest in exploring her masculinity. Does it also point to a gender identity evolving away from her sex assignment at birth? A conclusive answer seems unattainable.

In the end, all pronoun options fail Walker. She/her imposes normativity. He/him/his forces her to appear as a man without her consent, before she chose to transition. They/them allows for gender fluidity but contradicts Walker's lived experience before the coining of that alternative. She/her, in my reckoning, does the least harm, because it does the least amount of mind-reading, so I use this pronoun set to refer to Walker. It's the best of a poor set of choices. When referring to Ellwood, I use he/him.

Belmont's self-identification between 1878 and 1902 is clearer than Walker's. He created a man's identity for himself, dressed exclusively as a man, assumed the social roles of a man, and answered to he/him pronouns for twenty-five years. He defended his gender identity under public scrutiny in Minneapolis in 1880, acknowledging only briefly and under police pressure that he had been assigned a female sex at birth. For these reasons, I use he/him pronouns when talking about Belmont.

After leaving behind life as Belmont, Nova McClure Carr embraced the identity, dress, and pronouns of her chosen gender and stuck to them for twenty-five years. She did this in spite of the risks of transitioning publicly in Springfield, Missouri, in 1902. She introduced herself to neighbors as a woman and embraced her role as the mother of Kenneth McClure. When Kenneth went missing in 1922, she spoke to reporters as his mother, and she continued to identify as such until her death in 1927. The contemporary pronouns they/them might have appealed to Carr if she had lived in the twenty-first century, but there is no surviving evidence that she identified as what we might today call trans, nonbinary, gender-fluid, or genderqueer. For these reasons, I use she/her pronouns when talking about Carr.

Introduction
Making a Sensation

The title of this book is a bluff.

Leon Belmont does seem, at first, like a romantic sensation. Between 1878, when he started using the name Belmont, and 1902, when he retired it, he traveled through much of the United States. He rode horses across the Kansas plains. He eloped with a married sheriff to the gold mines of Dakota Territory. He engaged himself to two women in Minneapolis and married a third. He introduced himself to strangers as the illegitimate nephew of August Belmont, the New York millionaire, and lived in a style lavish enough to back up that claim. It wasn't true. For a few months in 1880, newspapers from Boston to San Francisco nevertheless hailed him as a celebrity.

It's easy, given these facts, to imagine Belmont as a trickster—a teller of tall tales to rival P. T. Barnum. And it's just as easy to cultivate a fantasy of Belmont as a queer hero. He was a man assigned a female sex at birth who endured invasions of his privacy to marry a woman. He resisted the pressures of Gilded Age gender conformity with panache, insisting on his right to live the life he chose in the identities that he determined.

But neither of these stories is true. In many ways, Leon Belmont was ordinary. He found himself in moments of drama, certainly. But he had no heroic qualities. As Addie Liona Walker (1853–1877), she[1] labored as a domestic servant; worked in a cotton mill; and spent eight months in a county jail. As Nova McClure Carr (1902–1927), she eked out a living for herself and her adopted son in small-town Kansas. In each era of his life, Belmont tried to survive in a particular time and place, with his own foibles, talents, and shortcomings. He made choices to protect himself from abuse, tedium, and poverty, and to make himself happy. Sometimes that involved lying about his past and seizing opportunities that ranged from guileful to shady to criminal. In that he was not alone; gender-normative people do these things as much as gender-variant ones.

In the middle of the media spectacles that sometimes engulfed him, moreover, Belmont was vulnerable. Whether real or imagined, the spectacular traits people attributed to him offered no protection from the realities of his time: labor exploitation, celebrity journalism, the second industrial revolution, Gilded Age gender codes, and legislation against gender variance.

The vision of Belmont as a romantic sensation comes from newspaper articles, and in particular from the *Minneapolis Tribune* profile published on October 30, 1880, which led to a cascade of national coverage. It ran with the headline, "IN DISGUISE: The Curious and Romantic Sensation That Was Developed in the City Yesterday Afternoon; How a Woman Lived in Male Attire for a Year and a Half."[2] In the late nineteenth century, calling something "romantic" referred to courtship, as it does today, but also to the literary genre of the romance, which covers early modern epics (e.g., *Orlando Furioso*), Shakespearean drama (*Cymbeline, The Winter's Tale, The Tempest*), and medieval chivalric poetry (*Sir Gawain and the Green Knight*). A romance in this vein deals with travel, fidelity, disguise, and unmasking—all of which featured in the stories reporters wrote about Belmont in 1880. These are recurring themes in Belmont's life. But he was not a knight, or a princess, or any other fictional character manipulated by an author to amuse readers. He was a real person with his own agency, affinity, and interiority, none of which were less real in his lifetime because they are unknowable for us today. His gender transitions are not in themselves sensational, just as they are not inherently sensational for any person. As you read this book, I encourage you to question sources that highlight Belmont's mystery at the expense of his humanity—to look with me for the evidence of his lived experience that remains visible through the fog of sensationalism.

We can't step across the chasm of time separating us from Belmont, but sometimes, in the right light, we'll see movement on the other side.

~

Belmont was born in Warren, Massachusetts, on June 1, 1853, given the name Addie Liona Walker, and assigned a female sex.[3] Her father made little money as a shoemaker, and Addie went to work in a cotton mill in 1867, when she was thirteen. This was at the vertiginous height of the second industrial revolution in western Massachusetts—after the heyday of the Lowell factory system but before the reforms of later decades improved safety for child laborers.[4]

After leaving the mill, Walker worked as a domestic servant and traveled, going to Springfield, Northampton, Boston, and New York. As Ernest Ellwood, he made it as far as Chicago by train before police intervened and (although Ellwood had committed no crime) escorted him back to Warren. A judge convicted Walker of money fraud in 1876, and she spent eight months in the Springfield city jail. She emerged afterward committed to a new life and another identity. Around 1878 she altered her middle name (Liona), added the surname Belmont, and began to live full-time as Leon A. Belmont.

After his first gender transition, Belmont left Massachusetts for good. He embraced Kansas as his new home at a time when the state had a reputation for lawlessness,[5] adventure, profiteering, and a relative tolerance of gender variance.[6] In 1879 he visited Dodge City, was jailed for fraud, escaped with the help of a married sheriff who'd fallen in love with him, and rode with him across the plains.[7] Together they traveled to Lead City on the western edge of Dakota Territory, missing the height of the Black Hills Gold Rush by a couple of years and the murder of Wild Bill Hickok in Deadwood by one more. After separating from the sheriff, Belmont landed in Minneapolis in 1880, ran afoul of that city's ordinance against dressing as "the opposite" sex, and became a celebrity. After marrying Melvina Campbell in Isanti County, Minnesota, in 1881, he fled the spotlight and returned south. He tried various careers: grocer, baker, cattle rancher, doctor. But he struggled to make a living in Missouri and Kansas in the 1890s, changing homes and jobs often.

At the age of forty-eight, while living with Melvina in Joplin, Missouri, Belmont chose to make a second gender transition and greeted her Joplin neighbors as a nurse named Nova McClure. She informally adopted an orphan boy named Kenneth before separating from her wife in 1913. During this period she started identifying herself as the widow of a man named Carr, though there is no extant evidence of their marriage. In old age, Carr found herself mixed up in the Great Railroad Strike of 1922, during which Kenneth planned to break a picket line in Parsons, Kansas, and then disappeared—suspected drugged and kidnapped. Carr and Kenneth eventually reunited but declined to give details to reporters. Carr lived out the rest of her life on Parsons's Main Street and died there at the age of seventy-three.

Even told in a nonsensational way, Belmont's life stories are entertaining, with episodes of peril, seduction, and conflict. But as a historian, I'm less interested in his entertainment value than I am in what he has to tell us about gender and sexuality in the United States between 1853 and 1927. Belmont gives us, first, an example of a nineteenth- and early twentieth-century American who went through two gender transitions. His romantic relationships with James Weakley, Grace Watts, Sarah Brackett, and Melvina Campbell reveal the historical appeal of what we might today call transmasculinity. His life's path traces the evolution of gender in the United States alongside trends in American history: industrial labor, rail transportation, settler colonialism, Manifest Destiny, sexology, and the legislation of gender variance. And his example offers evidence of someone who, at times, resembles a bisexual transgender man making a life for himself between 1878 and 1902.

"Resembles" a bi trans man? Why not "was"? For most historians of gender and sexuality, it's misleading to match historical figures with identity labels created after their deaths.[8] The concept of bisexuality, for instance, emerged from the medical writing that appeared in Europe in the 1870s, then solidified over the next three decades into the discipline called sexology.[9] Before sexology, plenty of people had attractions to and/or sex with both men and women. But they didn't take on an identity based on that feeling. "The bisexual" did not yet exist, just as "the heterosexual" and "the homosexual" had not yet appeared.[10] The word "transgender," meanwhile, evolved in the late twentieth century from "transsexual," a mid-century predecessor with similar sexological origins.[11] There had always been people who lived outside gender norms, and felt cross-gender affinities of various kinds.

But trans identity as we know it today was not an option for them.

Assigning bi and trans identities to Belmont after his death uses a vocabulary and an ideology that were not his own. It distracts from the project of interpreting his historical context, which is our best hope for understanding his lived experience in Gilded Age America. It also runs the risk of speaking for him. Self-identification is the cornerstone of both gender identity and sexual orientation. Trans and bi (like cis and straight) can't exist without interior desires and attachments, recognitions, and rejections. Since Belmont's interiority is unrecoverable, choosing a gender identity and sexual orientation for him is risky at best. Crucially, however, if Belmont was not bi and trans, he was also not straight and cis. If one set of sexological terms is anachronistic, its opposites are just as irrelevant.

Alongside the need to consider Belmont in his context remains an ethical duty to acknowledge that his experiences resonate with our LGBTQIA+ present. It may not make sense to label Belmont with letters from that acronym, but the people who claim them today can find affirming points of connection with his life story. Before she transitioned to living as Leon Belmont, nineteen-year-old Addie Walker carried out a strategic experiment in passing: outfitting herself in a man's suit of clothes, visiting a town near her own, and observing her reception.[12] The success of that first attempt encouraged her to become Ernest Ellwood and travel by train all the way to Chicago with only men's clothes in his suitcase.[13] This kind of incremental testing of public displays of masculinity away from home is familiar to trans men, nonbinary people, and butch lesbians, for whom the stakes of revealing a new gender presentation to family are high.[14] When Walker's second outing ended badly (police arrested her in Chicago and escorted her back to Massachusetts), she reacted by protecting her safety. She then kept a mostly gender-normative profile for the next five years.[15] After committing to a gender transition in 1878, Belmont chose a masculine name for himself and left behind his birthplace in order to embrace his identity as a man—two rites of passage with resonance for contemporary trans men. His habit of changing homes several times between 1880 and 1900 also speaks to the practices of contemporary trans men: itinerancy not as wanderlust, but as self-preservation amid transphobia.[16]

Belmont's encounters with doctors, meanwhile, are relatable for trans as well as intersex people. He submitted to two examinations to determine his sex in Minneapolis in 1880, with different results: one doctor declared him to be a woman, and the other to be a man. The *Minneapolis Tribune* speculated in print that he was a "hermaphrodite," using a word—a slur then as now—that has dehumanized intersex people for centuries.[17] The circumstances of Belmont's second exam are unclear, but the first happened while he was in police custody and therefore unable to withhold consent without endangering himself. This, too, is a relatable experience for trans and intersex people. It remains possible, given the doctors' conflicting reports, that Belmont had one or more of the gonadic traits, genital types, and/or genetic conditions that fall under the rubric of intersex. Even if he didn't, his challenge to the diagnostic/disciplinary regimes of doctors and police makes him an illuminating figure in intersex as well as trans history.[18]

In other instances, Belmont's choices and dismissive treatment by reporters resonate with contemporary bi, pansexual, and queer experiences. His overlapping romances with James Weakley and Grace Watts in Dakota Territory show a person who, in at least one season of his life, was attracted equally to partners of different sexes . . . or without regard to their sex at all. Then, during his first summer in Minnesota, Belmont's outing to Lake Minnetonka with a male friend led a reporter to ridicule him in a newspaper write-up as an effeminate dandy.[19] The writer touted the excursion as "a lakeside romance" and underlined its homoerotic potential in a satire of a failed same-sex seduction, complete with flowery, Aesthetic movement prose.[20] The takeaway was that two men in such a romantic situation were absurd, even if one of them was "really" a woman.

Two decades and a second gender transition later, Nova McClure Carr also made choices that upended heterosexual norms. By continuing her domestic partnership with the woman she had married (as Belmont) in 1881, Carr claimed an identity outside of a traditional family structure. She created a chosen family without men, first by living with Melvina (1902–1913) and then by adopting a child in the 1910s.

For all of these reasons, it's tempting to imagine Belmont as a queer hero—an anti-normative crusader thwarting convention at every turn.

It would be satisfying to stir up a second romantic sensation around him in the twenty-first century, this one to celebrate a long-lost role model. But does Belmont support that kind of reading? It's worth pausing to consider the implications of starting down that path.

In many ways, Belmont embodies the oppositional, transgressive, and undefinable ideal subject that emerged from queer theory in the 1990s. He presents to us, to use Eve K. Sedgwick's 1993 concept of queerness, "an open mesh of possibilities, gaps, overlaps, dissonances and resonances, lapses and excesses of meaning."[21] He is gay, bi, and neither; trans, cis, and something else entirely; he means too much and not enough at the same time. His gender and sexuality do not "signify monolithically."[22] He appears to stand, in David Halperin's words from 1995, "at odds with the normal, the legitimate, the dominant" and occupies "a positionality vis-à-vis the normative."[23] The idea of being "at odds with the normal" is crucial here; bell hooks echoed Halperin's words years later when she defined queer as anything "*at odds with* everything around it [that has] to invent and create and find a place to speak and to thrive and to live" (emphasis mine).[24] What was Belmont searching for when he moved across Massachusetts, and Kansas, and Minnesota, and Missouri, if not a place for himself to speak and thrive and live? What was he aiming for with his gender transitions if not self-invention? And who was more at odds with the world than Belmont in the fall of 1880, when he insisted in a crowded Minneapolis courtroom on his right to wear men's clothes?

Queer theory offers a useful way to think about Belmont because it insists on his transgressive appeal without assigning an anachronistic identity. The field's signature move—using "queer" as a verb—lets me name his disruptive power outside of the historical domain of sexual orientation and gender identity. Put another way: queer theory shows us that even if Belmont wasn't queer, he queered his environment.

A similar move emerged from trans studies in the 2010s, when scholars looking for a way to talk about historical figures who were "trans before trans" rallied around the concept of transing, first articulated by Susan Stryker, Paisley Currah, and Lisa Jean Moore.[25] For Clare Sears, to trans is to "[incorporate] insights from the burgeoning field of transgender studies . . . [with] a specific focus on the historical production and subsequent operations of the boundary between normative and nonnormative gender."[26] Transing is therefore a method of critical engagement—an interrogation technique.[27] Rachel Hope Cleves, writing on the educator Frank Shimer (1826–1901), aims "to trans Shimer's biography without imposing an ahistorical trans subjectivity upon her."[28] Scott Larson, investigating American religious revivals in the 1840s, transes analysis in order "to open up an archive of gender-transformative accounts of desires, expressions, and transing practices that do not necessarily demand a laying open of overexamined individuals."[29] Documenting female husbands (men assigned a female sex at birth who married women) in the United States in the 1800s, Jen Manion follows this model but contends that transing is also a practice visible in the historical record, since female husbands *themselves* transed gender. Jesse Bayker makes this helpful distinction: "For Sears 'trans-ing' is something that historians do, while for Manion 'transing' is something that historical actors do."[30]

The language of transing empowers an expansive mode of analysis that identifies historical subjects who moved away from their sex assignments at birth without confining that movement to a single moment, significance, or dimension.[31] For that reason, it's an ideal word for talking about Belmont, whose movements away from, through, and around gender proceed in multiple directions rather than a straight line. Belmont's life story reads, indeed, like a kind of instruction manual for transing and queering maneuvers. Ernest Ellwood transed gender in 1873 when he rode a train to Chicago while wearing men's clothes. Belmont transed class when he left behind his factory-worker origins in 1878 to pose as a millionaire's nephew, and when he toggled between that persona and his daily life as a middle-class striver in the 1880s and 1890s. Belmont queered Gilded Age parenthood when he became a stepfather to Maude Campbell in 1881 and again in 1903 when, having transitioned to a new identity as Nova Carr, she became an adoptive mother.

In all of these ways, Belmont looks like an ideal queer and trans subject, refusing to conform to social norms in the midst of surveillance, ridicule, and discrimination. But uncritically accepting this appearance risks yielding to what Kadji Amin has called the "queer romance of the alternative."[32] In his reappraisal of the queer icon Jean Genet, Amin points out that the drive to celebrate Genet's marginal identities (thief, dissident, prisoner) has led queer scholars to overlook his shortcomings, and sometimes to excuse his faults. Amin calls this impulse to flatten out the complexity of marginalized figures "the idealizing engine of queer studies," and it exerts as strong a pull on an interpretation of Belmont as it does on an understanding of Genet.[33] With Amin I believe that "complex personhood—the way in which we are all, even the 'queerest' or most subaltern among us, both good and bad subjects, imperfect, contradictory, and 'ordinary'—risks being the fallout of [queer theory's] institutional norms," and of its drive to produce objects of queer and trans veneration.[34]

In some episodes of his life, it turns out, Belmont was not a powerless subaltern but a beneficiary of his relative power over others.[35] Nowhere is this more dramatic than between 1878 and 1902, when he traveled across the Great Plains from Kansas to Dakota Territory and Minnesota, and from there back to Kansas, Indian Territory, and Missouri. At each stop on his journey, Belmont relied on the United States' dispossession of Native land—a process that in some of his new homes was not even complete by the time he arrived—to supply him with refuges advertised as "unoccupied" through settler-colonial sleight of hand. He relied, too, on his perceived entitlement as a white American to participate in the national project of Manifest Destiny without fear of reprisal. In this way, he was an agent of settler colonialism, empowered to start a new life for himself by the foreclosure of the lives of his Native neighbors. When Belmont camped outside Lead City (Dakota Territory) in 1879, he pitched his tent on land that had belonged to the Lakota Nation two years earlier.[36] The cattle ranch he bought in Kansas in 1882 stood on territory ceded by the Osage (Wazhazhe) Nation in the Drum Creek Treaty of 1870.[37] The Wahzhazhe and Cherokee people in Indian Territory to whom Belmont offered his medical services in the 1880s were susceptible to quacks, having few options for care on their reservations.[38] Even if "Dr. Belmont" treated them to the best of his ability, he was dubiously qualified, and would have had chances to overcharge his patients.

Earlier in his life, Belmont had seized opportunities to profit from other people in a less-than-ethical manner. In fact, he had engineered them. Addie Walker extracted cash from Columbus Orcutt, a farmer from her hometown of Warren, Massachusetts, while he acted as her surrogate father figure in the mid-1870s. Between 1873 and 1876 she forged checks and bonds that convinced Orcutt to give her $3,300—a sum worth more than $100,000 in 2026.[39] To afford this, Orcutt had to take out a mortgage on his farm.[40] A Springfield court tried Walker in 1876 for "obtaining money under false pretenses" from Orcutt, and she narrowly escaped conviction.[41] The charge of money fraud followed Belmont when he went to Kansas, and then when he went to Minnesota (though in that case, the accusation was mixed up with the perception of gender variance as its own kind of fraud).

Here it's important to stop short of villainizing Belmont, which is as dangerous as idealizing him. Belmont exploited people, lived on stolen land, and lied about his origins.[42] But he also assisted strangers, adopted an orphaned child, and helped an abused wife (Melvina Campbell) leave her marriage. The 1883 meeting minutes of the Winfield City Council (Cowley County, Kansas) reported Belmont's expenditure of $5.00 (more than $150 in modern currency) for "care of poor."[43] In 1895, a Missouri newspaper reported that after Belmont came across a panicked mother and her cholera-stricken baby in Galena, Kansas, he drove them in his surrey to their destination in Oronogo, Missouri, twelve miles away.[44]

Belmont was complicated. But for all his idiosyncrasies, he was typical. Although the newspapers exclaimed over his transing of gender as if it were unprecedented, Belmont was far from the only female-assigned American presenting himself as a man between 1878 and 1902. He wasn't even the only person transing gender in the Twin Cities in the fall of 1880. On November 13 of that year, the *St. Paul Globe* reported on "a man who has usurped the outward appearance of a woman" doing some shopping in the state capital.[45] The count grows exponentially if you widen the parameters of time and space. In my research, I've found documentation of more than twenty-five individuals who transed gender in some way between 1856 and 1930 in Minnesota alone.[46] And those are just the people who were written up in news articles and archival records that have survived to the present day.

Gender variance was more common in Belmont's time than stereotypes about uptight Victorians allow, and establishing this fact has been one of the accomplishments of historians working in trans, queer, and intersex American history since 2000. In surveys of gender variance in the nineteenth and early twentieth centuries,[47] scholars have studied scores of people who challenged sex and/or gender norms in various ways between 1850 and 1930—Belmont's lifetime. In *Bodies in Doubt: An American History of Intersex* (2009), Elizabeth Reis reviews the case files of medical patients from this period who might identify today as intersex. Viola Estella Angell, assigned a female sex at birth, sought the help of a New York doctor in the mid-1890s after a home for struggling women rejected her for having what they judged to be a penis.[48] In 1896, Dr. J. B. Naylor of Ohio examined a female-assigned patient who grew a penis and testicular tissue as a teenager and declared him to be "*both* and *neither* male or female."[49] Other patients resemble Belmont—especially the young woman who visited Dr. William P. McGuire of Winchester, Virginia, in 1884. The patient, A. B., was attracted to women. She had some secondary sex characteristics usually typed as female (short stature, breasts, lack of facial hair), but she also had a small penis (or large clitoris).[50] Although the two doctors who examined Belmont in 1880 left behind no written records, their opposing sexual verdicts (one male, one female) make sense if you imagine that Belmont had traits similar to A. B.'s.

Peter Boag's book *Re-Dressing America's Frontier Past* (2011) draws from plentiful examples to show that gender-variant people "were not simply ubiquitous, but were very much a part of daily life on the frontier and in the West."[51] They include Charley Pankhurst, a Wells Fargo stagecoach driver active in California between the 1850s and 1879; Tom Johnson, a flirtatious charmer who captivated the women of Waco, Texas, in 1876; Milton Matson, a Belmont-like traveler arrested in San Jose in 1895; Idaho cattle rancher Joe Monahan (1850–1903); the cowboys Jack Hall and Dick Wells, active in Arizona Territory in the 1890s; and a cast of bandits who ranged across the Great Plains.[52] Similarly, in *Arresting Dress: Cross-Dressing, Law, and Fascination in Nineteenth-Century San Francisco* (2014), Clare Sears offers a survey of gender variance inside a single city. They extend Boag's conclusion to urban areas, pointing out that cross-dressing was "far from a marginal practice" but instead "a central component of nineteenth-century urban life."[53] They revisit the examples of Pankhurst and Matson, whose experiences illustrate the competing perils (e.g., imprisonment) and incentives (e.g., income from performing in freak shows) of gender variance.

The historians Emily Skidmore, Jen Manion, and Jesse Bayker have also written surveys that add to the catalog of Belmont's peers. Skidmore opens *True Sex: The Lives of Trans Men at the Turn of the Twentieth Century* with anecdotal evidence from 1902 of ten men who might today identify as trans living in mutual recognition of one another in Buffalo, New York.[54] She reports having found at least sixty-five "stories of individuals who had been assigned female at birth but chosen to live as male" written up "in US newspapers between the 1870s and 1930s."[55] They are men like Frank Dubois, the "female husband" who inspired a media sensation as far reaching as Belmont's in the small Wisconsin town of Waupun in 1883.[56] Manion includes Dubois in *Female Husbands: A Trans History,* which teems with examples akin to Skidmore's. And Bayker's dissertation "Before Transsexuality: Transgender Lives and Practices in Nineteenth-Century America" also shows how "the experience of reinventing one's gender was not altogether uncommon in the nineteenth century."[57] To cover the variety of settings in which this experience played out, Bayker introduces the concept of gender migration: "the process by which ordinary individuals changed their gender socially" by negotiating new names, clothes, and identities, thus "mov[ing] across the gender border."[58] For Bayker, Belmont is a gender migrant—an apt term for someone who moved throughout his life, from woman to man to woman but also from east to west (geographic migration); from servant to businessman (class migration); and from prisoner to celebrity (social migration).

The scholarship of Reis, Boag, Sears, Skidmore, Manion, and Bayker proves that Belmont was not unique in Gilded Age America.[59] In a few ways, though, he was an outlier. As mentioned above, he had romantic relationships with both men and women—one man and three women, to name the documented ones. Although the sincerity of his affections is sometimes questionable, he seems to have chosen each partner freely. This makes him rare among the gender migrants of his era, who typically sought out women or men (or no one at all), but not both. Belmont also transitioned twice, without coercion, and in this he is even rarer. Many Civil War soldiers assigned female at birth reentered their lives as women in peacetime—but not after continuing on as a man for twenty-four years, as Belmont did.[60] More important, Belmont's second transition did not involve exposure and spectacle. He became Nova Carr quietly, at home, in 1902, and went on with her life in Joplin and Parsons until her death in 1927. Neighbors noticed, but they kept their suspicions to themselves.[61] In this way, Belmont shows that a gender migrant could transition in a place like rural Missouri in 1902 and walk away unscathed, raising the possibility that others transitioned in the same period and escaped detection (and documentation).

Belmont also stands out for his ability to validate a spectrum of trans, queer, and intersex experiences in the twenty-first century. He was surveilled by neighbors; examined by doctors; detained by police; interrogated by lawyers; evaluated by judges; and ridiculed by reporters, all for traits and behaviors that mark people as trans, intersex, bisexual, pansexual, and lesbian today. This makes him a unifying historical figure in a time of increasing division between these identities. It's impossible, because of Belmont's complexity, to claim him as an ancestor of one group but not others—of queer women but not of trans men, for example, or of dyadic trans men but not of intersex people. Queer, trans, and intersex scholars are mindful of these overlaps. Jules Gill-Peterson, for example, has remarked that "it actually takes a massive amount of work to make gays+lesbians and trans folks even appear to be separate groups. You have to rewrite the entirety of our shared history."[62] Hil Malatino, meanwhile, has argued that "intersexuality is a conceptual center of queerness, the figure that nonnormative genders and desire are, and have been historically, understood through and in relation to."[63] Belmont testifies to the hybridity of queer/trans/intersex history—a history that is visible (though not categorizable) before the identity formations of the early and mid-1900s.

Belmont is unique in one final way: he left a paper trail. That is, he left behind written imprints (in directories, censuses, depositions, payrolls, rosters, and news articles) in multiple decades of his life. Most people who transed gender in the nineteenth century figure in a handful of records clustered around a dramatic event like a death, an arrest, or a scandal. They appear in two or three sensational newspaper articles before the light of the historical record flickers out, leaving us in the dark about what happened to them before and afterward. But light shines on Belmont, Addie Walker, and Nova McClure Carr in every decade between 1853 and 1927, with only a few stretches of darkness. It is therefore possible to make out the shape of Belmont's life and consider it as a whole—not as a series of incidents, but as an integrated biography. That is the project of *Romantic Sensation.*

Modern biographies of gender migrants offer models, precedents, and cautionary tales for writing the life of someone like Belmont. Lou Sullivan's *From Female to Male: The Life of Jack Bee Garland* (1990) brought attention to a contemporary of Belmont's active in California between 1897 and 1936. Its publication was a first in trans historiography: a chronicle of a gender-transing man attracted to other men by a writer who was himself a gay trans man. Inspired by this affinity with his subject, Sullivan assembled dozens of newspaper articles on Garland and presented them almost word for word, creating a trove of primary source material.[64] But he stopped short of analysis, and of considering how sensational 1890s newspaper exposés might have distorted Garland's story. As Cameron Awkward-Rich admitted in an otherwise supportive reading of *From Female to Male,* "There is something peculiar about the form of this biography insofar as it is primarily an accumulation and transcription of archival material, with little reflection or pretense to coherent narrative."[65] With this in mind, I've aimed for *Romantic Sensation* to strike a balance between evidence and narrative that benefits from both.

One of the strengths of *From Female to Male* was Sullivan's respect for Garland's male identity. Sullivan never dismissed his subject's transing of gender as confusion, a scheme, or a plea for attention. Nor did he interpret it as fraud, a disguise, or a masquerade. In this he was rare among biographers both before and after 2000, many of whom assume that transmasc gender migrants identified as women. Betty T. Bennett's *Maria Diana Dods: A Gentleman and a Scholar* (1991) explored the life story of a Scottish writer assigned a female sex at birth who published short stories as David Lyndsay and presented himself in person as Walter Sholto Douglas. Bennett consistently referred to Lyndsay/Douglas as Mary Diana Dods, calling his identity a "deception" and doubting the likelihood that he was trans (to use Bennett's word, "transsexual").[66] She considered at greater length the possibility that he was a lesbian or a transvestite, but concluded that his male identity was a "pose" undertaken for practical reasons.[67] Biographies in this vein propose myriad reasons for transing gender but duck the simplest explanation: that the female-assigned people who lived as men for decades in the nineteenth century did it because they liked it. Many of them wanted to be men; indeed, they were men.[68] This seems to have been true of James Barry (ca. 1789–1865), an Irish surgeon who earned renown for his medical reforms during a forty-six-year career in the British Army. Barry never wavered in his presentation of himself as a man, and he took pains to prevent his identity from being disrespected after his death. In spite of this, biographers have declined to engage with Barry as a predecessor of people who identify as trans. English professor Ann Heilmann of the University of Cardiff has studied five modern (post-1970) Barry biographies and noted that four of them limn Barry as "really" a woman.[69] In the most recent example, published in 2016, "the potential of transgender is passed over and Barry is pathologized" as having a divided self.[70]

Romantic Sensation leaves behind the track described above and follows a different path. It sticks to the guidelines of life writing drawn by Jack Halberstam in his essay "Telling Tales: Brandon Teena, Billy Tipton and Transgender Biography," published in *Auto/Biography Studies* in 2000. Because he focuses on two people who lived in the mid-to-late twentieth century, Halberstam uses the word "transgender." His observations remain applicable, however, to the nineteenth-century gender migrants (like Belmont) who predate that word. He writes out of fatigue brought on by the wave of misleading depictions of trans lives that crested at the turn of the millennium, paying particular attention to media about Brandon Teena and Billy Tipton. Surveying these narratives, Halberstam finds a common thread: writers explaining away their subjects' gender variance as practically or coercively motivated. They assume, that is, that their subjects transed gender because they wanted to get something out of it, or because people forced them to do it.[71] Halberstam calls this move rationalization. He writes:

> Transgender lives often seem to attract enormous attention from biographers, film makers, talk show hosts, doctors and journalists, all of whom are dedicated to forcing the transgender subject to make sense. While one would not wish to assign the transgender life to the inauspicious category of nonsense, we should be wary of overly rational narratives about lives filled with contradiction and tension.[72]

Alongside the rationalizing impulse, Halberstam notices two parallel trends: stabilization and trivialization. In the stabilization process, biographers offset "the destabilizing effects of the transgender narrative" by portraying their subjects "as strange and uncharacteristic and even pathological."[73] In doing this they shore up—stabilize—the scaffolding of normative gender when it starts to wobble. In the case of *Romantic Sensation,* this could mean presenting Belmont as a freakish anomaly unrelated to his historical contexts (industrial Massachusetts, frontier Kansas, etc.). Through the trivialization process, biographers dismiss their subjects as "non-representative and interesting but without any real effects upon gender normativity."[74] *Romantic Sensation* could do this by, for example, assuming that the onlookers at Belmont's 1880 Minneapolis hearing left the courthouse without any doubts about the integrity of gender categories. Executed together, stabilization and trivialization push the act of transing to the margins of nineteenth-century history and obscure its role at the center.

Forcing trans subjects to make sense, denying their prevalence, and discounting their impact are the three errors that Halberstam warns against. But biographers make them in tandem with a fourth misstep—what Scott Larson has called the "laying open" of gender-variant people in history. A sometimes unintended effect even of scholarship rooted in trans studies, this public dissection of trans bodies adds to the scrutiny of an already hyperscrutinized group of people. Uncritical analysis, Larson shows, can end up bolstering the same "structures of examination, spectacle, and adjudication" that it tries to knock down.[75] To mitigate that risk, he calls on writers to do three things. First, to abandon the project of assigning gender identities to historical subjects. Second, to ask whether "detailing embodiment"—describing genitalia, hair, posture, scars, weight, and so on—is necessary for a project rather than gratuitous. Third, he asks writers to honor the mutability of gender in people's lives, recognizing that a person's self-concept as a young adult may not hold true for the rest of their life. The memoirs of an elder, by the same logic, don't necessarily cancel out their understanding of themself as a young adult. Gender identity expressed in coerced "moments of vulnerability, 'discovery,' or 'revelation'" does not cancel out feelings expressed more quietly and consensually over a lifetime.

Larson's and Halberstam's insights have guided my approach to understanding Belmont. Pieced together, they map out a route around the roadblocks to a respectful biography of an alternately gender-variant and gender-conforming person who lived between 1853 and 1927. They lead to five foundational positions:

1. *Romantic Sensation* does not force Belmont to "make sense."[76] It does not assign him to identity categories, whether modern or historical. It does, however, recognize him as an ancestor[77] of twenty-first century people who identify as trans, intersex, bisexual, and queer.
2. *Romantic Sensation* does not assume that Belmont must have transed gender because he wanted to get something out of it other than personal satisfaction. It separates the practical effects of his gender variance (mobility, money, freedom) from his possible motives.[78] Those motives may have multiplied, overlapped, evolved, and eroded over time.
3. Belmont was a product rather than an anomaly of history. He did not exist in some kind of air-sealed vacuum of gender variance, cut off from the rest of the world. He shaped and was shaped by the social contexts of industrial New England, settler-colonial Plains states, and small-town Kansas in the 1920s.

4. Belmont was not alone. Newspaper articles and the research of nineteenth-century historians point to the existence of dozens of gender-transing American contemporaries.[79]
5. Belmont was not a sensation, though reactions to him sometimes produced one. He was and is not a pretext for spectacle, astonishment, and unmasking. *Romantic Sensation* aims to present the events of his life without subjecting his body to dehumanizing scrutiny.

These assumptions stress the mundane aspects of Belmont's biography: he was not alone, and he was a product of his time. They also reveal the real romantic sensation of this book, the one promised in the title: the revolution in sex and gender ideology that played out in the United States between the 1850s and the 1920s.

In 1853, the year Belmont was born, the Cult of True Womanhood reigned, pressuring women to live up to saintly ideals of innocence, piety, obedience, and femininity.[80] American society expected them to cleave to the private sphere—hearth, home, and child-rearing—and to reserve public life for their male relatives. At the same time, a woman who wanted to express passionate and even sexual love for another woman could find a measure of freedom in the concept of romantic friendship. Communities increasingly saw adults we would today consider intersex as impostors—fraudulent tricksters whose "disguises" demanded unmasking for the public good. And when a baby was born with genitals that were both phallic and vulval, or when a girl reached puberty and grew a beard (for example), families sought out doctors for an appraisal of the child's "true" sex—but did not intervene surgically.[81]

In Belmont's middle age, the Cult of True Womanhood was eclipsed by New Womanhood, a sometimes demonized concept embodied by women who attended universities, published books, started businesses, and otherwise claimed the public sphere for themselves.[82] Boston marriage (a term used more often by outside observers than by couples themselves) gained currency alongside romantic friendship as an option for women who wanted to live together as intimate partners.

Doctors, meanwhile, began linking such women to the emerging "disease" of homosexuality. The homosexual diagnosis offered an explanation for gender migrants, too, and adhered to the children and adults who had previously been called hermaphrodites.[83]

By the time of Belmont's death, in 1927, the New Woman had assumed the form of the flapper, the archetypal liberated woman of the Jazz Age. Women who had intimate relationships with other women, however, now risked the rejection of their families, the suspicion of police, the scrutiny of doctors, the "cures" of psychiatrists, and the stigma of homosexual "perversion." Surgeons operated on infants deemed sexually ambiguous in procedures that became routine, and medical intervention emerged as the standard rather than the exception.[84] Americans looking to transition or otherwise align their bodies with their identities lacked access to care in their own country, but word was beginning to travel across the Atlantic of Magnus Hirschfeld's Institute for Sexual Research in Berlin, which offered cutting-edge surgeries, hormonal therapies, and affirming counseling.[85]

The thread of Belmont's life runs through this tapestry of changes. The association of gender variance with fraud fueled the Belmont Sensation of 1880, priming onlookers to participate in the spectacle of his public "unmasking." Without it, they might never have assumed that Belmont's gender presentation amounted to a mask. The Cult of True Womanhood and the later flowering of New Womanhood, meanwhile, affected Addie Walker and Nova Carr, subtracting and then multiplying their viable life paths. Each change contributed to the overhauls of sex and gender that produced Belmont, Walker, and Carr: the true sensation hiding behind an imagined one.

The project of unsensationalizing Belmont has a final step. It leads to Virginia Woolf, whose 1925 essay "Lives of the Obscure" animated lesser-known historical figures, including the poet Ann Taylor Gilbert (1782–1866). At the time Woolf wrote about Gilbert, she was closer to her than we are to Belmont today. But even with that advantage, she accepted her inability to make contact. Woolf was sanguine about her role as an excavator of lives, and she refused to turn her subject into a romantic sensation. As much as we may cling to it, she suggested, we must resist the fantasy of "rescue":

> For one likes romantically to feel oneself a deliverer advancing with lights across the waste of years to the rescue of some stranded ghost. . . . They shuffle, they preen, they bridle. Old secrets well up to their lips. The divine relief of communication will soon again be theirs. The dust shifts and Mrs. Gilbert—but the contact with life is instantly salutary. Whatever Mrs. Gilbert may be doing, she is not thinking about us.[86]

Like Ann Gilbert, Belmont is not waiting in the dark for us to find him. Whatever he is doing, he is not thinking about us.

Part I

Addie Liona Walker

1.
The Child, 1853–1867

She "ran wild" till she was about 14 years old[,] when she went to work in the Warren cotton-mills. She was always a romping sort of girl, fonder of playing with the boys than the girls, and there were incipient scandals about her even then.

—"'The What Is It,'" *Minneapolis Tribune,* February 21, 1881

Leon Belmont's story begins where it does because of a river.

The water that emerges from the earth at a place called Quaboag Pond flows for 150 miles into Long Island Sound. For nearly twenty-six of those miles, before that water joins the Ware River, and then the Chicopee, and then the Connecticut, it is its own river: the Quaboag. This is the homeland of the Nipmuc, an Algonquian nation whose relationship to inland waterways is written into its name: freshwater people.[1] "Quaboag" is a Nipmuc word, and Nipmuc people were the first known to live along the river's path through the rocky, forested hills of what was later called central Massachusetts.

The English colonists who encroached on Nipmuc land beginning in the 1640s established a series of plantations to the west of their original settlement at Plymouth. They benefited from the outcome of King Philip's War (1675–1678), a multinational conflict fought across New England that led to tighter control of Nipmuc country by outsiders.[2] A few Nipmuc families, however, held on to their land.[3] The Worcester Plateau remained—and remains today—a Nipmuc landscape.[4]

Colonists founded Quaboag Plantation at the site of present-day

Brookfield in 1660, and over the next hundred years it fractured into a cluster of independent villages that gradually grew into incorporated towns. One of these towns, Warren (called Western in its earliest days), spread out on the northern bank of the river alongside energetic waterfalls.[5] Industrialists seized on the falls for their ability to power a variety of factories—wool, cotton, and powder mills as well as an ironworks.[6] By the time the Western Railroad built a depot in town in 1839,[7] Warren had everything it needed to attract migrants from around New England: housing, transportation, expanding companies eager to hire workers, and the energy of a town resolved to make something of itself.[8]

Two of the newcomers to Warren in the 1840s were Albert and Achsah Walker, a married couple with three young children.[9] They moved to West Warren, the smaller of the town's two villages, downstream from Warren proper. Albert was a shoemaker by trade, and Worcester County's growing reputation as a center of shoe and boot manufacturing may have coaxed him and Achsah away from Upton, their home in the 1840 US census.[10] In 1850 the census taker counted them in their new West Warren home, and on June 1, 1853, the couple had a child they named Addie Liona Walker.[11] When he completed the baby's birth record, town clerk J. F. Hitchcock wrote "female" in the "sex and condition" column of his register.

Addie Walker's sex assignment at birth was the first of a lifetime of reckonings with sex and gender. It was also the most impactful. When the town clerk recorded that the baby had a female sex, he set her future. The fate of a female-assigned child born in 1853 was constrained by the binary gender system—its formidable Victorian version. From the assignment of a female sex, a cascade of assumptions flowed. The baby would become a woman, and only a woman. She would become a wife and mother, and only a wife and mother. She would naturally desire men, and only men. She would be feminine, not masculine, and her femininity would remain unchanged in each decade of her life.

The adult Addie Walker ended up shattering each of these assumptions. Leon Belmont, into whom Walker transitioned, was a husband and stepfather who had romantic relationships with both men and women. When two doctors examined him in 1880, the first declared him female, and a woman. The second pronounced him male, and a man.[12] One possible explanation of their disagreement is that Belmont, and thus the baby born to Achsah and Albert Walker in West Warren in 1853, was what we would today call intersex.

The twenty-first-century category of intersex covers a range of genital forms, gonadic traits, hormonal metrics, and genetic conditions deemed "abnormal" by doctors. The word was not yet in use in 1853; modern intersex identity as we know it depends on a set of post-Victorian cultural/medical developments, including bioethics, psychology, endocrinology, genital surgery, chromosomal analysis, and the patient-centered care movement of the 1970s.[13] But intersex history avant la lettre is, like queer and trans history, as old as sex itself. For as long as people have expected bodies to conform to one of two categories, male or female, they have found examples of individuals who are not entirely one or the other.

Responses to intersex bodies evolved dramatically between the beginning of the nineteenth century and the twentieth. In the 1700s, endosex people had tended to regard their intersex peers as monsters worthy of pity at best, and of horror at worst.[14] In the decades between 1800 and Addie Walker's birth, their thinking changed to match an increasing confidence in the gender binary. Unable to find examples of people who had "complete" sets of male and female genitalia—true hermaphrodites, in the language of the time—doctors set aside the logic of monstrosity in favor of the logic of fraud.[15] Accordingly, they stopped seeing their sexually ambiguous patients as freakish and started seeing them as dishonest, or at least confused. If a community discovered that one of its citizens living as a man menstruated, it thought of him not as a mutant but as an impostor trying to enjoy male privilege through subterfuge.[16]

What remained consistent through the early nineteenth century and until Walker's birth was the custom to keep quiet when an infant was born with an "ambiguous" sex.[17] Adults could pass as imposters, but it was harder to see a baby as a mastermind of fraud. Babies were also easier to control, and to socialize in the dyadic sex chosen by a midwife, doctor, or parents. Their adolescence was reassuringly distant; until that far-off time, they couldn't disrupt the social order by making someone pregnant unexpectedly, or by becoming pregnant themselves.[18] The relatives of newborns thus had much to lose, and little to gain, from disclosing intersex genitalia to an official at the time of the birth.[19] Advertising a baby's sexual "abnormality," particularly in rural communities, risked bringing judgment upon its family.[20]

Fear of ostracism motivated families to leave behind no written trace of a newborn baby's intersex traits, and it's for this reason that the word "female" next to Addie Walker's name in the birth register is less conclusive than it appears. It's possible that Walker had dyadic genitalia at birth, and did not develop intersex characteristics until puberty. What's clear is that regardless of her physical state at birth, Walker's family, neighbors, and town officials inscribed a female sex onto her body that persisted throughout her childhood. By treating her as a girl, the citizens of West Warren made her into a girl, and they reinforced that action when they interacted with her.[21] Over time, they had so committed themselves, as a group, to enacting Walker's femaleness that questioning it would have maligned the judgment of the entire community.[22] Having received her assignment as female, infant Addie Walker was, in the eyes of West Warren, female.

Between 1853 and 1867, when she went to work in a cotton mill, Walker left the faintest of traces in the historical record. In addition to the birth register, her name appears only in the Massachusetts state censuses of 1855 and 1865. This is unsurprising, since recordkeeping at the time tended to focus on property-owning adult men. It's still possible, however, to limn the contours of Walker's life during this period, affected as it was by better-documented topics: her relatives; the town of West Warren; and Victorian ideologies of gender and childhood. If we consider each of these alongside the writings of Walker's contemporaries—some of whom kept diaries when they were children—a picture emerges of what it might have been like for a female-assigned child to grow up working class in central Massachusetts at the start of the new half century.

The family into which Addie was born was not big by 1850s standards. In her first year of life she had five older siblings: Harriet (thirteen), George (eleven), Asahel (five), Clara (three), and William (two). While enjoying these built-in playmates, the Walker children consistently lived alongside more than a dozen other children under the age of fifteen.[23] But the family appears to have moved throughout the decade. The state and federal censuses of 1850, 1855, and 1860 show them living among different sets of neighbors. In 1850, these neighbors included a doctor and a butcher as well as a merchant, a carpenter, and laborers. By 1855, when Addie was two years old, the family had moved to a new area, where their neighbors were all laborers and farmers. And by 1860 they were in a third location, surrounded by factory workers, day laborers, and scythe makers. Albert Walker has no listed property in the censuses of 1850 and 1855, but the 1860 census lists his net worth at $200.00.[24]

On January 24, 1856, four months before Addie's third birthday, Achsah Walker died.[25] She was forty years old. The town clerk recorded "bed ridden" as her cause of death, but he also wrote "debil." (debility) in tiny letters above the primary explanation. These two causes are catch-all categories—many circumstances keep a debilitated person from getting out of bed—and they leave the real reason for Addie's mother's death unclear. Other adult residents of Warren who died over the winter of 1855–1856 suffered from consumption, scarlet fever, typhoid, and dysentery;[26] Achsah may have had an undiagnosed form of one of them.

Less than a year after Achsah's death, Albert Walker married Caroline Isabel Howard, a nineteen-year-old widow.[27] The five Walker children now had a stepmother. Census records of the following ten years, however, suggest that the household became more rather than less fluid after the marriage. The US census of 1860 lists only three children living with Albert and Caroline: Isahel, Lydia, and a newborn baby (Emily). Addie's name, and her other brothers' and sisters' names, do not appear. Five years later, an enumerator of the Massachusetts state census counted seven Walkers living in Warren in the household of Almus Bliss, including Isahel, Adelaide (Addie), Lydia, Emily, and two-year-old Charles.[28]

Albert Walker's role (or lack of a role) in his children's upbringing is hard to make out. The few sources that mention him point to chronic struggles with poverty and alcoholism. In 1880, when a visitor from Northampton interviewed Warren residents about the Walkers, he reported that Albert was "drunken" and "shiftless," known around town for his debts and his failure to provide for his family.[29] A newspaper item published in 1877 noted that he moved often, living in Warren only "off and on."[30] And in 1852, the year before Addie was born, Albert owed so much money to the town of Palmer that it petitioned a second town to cover his debts.[31] His chosen trade did not always pay well; in 1861, a Massachusetts shoe cutter could make as little as sixty cents a day.[32] Albert supplemented that income in the 1860s by selling horses to his neighbors, but the business petered out after 1866.[33]

Addie's father's greatest impact on Worcester County was probably an incident that almost killed him. While living in Blanchardville (Palmer), he went out one Sunday to pass the time doing a kind of target practice with friends. They gathered at the site of a burned-out mill and shot at the rats attracted by lingering flour dust. Albert spotted a rat sitting on a powder keg, took aim, fired, and set off a violent explosion. He survived to nurse his burns, but a boy who had tagged along with the group did not.[34] The child's death cemented Walker's reputation as a deadbeat—an idler with too much time on his hands who led others to a tragic end.

The powder-keg incident hints at the unique situation of Warren and neighboring towns in the years surrounding the Civil War. The area was industrial enough to have ruined flour-mill complexes, but rural enough for citizens to turn to shooting rats out of a lack of entertainment. In some ways, Warren's pocket of central Massachusetts had modernized. Factories dotted the landscape, churning out mass quantities of wool, cotton, lumber, and paper, and employing nearly half of all of the county's adult men.[35] Only a fifth of these men remained at work on family farms. But in other ways, towns like Warren, Palmer, Spencer, and Brookfield held on to the pastoral, colonial character they had honed since the Puritans set up their plantations in the 1600s. Warren's central feature was an open meadow that served as a town common, in the tradition of rural English villages.[36] A classic New England meetinghouse (built circa 1797) anchored the common's western edge.[37] Just 1,793 people lived in Warren in 1855, placing it in the midrange of Worcester County towns in terms of population.[38] Most of them, however, lived in Warren Center; Addie and her family lived two miles away, in a physically (though not politically) separate settlement called West Warren, where it's likely only a few hundred of the town's total residents had homes. In 1855 it was little more than a single residential street that followed the path of the river, with a cotton mill on the south bank.[39] That footprint barely expanded over the next fifteen years, as Addie grew up. The mill complex, meanwhile, doubled in size and provided a majority of the community's housing and employment.[40]

What West Warren lacked in amenities in the 1850s it made up for in natural beauty. If there were no general stores, no festivals, dances, or fairs, there were plenty of opportunities for a child to "grow wild," as a newspaper article later reported Addie did.[41] The Quaboag River was steps away from Main Street and shallow enough for wading, paddling, splashing, and catching turtles. In the spring, when snowmelt trickled down from the hills, there was mud for playing in, and it was common for girls as well as boys to go without shoes.[42] Older and bolder children could climb Marks Mountain for a view of the valleys below and even a glimpse of Mount Greylock, the tallest point in Massachusetts, rising forbiddingly in the western distance.[43]

The idea of a barefoot Addie Walker traipsing through Warren's muddy streams sits at odds with the twenty-first-century stereotype of a demure Victorian child—particularly one socialized as a girl. But imagining Walker's childhood requires setting that stereotype aside, and focusing on the realities of class and gender that structured her life. American girls and young women in the mid-1800s did face pressure to conform to an ideal of femininity.[44] In their earliest years, they learned that questioning the patriarchs who surrounded them (fathers, uncles, religious figures) could bring punishment and shaming. The women in their lives, too, cultivated obedience to male authority. They raised girls to be chaste, pious, submissive, and domestic, rewarding them when they displayed these qualities and correcting them when they did not.[45] Many girls who expressed interest in so-called "masculine" activities like running, shouting, and rough play adapted in order to fit gendered expectations.

Many conformed—but not all. Strict though they were, mid-Victorian gender ideals were still ideals, enforced inconsistently. Some girls found ways to resist. The diaries and memoirs of Addie Walker's contemporaries offer a clarifying perspective, showing 1860s gender orthodoxy not just as it appeared on paper, but as girls negotiated it in real life. The teacher Corabelle Fellows, for example, recalled in a 1938 memoir an act of rebellion against her father that stayed with her as an adult. After Corabelle told him a lie in 1865, Homer Fellows spanked his daughter and locked her in a closet. Her response was not regret or tears but protest:

> With a sudden rush of anger and revenge I felt up in the dark. On tiptoe I managed to reach, yank and tug from their hooks and hangers all the best clothes of the family and let them fall about me as they would. When my fifteen-minute incarceration was ended and Mother came to release the prisoner, she found a tearless and defiant face turned up to hers. Her spanking was without restraint and left me humiliated.[46]

Corabelle's closet rage is a tantrum that any young child would use to test parental limits. But it's also a snapshot of Victorian girlhood at odds with the status quo. In the face of her father's discipline, Corabelle is angry and vengeful rather than meek and obeisant. And although the adult Corabelle remembers her punishment as a humiliation, the child Corabelle did not change her behavior after the incident. Instead, she disobeyed her father's orders to stay in his sight and ran across a busy street, alone, to visit a circus.[47]

At the same time Addie Walker was growing up in West Warren, a little girl living on the other side of Massachusetts was creating a record of her daily life. Sarah Gooll Putnam lived with her parents and siblings in Boston and kept a diary beginning in 1860, when she was nine years old. Eager to practice her skills at drawing and watercolors (the adult Putnam worked as a professional painter), Sarah included sketches of herself at play between cascades of cursive text. She drew herself at dancing school, learning the cotillion in a child-sized crinoline. Just as often, she recorded herself wearing the same hoop skirt while doing things usually associated with Victorian boys, including throwing a ball and sledding.[48] On one illustrated page, Sarah and her friend Helen stab at a frozen stream with sticks; on the next they hoist up an ice block between them to move it out of their play area.[49] In another, Sarah holds herself aloft on a pair of parallel bars as part of an exercise routine at a gymnasium.[50] The lack of commentary surrounding the sketches suggests that these activities were noteworthy but not necessarily forbidden.

On February 11, 1860, Helen invited Sarah to attend a dance. It was a middle-class event typical of the period, with children trying on the adult roles of ladies and gentlemen and following the behavior conventions for each. But in one way it was unique. Sarah wrote in her diary:

> In the first part of the time Helen, and a few other girls acted a little french play. Helen acted the part of a waiter, and was dressed in a boy's coat, and pantaloons. She looked so funnily. In the last part of the time we danced, and I had a very nice time. Then we all went into supper, and Helen was my partner. I called her Robert, for that was her name in the play. I think after supper we danced again, and at eight oclock I went home.[51]

Helen's cross-dressing registers with Sarah as unusual; she comments that there is something "funny" about a girl dressed as a boy. But Helen's continuation of her role past the end of the play is accepted by the group, and Sarah accepts it, too. Even in the 1860s, opportunities to trans gender could arise in the middle of conventional social exercises—rehearsals of the gender binary and opposite-sex romance. A theatrical context, as well as the children's age, softened the transgression. For the children, however, this blip of permissiveness allowed them to imagine new gender possibilities. A child like Helen, acting the part of a boy in public for the first time, might have realized that such a thing was possible and that she enjoyed it. A child like Sarah, meanwhile, might have noticed that there was room for someone like her in that kind of couple, and that *she* enjoyed it. Sarah seems to have done exactly that, chronicling the evening in her diary with three illustrations: one of dancers in silhouette, one of Helen as Robert, and one of the two of them dancing arm in arm as a couple.[52]

Sarah Gooll Putnam *(right)* dances with her best friend, Helen, dressed as "Robert" *(left)*, on January 11, 1861. Volume 1, November 26, 1860–June 26, 1861, image 35 of the Sarah Gooll Putnam Diaries, 1860–1912. Collection of the Massachusetts Historical Society. https://www.masshist.org/collection-guides/digitized/fa0176/vol1#35.

The diary of M. Carey Thomas documents a young teenager's frustration with gender rules as she comes of age in Baltimore during the 1860s. At thirteen, Thomas rejected the imperative to be "ladylike" as she approached a marriageable age, enlisting a friend to join her in acts of rebellion like climbing to the top of a stable in front of a crowd of people.[53] At fourteen she responded privately, with frustration, to a sermon on True Womanhood she received from a family friend:

> Dr. Morris walked home with us and talked all the while about the "sacred shrine of womanhood" and that no matter what the splendid talents of a woman might be she couldn't use them better than by being a wife and mother and then went off in some high faluting stuff about the strength of women's devotion completely forgetting that all women ain't wives and mothers and they I suppose are to fold their hands and be idle waiting for an *eligible offer*. Bah! Stuff and nonsenses! Well

> when we got undressed we skedaddled around went over in the laboratory, ate candy and talked until I happened to look at my watch and found it was half past one.[54]

This was the gender ideology that Addie Walker had to navigate in the 1860s: sentimental, punitive, patriarchal, and binary. But even at its most rigid, it offered routes of resistance—as well as consequences for choosing them. Thomas's diary entries, for example, show a young woman simultaneously committed to finding her own path and worried about where it might lead. In the same entry that celebrates her power to rebel in small ways, like visiting the laboratory after Dr. Morris's lecture, she remains aware of the punishment coming to her if she's caught. During the roof-climbing incident, too, she is both defiant and thinking of the judgmental faces staring up at her, aware that climbing down will ruin her white dress.[55]

The examples of Fellows, Putnam, and Thomas are helpful only to a point. Each of them was middle class; Addie Walker was not. Class, as much as gender, dictated the expectations that Walker faced. She didn't have in-home laboratories to sneak off to or closets full of clothes to ransack. Her parents couldn't afford to send her to dancing lessons, as Sarah Gooll Putnam's did. At the same time, she grew up free of the commandment to be a "lady," with all of the benefits and burdens that entailed. Working-class girls, like working-class women, were less constrained physically, in part because they were required to produce labor. They wore simple dresses without the crinoline cages that reached their peak width in the 1860s, both because fashion was prohibitively expensive and because they needed a full range of motion in order to scrub floors, wash clothes, and operate machines.[56]

Understanding Addie Walker's obligation to provide labor is the key to understanding her childhood. In this respect, working-class Victorian childhood was its own phenomenon. Before the turn of the twentieth century, households followed a family-economy model that enlisted children to help their parents at home, on farms, and in factories as soon as they were physically able to do so.[57] Preteens chopped wood and hauled water; eight-year-olds built cooking fires; their younger siblings gathered coal or kindling. And they had to do it every day, before the family could eat or drink or wash. They still found time to play, but they did so within the limits of a daily routine that centered on work.[58] Addie's stepmother, Caroline, was burdened by childcare. Her stepchildren Harriet and George Henry were adults by 1860, but Addie's brother Asahel (Asel) was twelve, and her sister Clara was ten. Caroline gave birth to six children of her own between 1857 and 1868, and for much of the 1860s she was both pregnant and responsible for multiple children under the age of five. As a middle child, Addie would have been easy to lose track of—but also useful as a caretaker for her younger siblings as the decade worn on.

The timing of Addie's childhood did give her a partial reprieve from working as an adult. In 1852, the year before Addie was born, the Massachusetts legislature passed the nation's first compulsory school law.[59] It required two things: first, that every town in the state provide residents with at least one public primary school, and second, that children between the ages of eight and fourteen receive elementary instruction for at least three months out of every year.[60] Even the poorest families in Warren, like the Walkers, released their children from work at home for a modest amount of time. Nine school districts provided locations for students to learn in all the corners of the town.[61] After leaving primary school, children could attend the high school repurposed from its original use as Quaboag Seminary.[62]

Addie's hometown benefited, too, from the wider wave of reforms that pushed Massachusetts to the leading edge of progressive public education in the nineteenth century.[63] Horace Mann had grown up in Norfolk County, Worcester County's neighbor to the west, and served as the secretary of the first Massachusetts State Board of Education between 1837 and 1848. Among his accomplishments were the Common School movement; the word method of teaching reading; and the normal school system, which standardized teacher training. Mann's push for graded classrooms ended the practice of instructing students of different ages and abilities in the same room—a reform that accelerated learning. And it was Mann, in part, whose influence brought about the compulsory attendance law that kept Addie in school until the age of fourteen.[64]

The reformist and even egalitarian spirit of Massachusetts public education in the 1850s connected working-class children like Addie to resources that their peers in other states couldn't reach. That education supplied the verbal poise and cultural savvy that Belmont used to blend into middle-class society in 1879, and to present himself as an eligible suitor. Intellect was a feature of Belmont's charm; the *Minneapolis Tribune* reported approvingly in 1880 that he "speaks with fluency, uses excellent language, and is to all appearances a remarkably shrewd individual." It was schooling in Massachusetts that set Belmont on this path—one that led to an appreciation of art, poetry, and medicine,[65] and the ability to use that insight to his social advantage.

On May 1, 1867, exactly one month before her fourteenth birthday, Addie Walker took a step away from her childhood. It was probably not by choice. Her stepmother, Caroline, had six children to manage in addition to Addie. The youngest, Mary, was less than a year old, and her brother not much older than that. The Walker brood would have been hard to clothe and feed under any circumstances, let alone with only one parent earning wages. When the US Treasury Department published an 1869 report on Americans living in manufacturing towns like Warren, it noted that two-parent families with seven children spent an average of $23.78 a week in 1867 on rent, food, and fuel, with an additional $1.22 used for "clothing, housekeeping goods, &c."[66] The average Massachusetts shoemaker in the same period made about $17.00 a week.[67] It's likely that Caroline faced a household deficit as she took stock of the family's situation in the spring of 1867. If Addie really was "running wild," as the newspapers later claimed, sending her to work made practical and financial sense. She was close—only weeks away—to aging out of the education requirement. With child labor a fact of life all around her,[68] and Massachusetts thriving as its factories helped the nation recover from the Civil War, Caroline's solution was clear: find Addie a job.

West Warren's biggest employer of men, women, and children for several decades in the 1800s was the Warren Cotton Mills Company, which stood in the middle of the village. In some ways, it was the village.[69] At the peak of its production, it had 900 people on its payrolls at a time when the population of Warren proper was only a handful of thousands.[70] A map of West Warren created in 1870 shows a sprawling complex of thirty-five mill buildings straddling both sides of the Quaboag River, with the complex accounting for more than a third of the village's overall footprint.[71] Seventeen of those buildings were boarding houses,[72] which allowed workers to live inside the mill complex itself; the company therefore provided more housing than any other single entity in the village. By 1867 it operated two different mills: Mill #1, built in 1854, and the more technologically advanced Mill #2, completed in 1866.[73] Due to high employee turnover, overseers looked for replacements on a regular basis, and this steady demand for labor made the Warren mills the surest option for an untrained child worker.

Warren Cotton Mills Company hired Addie to work in the carding room at Mill #1 during the month of May 1867. The scene that met her there on her first day would have been physically overwhelming. First, there was the noise, which roared into mill workers' ears before they had crossed a building's threshold. It was a cascade of hums, whirs, and shrieks—a relentless drone that sent such strong vibrations through their bodies that they felt the sound as much as they heard it.[74] Then there was the spectacle of the space itself, a barn of a room filled with rows of people and machines stretching to a vanishing point on the opposite side. Even the ceiling was crowded, with whirling line shafts, pulleys, and belts feeding power to the machines.[75] As the carding rollers lurched into action and workers fed them with fiber, the air filled with cotton dust that settled on every surface. Before long, they couldn't see what was happening on the other side of the room. Finally, there was the heat. Cotton fibers are more pliable at high temperatures and levels of humidity, so overseers kept mill rooms hot and sticky.[76]

This was the place in which Addie was now expected to spend up to twelve hours a day.[77] But there was no time for reflection. Once the machines started up, they ran without stopping until the midday break, and they required uninterrupted tending to prevent jams. Like every worker in her department, Addie's task was to provide a constant flow of cotton through the processing chain as it evolved from lumps of fiber (laps) into uniform strands (slivers) and then rovings, ready for spinning. Standing in front of the machine assigned to her—a wood-and-iron beast nearly as tall as Addie herself—she heaped the

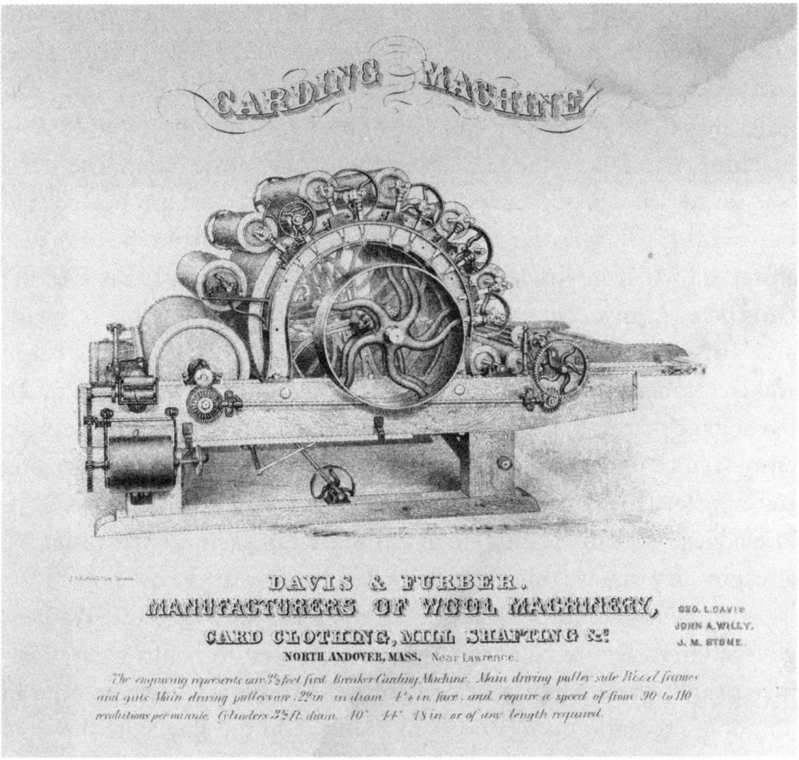

A carding machine similar to the one Addie Walker would have operated at the West Warren Cotton Mill in 1867. From the Collections of The Henry Ford (Henry Ford Museum). https://www.thehenryford.org/collections-and-research/digital-collections/artifact/148569.

laps onto a rotating conveyor belt that fed them into a set of rotating cylinders. They emerged from the machine in smooth strands that piled up in cylindrical containers, which were then carried to the next station on the carding-room floor.[78]

New workers learned their jobs by doing them; training was brief bordering on nonexistent. Addie would have figured out what to do by watching those around her, and at her own peril.[79] It was in those first attempts to squeeze a hand between the toothed cylinders to wipe away the cotton fuzz that the risk of injury was greatest. And even for someone who understood the machine's inner workings, its reactions were hard to predict. When the Massachusetts Bureau of Statistics of

Labor published its first annual report in 1870, one cotton miller admitted that on-the-job injuries at his factory often befell "boys, girls, and older persons getting their fingers nipped in the gearing."[80] Another described how a boy "got one of his hands caught in the carding machine, which tore the flesh from the inside of the hand. The hand was saved, though somewhat stiff."[81] An employee even reported that one of his carding-room coworkers eventually died from the injury he sustained when a cylinder mangled his hand.[82] But the hazards didn't end there. A mist of cotton dust filled the air, coating workers' heads and arms and working its way into their lungs.[83] The carding room was a cotton mill's dustiest area, with the machines producing so much particulate matter that tending them was like working in a fine rain. An employee of one Massachusetts mill referred in 1844 to "the carding room, where the cotton flies most, and the girls get the dirtiest."[84] Prolonged exposure to the dust led to asthma, emphysema, and byssinosis, a respiratory disease unique to workers in cotton and wool mills.[85]

As the worker's observation from 1844 shows, Addie Walker's generation of women and girls was not the first to confront the realities of industrial labor in Massachusetts. Addie was participating in a double revolution of gender and industry in the Bay State that had started decades earlier, in the 1830s. Before he died in 1817, Francis Cabot Lowell had made headway in bringing the vertically integrated system of textile manufacturing he observed in England to Middlesex County. He added a key innovation: recruiting young women (some of them in their early teens) to leave their rural hometowns, sign on to the company payroll, and move into boardinghouses next to factories. His business partners refined the system in the 1820s and 1830s at the Boston Manufacturing Company, based in Waltham, and then at the Merrimack Manufacturing Company, in the town that became Lowell.

The Waltham–Lowell system, or Lowell system, as it came to be known, invited Massachusetts women to enter public space as independent wage earners outside the control of their fathers and brothers. This was at a time when separate-spheres gender ideology—the belief that women ought to stay at home (the private sphere) while men ventured out to work (the public sphere)—was held up as the natural, moral, and ideal arrangement of social life. In order to quash the concern that working in factories tarnished women's purity, mill owners offered amenities that appeared to protect it: zero-tolerance codes of conduct; classes, concerts, and lectures in Christian ethics; even matrons installed in the boardinghouses to surveil residents' behavior. The system's educational component (as well as periodicals like the *Lowell Offering*, which published the writing of women workers) led to the public image of "Lowell girls" as studious, striving, and upwardly mobile, and their bosses as benevolent. Some of the workers themselves agreed. When Lucy Larcom wrote a memoir of her years in the mills in 1881, she hailed the Waltham–Lowell system as "a new industry for American women, offering them an opportunity for self-support with self-respect, the guarded freedom of a home, and a social atmosphere wherein heart and soul might helpfully breathe." She emphasized that workers "were never unkindly treated. We had homes and careful guardianship; none of us knew what real poverty meant; and everything about us was educating us to become true children of the republic."[86]

Letters written by mill laborers during their employment show that the reality was more complicated.[87] A worker named Susan admitted in 1844 that standing all day made her feet ache, and the tedium of tending the machines tried her patience, but she concluded that "in general, I like it very much. It is easy to do, and does not require very violent exertion, as much of our farm work does."[88] At the other end of the spectrum were those who decried mill labor as a "death-spreading monster" and "a deep, festering rotten system, which is sapping the life-blood of our nation."[89] One unnamed woman and mill worker wrote in an 1847 letter to the periodical *Voice of Industry*:

> These lovers of the Romance of Labor—they don't like the reality very well—see not the pale and emaciated ones. They see not those who wear Consumption's hectic flush. They think little of the weariness and pain of those fair forms, as they stand there, at the loom and spindle, thirteen long hours, each day! . . . A dizziness in the head or a pain in the side, or the shoulders or the back, admonishes them to return to their country homes before it is too late. But too often these friendly

> monitions are unheeded. They resolve to toil a little longer.— But nature cannot be cheated, and the poor victim of a false system of Industrial Oppression is carried home—*to die!*[90]

If the number of days Addie chose to work in her first month at the Warren Cotton Mills is an indication, her feelings about factory labor were closer to this unnamed writer's than to Susan's, and a world away from Lucy Larcom's. By the time she entered the labor force in Warren in 1867, Massachusetts cotton mills had jettisoned the Waltham–Lowell system's perks while maintaining its paternalism.[91] There were no after-work lectures for Addie to attend, no employee journals like the *Lowell Offering* to publish her writing.[92] But the rules remained strict, and the benefits meager; some mills refused to compensate workers injured on the job, whether by covering medical bills or by paying for time off during recovery.[93] In 1866, Boott Mills in Lowell warned its employees (by way of an intimidating list of regulations, posted on-site) never to leave their stations "except in cases of absolute necessity."[94] The arrangement failed to impress Addie. At the end of May, she signed the company's payroll register to show that she had worked for just two and a half days (thirty hours). No one in the carding room had worked less in that pay period, with most putting in more than twenty and as many as twenty-seven working days in the month. Her rate of pay had been less than five cents per hour, so she had earned a total of $1.25.[95]

In a testament to her education, Addie signed her name to the company payroll in her own handwriting. It's the signature of someone taught penmanship in school; her capital A and W show off the curlicues and flourishes of cursive style in the 1860s. The majority of Addie's coworkers, who could not read or write, had the supervisor sign on their behalf before adding an X. The divide between literate and illiterate laborers was another sign of the new status quo in the wake of the Waltham–Lowell system. The first Massachusetts cotton mills had relied on American-born young women and girls like Addie, but by 1867, they hired immigrants who accepted lower wages than their predecessors.[96] The Warren Mills' carding room staff skewed Irish, as shown by the names recorded alongside Addie's in the payroll:

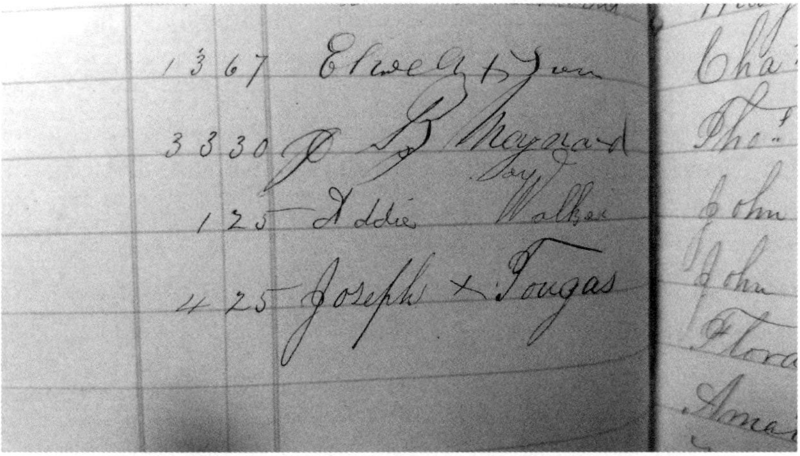

Addie Walker's signature in the Warren Cotton Mills Company's payroll register for the month of May 1867. From Volume 100 (Payrolls, 1865–1870), Thorndike Company records (MSS:442 1836–1918 T455), Baker Library, Harvard Business School.

Hallihan, Dougherty, Bresnahan, Shay, Leary, and Shehan. The ratio of men to women shows a parallel shake-up of the Waltham–Lowell system along gender lines. Of the twenty-four people working beside Addie in May, thirteen were men or boys and eleven were girls or women.[97]

Whether because of pressure from her parents or a change of heart, Addie showed more commitment to the job in her second month at the mill. In June, she was still among the carding-room employees who worked the least, but this time she put in thirteen and a half days—162 hours—in the four-week pay period.[98] Her rate of pay was once again less than five cents per hour, and she earned a total of $6.75. Although this was a leap forward from her May earnings, it was a pittance compared to the hours required to get it, and barely enough to buy a pair of boots.[99] It's unlikely she got to keep even that. In June, she did not sign her name in the payroll; her stepmother, Caroline, signed for her.[100] The change suggests that Caroline Walker was now receiving Addie's wages, or at least collecting them.

By the end of June, Addie had spent 192 hours in the carding room of the Warren mills, staring at the same spots on the wall and walking the same tired routes around the roaring machines. Her mind was numb from the unceasing repetition of a handful of tasks. She faced the prospect of more of the same, month after month, and of turning over the money she earned to someone else. She saw the future her background had laid out for her and rejected it. At fourteen, she was about to move beyond Warren and make a place for herself in the wider world.

2.

The Youth, 1867–1873

She is rather petite in figure, and abrupt in manner, with short hair and a not very unpleasant face. There is no romance about her, nor would she be especially interesting in the garments generally worn by her sex. A gentleman remarked that her disguise was very good, which she appeared to regard as a compliment.

—"On Her Travels. A Springfield, Mass., Girl Dons Male Attire and Goes West—She is Detected and Brought to Grief in Chicago," *Chicago Daily Tribune,* January 11, 1873

When Addie Walker left the Warren Cotton Mills in July 1867, there were few other paths she could pursue. Her childhood was effectively over. Having entered the work force and established herself as an earner, she could not return to her former role outside the wage economy. She needed to get another job. One choice was to sign up with another textile mill—one of the dozens of cotton manufacturers across Massachusetts ready to hire girls and young women. There were options within Warren itself, including J. S. Tidd's mill, which made cotton batting,[1] and the Western Cotton Manufacturing Company.[2] If she had wanted to, Walker also could have worked at any number of cotton mills across Worcester County, which employed a total of 2,851 women in 1865, or in next-door Essex County, which employed 3,125 women.[3] But each of these would have meant more of the same. The working conditions, tasks, and schedule that Walker had experienced at the Warren Mills were standard across the state.[4]

Walker chose to leave factory life for good and try her hand in a new industry: domestic service. Her decision shows how determined she was to get out of the carding room, regardless of whether it made financial sense. In 1869, women domestic workers in Massachusetts farm country made an average of $10.20 a month, including board. Even the lowest-paid mill workers made more.[5] Scrubbing floors, moreover, was as backbreaking as keeping a carding machine running for fourteen hours a day, if not more so. And there were other disadvantages. When the Massachusetts Bureau of Statistics of Labor issued its first annual report, covering the period of March 1869 through March 1870, it offered this grim assessment from a women's labor advocate based in Boston:

> Domestic servants receive all the way from one to five dollars a week, which is supposed to include food and lodging; great complaint is, however, made by the servants that in many cases all food is kept under lock and key, and very insufficient amounts of unfit food dealt out to girls who have to labor fourteen hours a day with only one evening out each week. Domestic work in genteel families, where the labor is described as "light," and offering the "advantages of a home to the girls," is so exhausting to the nervous and physical system, that very few women can work more than one or two years without "breaking down," and being obliged to leave work, for a time at least.[6]

By moving from a cotton mill into domestic service, Walker was leaving behind one punishing domain of women's work for another. She may have done this casually at first, offering to "help out" at her neighbors' farms. This seems to be the arrangement she fell into with Columbus Orcutt, the South Warren farmer who was her first employer after the Warren Mills. But her role in the Orcutt household was complicated, straddling the line between servant and adopted daughter. It was this relationship, and in particular Orcutt's trust in Walker, that spared her from the kind of overwork reported to the Massachusetts Bureau of Labor. It influenced Walker's life after 1867 in ways subtle and dramatic, propelling her toward a decision, in 1878, to leave Massachusetts behind.

~

The grandly named Columbus Christopher Orcutt lived with his wife, Mildred, at the foot of a hill in Warren's southeastern corner.[7] As the 1860s drew to a close he was in his seventieth decade, and a grandfather. He continued, however, to manage a prosperous farm. On three hundred acres of land he grew corn, wheat, oats, and potatoes, while twenty-eight cows provided milk for cheese and butter. In addition to the milch cows, he had three horses, eleven working oxen, seventeen cattle, an orchard, and farming machinery. When census enumerators visited in 1870, Orcutt valued his livestock at $3,413, his farm at $10,000, and his total real estate at $11,700.[8] As his children grew up, he hired local youngsters—including, in 1870, Walker's younger sister, Lydia—to cover the deficit in labor.[9]

How often and for how long Walker stayed with Orcutt is unclear. In the mid-1870s, when out-of-town reporters snooped around Warren for the details of her backstory, they contradicted themselves. "The [Walker] girl was of humble origin," one announced, "and seems to have lived in Orcutt's family from the age of thirteen till she was about seventeen, when apparently she went to seek her fortune, he having become her guardian."[10] Another claimed that she had lived with the farmer for no more than a year.[11] Whatever her location in specific years, Walker seems to have moved often between 1867 and 1873, working as a servant in Warren but also in Athol, in the household of a deacon.[12] This move would have given Walker a change not just in scenery but also in work, since a deacon's home kept to a different routine than a farm like Orcutt's. There were no cows for Walker to milk or potatoes for her to hoe in her second position. There was, however, a high school, and the deacon allowed her to continue her secondary education while she worked for him.[13] She was thus able to break up the long hours of domestic service by making her way to a building at the end of School Street.[14] The institution was not graded, meaning that students of all ages learned together, and it lacked formal courses of study for consecutive years.[15] Even so, attending Athol High School gave Walker a chance to bring her education past the rudimentary level she had reached in Warren. Fitting in with well-educated people was important to her later in the 1870s as well as in Minneapolis in 1880, when Belmont studied—or at least appeared to study—at a doctor's office.[16] The *Springfield Republican* investigated a related bluff in 1876, when it discovered that "[Walker] has claimed a sojourn at Westfield normal school, and a membership at one time of Lawyer Gillett's class; but inquiry shows that she was simply at Westfield a week, several years ago, visiting a school friend."[17]

In December 1872, still supporting herself as a domestic worker and continuing her education, Addie looked at the life path before her and changed her route. This time, her resolve was to dress as a man. That decision appears at first to be the most dramatic of her life—the expression of a unique sense of self that culminated in the Belmont sensation of 1880. But gender migrants were far from rare in the United States of Walker's youth. In some arenas, they were features of popular culture. It was the golden age of the dime novel, the cheap wood-pulp paperback that specialized in stories of adventure, violence, and romance, often with cross-dressing mixed in. Their price made them affordable to a wide swath of readers, including working-class youth like Walker. *The Female Marine, or the Adventures of Lucy Brewer,* published as a pamphlet in 1815, had sold so rapidly that it served as a model for the writers who established the dime novel formula over the next five decades.[18] *Female Marine* told the path of a young woman (later proved to be fictional) from Massachusetts who lived as a man for three years after being inspired by the real-life example of Robert Shurtliff (also spelled Shirtliff), a Revolutionary War soldier who was himself a female-assigned native of Massachusetts.[19] Later hits of the genre included *Fanny Campbell, the Female Pirate Captain* (1844);[20] *The Deserted Wife's Revenge* (also titled *Jealousy and Murder*; 1852), whose main character infiltrated a thieves' hideout while passing as a man;[21] and *Sue Munday: The Guerilla Spy* (1865), about a Confederate-allied Civil War marauder who turns out to be a man posing as a woman dressing as a man.[22] Tales like these, though sensational, spread through Walker's world the idea that a sex assignment at birth did not have to be the final word on a person's fate.

Alongside dime novel narratives, Victorian burlesque theater showed off the possibilities of cross-dressing to mainstream, working-class audiences. Popular in the United Kingdom since the 1850s, burlesque conquered America in the late 1860s, just in time to catch the attention of Walker's generation in Massachusetts.[23] The London-based Lydia Thompson Burlesque Company performed burlesque shows at the Springfield Opera House on September 5, 1870, and at the Boston Theatre on September 12.[24] On the programs were "Lurline" and "Sinbad the Sailor," both of which featured Thompson in the leading (cross-dressed) role.[25] The troupe returned to Boston in 1872 with "Kenilworth"—an Elizabethan drag fantasia with Thompson as the Earl of Leicester, Harry Beckett as Queen Elizabeth I, Camille Dubois as Sir Walter Raleigh, and three additional gender-bent roles.[26]

Dime novels and burlesque shows, transgressive though they were, could only plant a seed of possibility in their fans' imaginations. It was one thing for a fictional woman to put on pants in the middle of a book or a play, and another for a real person to do it. Here a second emerging medium of popular culture, the mass-circulation press, stepped in to provide true, if sensationalized, examples of Walker's peers transing gender in their day-to-day lives.

Multiple events converged in the decade between 1863 and 1873 to bring cross-dressing into the American public's imagination via newspapers. First, hundreds[27] of female-assigned individuals dressed as men to enlist in the army during the Civil War, inspiring newspaper editors, eager to attract readers with "girl soldier" exposés, to jump on the reports coming in from across the country.[28] Wire services, meanwhile, enabled the national sharing of local stories. They allowed Kentucky's *Owensboro Monitor,* for example, to carry an interview with a former private originally conducted by the *Rochester Union* in New York:

> She has the instincts of a boy—loves boyish pursuits, and is bound to become a man. She declares that she may yet be a gentleman, but that she can never be a lady. . . . She would not promise to make a change—indeed, she insisted that she would prefer any punishment, death even, rather than be compelled to act the part of a woman.[29]

The soldier girl narratives of the 1860s broadened the public's understanding of what was possible for young women, as well as the options that young women themselves could imagine.[30] Transing gender remained a marginal act, associated with risk and eccentricity. But it was possible in the Civil War years for someone like Addie Walker to open a newspaper and read about a "woman" who not only lived as a man, but rejected womanhood, and took steps toward claiming a male identity.

The second event that brought gender migration into the public eye in Walker's youth was the arrest of Ernest Boulton and Frederick Park in London in 1870. In April of that year, London police seized four people leaving a performance at the Strand Theatre and detained two of them (Boulton and Park, dressed as Stella and Fanny) on suspicion of being men in drag. At a subsequent trial, a jury acquitted them of conspiracy to commit a felony, but media coverage made them into household names, in the United States as well as England.[31] Journalists used the interest in gender transgression piqued by the case as a pretext for additional stories in the United States—many of them without much connection to the news from London. One multicolumn feature in *The Days' Doings* hurried to "call attention to some cases in New York in which the Boulton masquerade is reversed," complete with historical precedents, praise for "the poetry of female manhood," and a discussion of cross-dressing in Shakespeare, all delivered in a nonjudgmental tone. ("The question of morality," the writer winked, "is not ours to decide.")[32]

At the same time they were following Boulton and Park, newspaper readers were finding stories about Mary Edwards Walker (no relation to Addie), a New York–born doctor and suffragist who had won a Medal of Honor for treating soldiers during the Civil War. Reporters had commented on Walker's clothing (pants under a short skirt, then later, pants alone) as early as the mid-1860s,[33] but she attracted new attention in 1871 when she published *Hit: Essays on Women's Rights*. Reactions ranged from dismissive to excoriating but ended up spreading the same ideas they condemned. One reviewer wrote:

> She now insists that women everywhere shall imitate her example and, emancipating themselves from skirts, array themselves in the bifurcated bliss of manly clothing. With this purpose she has lectured, written, and talked. Now she comes

Dr. Mary Edwards Walker, circa 1880s. Dr. Mary Edwards Walker Collection, Oswego County Historical Society via New York Heritage Digital Collections. https://nyheritage.contentdm.oclc.org/digital/collection/p16694coll147/id/7120/rec/14.

> before the public as the author of a book, in which her cherished hobby is urged upon the women of America. . . . Not content with thus assuming the characteristics of both sexes she speaks of herself as though she belonged to a third sex.[34]

Unlike dime novels, which were fantasies; burlesque shows, which were entertainment; girl soldier exposés, which fell back on practical motives for cross-dressing; and the Boulton and Park story, which was too foreign and theatrical to threaten the American status quo, Walker's book urged readers to trans gender in their own lives.[35] The reviewer quoted above went a step further, interpreting Walker's choice of dress as an expression of self—what we might today call a gender identity.[36]

All of these examples of gender variance were circulating through Addie Walker's world in the 1860s and 1870s.[37] She did not make the decision to wear clothes associated with men in a vacuum; her choice had a context and precedents. Walker was less an anomaly than she was a product of her time, choosing to participate in an established, if marginal, tradition. But it was a choice with consequences. In 1843, St. Louis became the first of more than a hundred US cities to outlaw cross-dressing before 1900.[38] This cascade of restrictions was, in part, a reaction to the rise of the American metropolis in the middle of the nineteenth century. The nation's emerging megacities crammed together strangers who could not, as they had in small towns, be sure of each other's identities, raising anxieties about fraud.[39] City leaders responded to those anxieties with legislation, and soon, for the first time in American history, police could arrest citizens on sight based on judgments of their gender.

Why, at the age of nineteen, did Walker choose to change her gender presentation in spite of this risk?[40] The unavoidable answer is that we can't know. Motivation is hard enough to pin down in our own lives, let alone the life of a person born two centuries before us who left behind no diary or journal. Motives can be multiple, conflicting, ephemeral, and obscure, even to the people who have them. So may they have been to Walker—though it's just as possible they were crystal clear. The best response, especially in the realm of trans and queer history, is to stay open to possibility and resistant to the practical fallacy.[41] It's easy, from a twenty-first century position, to assume that Walker chose to trans gender not because of how it made her feel but what it allowed her to do: find work; escape boredom; gain independence. Just as possible, however, is the explanation that Walker felt happier, more comfortable, and more at peace when presenting as a man. When asked why he dressed as a man during his arraignment in Minneapolis, Belmont told the gathered crowd, "I cannot wear women's clothing and couldn't go naked."[42] He then proceeded to continue wearing men's clothes and to claim his identity as a man for the next twenty-two years. In the end, this is the most direct evidence of motivation that exists.

In the winter of 1872–1873, Walker was living in Springfield and working as a servant for Dwight Foster Orcutt, the second son of

Columbus Orcutt.[43] Orcutt Sr. had by this time made Walker his ward, and her relationship with the family was closer than ever.[44] She got on well with Orcutt Jr.—his family described her to a reporter a month later as "a very active and faithful servant"[45]—but she had other ambitions. One day in December she went to a Springfield clothing store, announced she needed to buy a suit for her "husband," and explained that since she was the same size as him, she might as well try on the outfit herself.[46] The ruse worked. The tailor asked no questions, and Walker left the store with her new duds.[47] After cropping her wavy hair she presented herself—now himself—as a man in public for the first time.

Walker took on the identity of Ernest Ellwood,[48] the debonair scion of a wealthy family in Worcester. He claimed to have attended a college in Boston since the fall, and to be planning for his Christmas vacation in Hampden County. He had had enough of Springfield and returned, in a move that shows his continuing connection to his real hometown, to Warren.[49] After he exhausted Warren's charms, he set off for the next-door village of Palmer, five miles downstream along the Quaboag River. On December 28, he signed the register of the American House hotel in Palmer as "E. Ellwood, Boston."[50]

Ellwood stayed in Palmer long enough to see December 1873 pass into January 1874, and to suffer through an unusually cold first week of the year.[51] But the weather came with a silver lining: ideal conditions for sleigh rides. Teenagers and unmarried young adults, including Ellwood, jumped at the chance to socialize outdoors. An editorial item in the *Palmer Journal* from January 4 painted the picture:

> This is an old-fashioned winter, and no mistake. There is plenty of snow, plenty of sleighing and an abundance of right down stinging weather. It is the harvest of the sleigh builders, and liveries, and in all the biting frost the young people find pleasure in sleighriding. The thermometers have been struggling among the zeros for a fortnight, sometimes indicating from 10 to 18 below the cipher. That will do for this latitude, and if any person desires a colder experience he had better remove within the arctic circle at once.[52]

At the center of this social scene was Ernest Ellwood, who carried on what a newspaper later described as "desperate flirtations" with multiple young women by inviting them on sleigh rides.[53] It helped that Ellwood had his own sleigh, horses, and livery, and spent his money with no concern for running out of it.[54] After two weeks, however, Palmer residents began to question him about his "girlish appearance," and he planned a more elaborate trip.

He had options. By 1874, Warren, Palmer, and Springfield were all stops on the Boston & Albany Railway.[55] Via Boston (as on the modern Amtrak line), you could reach New York, Philadelphia, Baltimore, and Washington, DC. Via Albany, you could visit Toronto and Detroit. Ellwood chose to go west, but with a different city as his goal: Chicago. Although this trip took more than twenty hours from start to finish, its route allowed him to see through a train window five states that he had never seen before. At a time when there were only ten states west of the Mississippi, this stretch was considered the heart of the Middle West.

Ellwood boarded a westbound B&A train to Albany on Wednesday, January 8, 1873. His suitcase contained only men's clothes[56]—a sign of his commitment. He had spending money, too, after pawning a trunk of his possessions for forty-five dollars.[57] After arriving in Albany he transferred to the New York Central Railway, which took him across the Mohawk River Valley. At Rochester, a woman embarked who was also headed to Chicago and struck up a conversation with Ellwood. The pair got on well—so well that they decided to stay in the same hotel once they reached the Windy City. At Buffalo they transferred to the Michigan Southern, which took them across a brief stretch of Pennsylvania and then on to Ohio, Indiana, and Illinois.

As the train was rounding the southern tip of Lake Michigan, a passenger discovered that twenty-five dollars was missing from his wallet. He reported the theft to a conductor, who walked through the cars looking for suspects. The conductor paused when he came across Ellwood and his companion, noticing Ellwood's androgynous appearance and his nervous reaction to being watched.[58] But with the train still in motion, he decided to bide his time and watch the couple to see where they went.

The Michigan Southern pulled into Chicago's Central Depot at around 7:00 in the evening on January 9. Ellwood and his companion got off and proceeded to the nearby Gault House, a "second-rate" hotel on South Water Street.[59] They were followed, secretly, by the conductor, who took note of their destination and then conferred with officers at the Harrison Street police station, who decided not to intervene until the next day.

When Ellwood woke up in his bedroom in the Gault House on the morning of January 10, he had a grand holiday ahead of him. He was at the center of not just the biggest city he had seen in his young life (Chicago in 1873 was bigger than Boston), but one of the biggest cities in the country, growing rapidly even after the Great Fire of 1871.[60] Tantalizing opportunities for entertainment, recreation, and exploration beckoned from every street corner, and he had a new friend—perhaps a romantic partner—to share them with.[61] He dressed in his finest clothes, choosing boots, a stylish hat, a blue pilot-cloth cape, and a gray muffler with colored fringe.[62] Then he went downstairs to join his companion for breakfast in the hotel's dining room.

The couple were in the middle of their meal when a policeman entered the room and approached their table. They listened, stunned, as he told them that he was taking them to the Harrison Street police headquarters under suspicion of the train theft. He laid an additional charge against Ellwood: violating Chicago's ordinance against appearing "in a dress not belonging to his or her sex."[63]

With that, Ellwood's vacation was over. What followed was his first experience with gender interrogation—a scene that became familiar in the later years of Belmont's life, but that would have struck Ellwood as frighteningly new.[64] In spite of his fears, he projected bravado, remarking, "It was a pity that a person who had been sick could not travel from one city to another without being arrested."[65]

The officer escorted the two suspects to the police station and delivered them into the custody of Police Superintendent Elmer Washburn.[66] *Chicago Post* and *Tribune* reporters in search of a story, as well as officers from around the station, gathered in the chief's office to witness the questioning. Ignoring the question of the robbery for the time being, Washburn first asked Ellwood if he were a woman. Ellwood said no, and stuck to his answer. ("She stoutly denied she was anything other than she appeared," the *Chicago Tribune* put it the next day.)[67] Washburn then threatened him with a physical examination, and under this duress he admitted to having lived as a girl in Massachusetts. His Rochester companion stressed that she hadn't known him before their chance meeting on the train, stating that she "had her suspicions about 'his' sex, but did not inquire."[68] Both of them denied involvement in the robbery.

Superintendent Washburn sized up Ellwood and decided to believe him. But he wanted him out of his hair and as far away from the state of Illinois as possible. He withdrew the accusation of theft and offered to look the other way on the cross-dressing charge—so long as Ellwood separated from his friend and returned to Massachusetts immediately. To ensure that Ellwood made it all the way home without incident, Washburn enlisted one of his officers, Detective Simonds, to escort him by train back to Springfield, and from there to his guardian in West Warren.[69] Simonds had already been planning a trip to visit relatives in Boston and would not have to go out of his way. Ellwood's companion, meanwhile, was released from police custody.

Washburn allowed Ellwood to stay at his family's home over the weekend, but on Monday morning the youth boarded an eastbound train with his detective chaperone. Through the window he watched the same Indiana and Ohio landscapes pass by that he had just seen in reverse order. Leg by leg, he and Detective Simonds undid his original journey, transferring at some point to a line leading through Pennsylvania. But they were not alone. Since Chicago, a young man had been following them at some distance behind. The whispers of other passengers suggested that rumors were already flying. When the man tried to start a conversation, Ellwood ignored him, and Simonds told him to mind his own business. All three of them got off at Pittsburgh to eat dinner at the Union Depot Hotel.[70]

When Ellwood and Simonds entered the hotel lobby, the young man was already there, waiting by the register to see how they signed their names. Perhaps to protect Ellwood, the detective inscribed the two of them as "Simonds and Son." This only stoked the stranger's curiosity, and he tried again to speak to Ellwood, both in the restaurant and after they had all reboarded the train. But by now, Simonds was fed up, and he told him pointedly that unless he left Ellwood alone, "there would be a collision, resulting in the young man's inability to travel by rail for some time."[71] He got the message and left.

What he did not do was stop gossiping. He told anyone who would listen, including the hotel clerk, his suspicions about the alleged father-son duo. The clerk passed on the story to a reporter, and so it was that the *Pittsburgh Weekly Gazette* ran the following article a few days later:

> **ELOPEMENT EXTRAORDINARY:**
> A Union Depot Adventure
>
> Simonds and Son—that signature can be found upon the register of the Union Depot Hotel. . . . The youth was handsome, his appearance as to dress comme il faut, he had hair of a beautiful auburn hue that hung in its elegant wavy ringlets covering his neck. His nose was regular, and a most superb mouth with dainty dimples in his chin, and a set of teeth like pearls, so pure and white. Suspicion was occasioned from the fact that "Pere" showed extraordinary affection for his garçon, who undoubtedly showed many symptoms of effeminacy. . . . The father, Mr. Simonds, so called, was a well-to-do merchant in that little burg, a batchelor who fell in love with the daughter of a dentist. It was love at first sight. They met in [a] Wabash avenue stage. Their eyes proclaimed the glance of cupid's unmerciful sting, cards were exchanged and the gentleman was invited to the young lady's house. For some time things went "merry as a marriage bell," and they "billed and cooed," finally becoming engaged.

The *Gazette* fantasy, in addition to showing the danger of relying on newspapers for facts about people who transed gender in the 1800s, reveals the storytelling gymnastics required to twist Ellwood and Simonds into a normative shape. In an effort to get the pair to "make sense" as a cishet couple, the writer transplanted them not just into a melodrama (inventing several plot points in the process) but onto an actual stage. In this way Ellwood's gender variance, drained of its transgression, reappears in the tamer guise of theatricality, with the French idiom hinting at something decadent and un-American at work behind it all. The pride of place given to an evaluation of Ellwood's body (clothes, hair, eyes, teeth) anticipates the objectifying descriptions of Leon Belmont published in newspapers in 1880. But as it does in those later articles, the focus on his androgynous beauty introduces a spark of homoeroticism, making the relationship between the beautiful, effeminate youth and the doting older gentleman appear pederastic as much as anything else.

Like the fabricated report in the *Gazette*, other newspaper articles documenting Ellwood's trip to Chicago reveal writers struggling to place gender variance in a context that made sense to them. They found reference points in odd places. The headline of the *Chicago Evening Post*'s "Donning Doublet and Hose" reached all the way back to Elizabethan theater (in particular, Shakespearean heroines who put on men's clothes) in order to explain Ellwood's dress.[72] The same writer also referenced "Fair Ines," the 1827 poem by Thomas Hood, saying that Ellwood "resolved to abandon home and friends, and like fair Ines, go to the West. For this purpose she donned pantaloons, and started for Chicago."[73] His counterpart at the *Chicago Daily Tribune* quoted from the Bible to explain Ellwood's decision not to lower the pitch of his voice to assist his "disguise": "The hands were the hands of Esau, but the voice was the voice of Jacob."[74] In a follow-up article, he speculated that Ellwood carried men's shirts in his suitcase "for the same reason that the Vassar College young ladies smoked poor cigars—to sustain the allusion 'that there was a man around.'"[75]

Nods to Shakespeare, the Bible, and poets like Thomas Hood were common enough in newspapers in 1873, drawing as they did from tropes familiar across social classes. But in Ellwood's case, they underscore the reporters' failure to see someone transing gender as a real person. Ellwood makes sense to them as a mythical character first, and as a stereotype (the mannish Vassar student) second. The narrowness of their imaginations, and their disinclination to come up with a real-life analogue (e.g., Dr. Mary E. Walker), point to the limited influence of newspaper exposés on the public's understanding of gender variance. Gender variance may have been visible in mainstream culture in the 1870s, but as the reaction to Ellwood shows, in the eyes of gender-normative people it remained the domain of theater, spectacle, and sensation.

Ellwood and Simonds continued their train journey to Massachusetts without further harassment. Simonds, free to spend the Chicago Police Department's money, spared no expense on food and transportation.[76] At Palmer they disembarked, and Simonds hired a carriage to take them the rest of the way to West Warren.[77] He dropped off Ellwood at a hotel, where he changed into a dress and returned to being Addie Walker.

Simonds then paid a visit to Columbus Orcutt's farm. The old man listened to the story of his ward's adventure, but he refused to accept her back into his household. "She had forfeited her claim to his care," the *Chicago Daily Tribune* declaimed on January 24, "and must now rely upon herself or others, in case her relatives were indisposed to overlook her follies."[78] Simonds relayed the news back to Walker at the hotel. But he had promised Superintendent Washburn that he would return the "lady" to her family, so return her to them he would, regardless of how they felt about it. The two of them got on yet another train—this one to Springfield, where Walker's sister Harriet lived with her husband, Dexter Smith.[79] The Smiths took in Walker, and Simonds' duty was at last discharged.[80]

Walker's experience as Ernest Ellwood exposed her to the potential consequences of transing gender in the 1870s: surveillance, arrest, detention, stalking, publicity, caricature, and the threat of an examination. This reality was a world away from vaudeville, dime novels, and even the liberationist gender message of a writer like Mary E. Walker. Addie Walker had tested the waters, and they'd been cold. She did, however, get a measure of revenge, and the last word on the story of Ellwood in Chicago.

On January 22, Walker sent a letter from South Brookfield, just outside of West Warren, to Police Superintendent Washburn in Chicago. With the utmost politeness and only a hint of snark, she thanked him for entertaining her at his home before sending her back to Massachusetts with Detective Simonds. This appeared to button things up; she was ready to stay at home. But it was a joke. Immediately after posting the letter, Walker boarded a westbound train (wearing a dress this time) and was in Chicago again by January 24.

In a baffling coincidence, the officer who had arrested Walker at the Gault House happened to be at the rail depot when she arrived. He did a double take, recognized her, and caught up with her, demanding to know her destination. She replied, unruffled, that she knew where she was going, even if he did not. Having no pretext for detaining her, he let her go. He did, however, tell a reporter at the *Chicago Tribune,* who wrote up the story with glee. He also finagled the letter away from Superintendent Washburn, allowing the paper to print Walker's parting words on its front page the following day.

> [Brookfield], Mass.
> Jan. 22, 1873
>
> Mr. Washburn—Dear Sir:
>
> I thank you very much for sending me home. The gentleman you sent with me was kind but stern. Otherwise I have no fault to find with him. I shall always remember you with pleasure, though I do think you transcended your duty. Give my compliments to * * * * and accept my thanks for the kind treatment I received from your family. I shall always entertain a high regard for Western ladies,—but, by the way, not for the reporters. I will not tire you with any more, but bid you a pleasant afternoon, though it is storming.
>
> Respectfully yours,
> [Addie L.] Walker[81]

3.

The Con Artist, 1873–1878

To-day the picture was shown to the town treasurer of Northampton, a greatly esteemed gentleman whose misfortune it was to have the girl as a boarder at his house for some time. He, too, was given no hint as to the sex of the party but he feelingly exclaimed at once: "Good heavens, what have you brought her up again for? That is Addie Walker, and she is a devil."

—"'The What Is It,'" *Minneapolis Tribune,* February 21, 1881

At 11:45 a.m. on January 26, 1876, a crowd of people gathered around the entrance to the vault of the Northampton National Bank in Northampton, Massachusetts. They had been waiting there since the early hours of the morning for a lockmaker to fix the dial on the vault's door, allowing them to open the bolts and see inside. There was reason to believe that thieves had tampered with the dial, but the onlookers doubted anyone had forced a way inside. The vault's state-of-the-art technology (a Dexter double-dial combination lock) seemed more than capable of preventing a break-in. The bank's vice president at last did the honors, swinging open the massive steel slab to reveal what no one had expected: nothing. The vault was empty, except for a few stray papers on the floor. The new safe inside the vault was also empty. Robbers had stolen a combined total of $1.6 million dollars in cash, stocks, and bonds, and fled Northampton. It was the biggest bank heist to date in American history.[1]

In the weeks after the robbery, Northampton police hurried to identify locals who might have been involved. The core members of the gang, they suspected, were from out of town, but they would have needed a local accomplice to pull off the job. By March their list of suspects included a woman named Mrs. Stanley, a boarder in the home of Town Treasurer Hiram Day who'd attracted attention for spending lavish amounts of money at Northampton stores.[2] Mrs. Stanley "seemed to have unlimited money at her disposal," a newspaper later noted, "without any well-defined source of supply."[3] She claimed to have been married in 1875 and then widowed, but no one had ever seen her husband. Her name before the marriage had been Addie Walker.

In the years since Ernest Ellwood's train escapade in 1873, Walker had continued to travel around New England. But she also moved her home base from Springfield to Northampton, twenty miles to the north. In 1874 she worked as a housekeeper in the home of David Shields of Florence, a village outside the city limits, before finding a place in the household of Hiram Day. Day made his living collecting tolls from travelers crossing the bridge over the Connecticut River that linked Northampton to Hadley.[4] When Day moved up in the world, winning an April 1875 election for town treasurer, Walker moved up with him, relocating with the family to a house on West Street.[5] In this way she managed to ride out the effects of the Panic of 1873, a yearslong international depression that particularly hurt working people.[6] But Walker also had personal hardships to bear. On February 3, 1874, her half-sister Mary died in Brookfield of morbus coxalgia (hip disease).[7] She was eight years old.[8] Another half sister, Lydia, contracted tuberculosis later that year, as did her father, Albert. Albert Walker died from the disease on November 3, and Lydia on December 7.[9]

At twenty-one, Walker had outlived both of her parents and two of her siblings. But she did not lose all connection to her blood relatives. Her older half sister Harriet, married since 1860, continued to live in Springfield with her husband, whose father co-owned the Smith and Wesson Revolver Company.[10] The couple valued their estate at $20,000 in 1870,[11] and Walker seems to have known about and benefited from that wealth. In 1872, when she handed over a cache of money ($4,450) to Columbus Orcutt for safekeeping, she explained that she had received $1,000 of the hefty sum from a senior partner at Smith and Wesson.[12] That partner was probably her brother-in-law.

What Walker did in return for the $1,000 is unclear, as is how she came by the thousands of dollars she had on hand between 1872 and 1875. Northampton police noticed her ready cash and mentioned her to state detectives, but without evidence of criminal wrongdoing, their hands were tied. Then came the bank robbery. The detectives still had no evidence, but they did have an excuse for questioning Walker: solving the unprecedentedly high-profile[13] case that remained unsolved at the end of January, and throughout February, and into March. When they failed to get anything definitive out of Walker herself, they turned to Columbus Orcutt, whose finances seemed tangled up with their suspect's.

What Orcutt told the detectives, reluctantly,[14] offered no leads on the robbery. It did, however, open up a new line of investigation: a pattern of frauds and forgeries through which Walker seemed to be taking advantage of her old guardian at best, and fleecing him at worst.

The pattern involved three major incidents. In the first, Walker had approached Orcutt in March 1875 with the news that she was about to realize several thousand dollars in a defamation suit against a Chicago lawyer.[15] The payout was a sure deal, she said, but in order to finalize it, she first had to pay her own lawyer's fee of $1,200. She asked the farmer to advance her that amount and promised to bring him a check from said lawyer, district attorney George M. Stearns, as repayment. Orcutt obliged. When he examined the signature days later, however, he noticed that it read "George E. Stearns" rather than "George M. Stearns." By the time he tracked down Walker and asked for his money back, she reported that the $1,200 was gone, stolen from her during a holdup in Brimfield.[16]

In the second incident, Walker visited Orcutt en route from Boston, where she claimed she had met with a moneylender to repay a debt. After she had given up the money owed, the man refused to give up the bond; she had knocked him on the head with a club and fled the scene. He was a Jew, she added, and allowed the antisemitism of the 1870s to fill in the rest. She now needed $300 in order to evade police, but would return soon with a check to cover both this new payment and the outstanding $12,000 from March. Again, Orcutt obliged.[17]

The third scam was the most elaborate. On October 27, Walker appeared at Orcutt's farm and announced that the man she had married only a few months earlier, a Mr. Stanley, had died, leaving her a widow.[18] But her husband's meddling mother threatened to write her out of the will, and to stop her, Walker needed $1,400 immediately. To back up this third transaction she produced a bond in the amount of $3,000 signed by James Snow of Worcester, her husband's executor. By now Orcutt was suspicious, and he remained so even when a telegram from Snow turned up promising that "the money is ready for Mrs. Stanley."[19] He got Walker to take the matter to a trusted friend of his, a judge named Allen with an office in Palmer.

At Palmer, Walker handed over the $3,000 bond from James Snow to Judge Allen. As later reported in the *Palmer Journal,* the following scene then took place.

> The bond was very neatly executed, on "Boston deposition paper," and wholly written, and signed by the drawer. It assured C. C. Orcutt that within five days after payment by him of $1400 to Mrs. Stanley[,] James Snow would deliver to him $3000. After careful examination Judge Allen found the words "in consideration for value received" had been omitted, and then pronounced the bond of doubtful value. All through the interview Addie was very much excited, and repeated from forty to sixty times, "Don't you believe it's good?" and "Can't I have the money on it now?" The judge suggested that Mr. Orcutt visit Worcester, and see if Mr. Snow was good. But Addie beckoned the old man out, and, after ten minutes, they returned, and Mr. Orcutt handed the judge the money to count for the woman, after which a memorandum obligation to Mr. Orcutt was signed by her.[20]

The mysterious ten-minute pause in which Walker convinced Orcutt to accept the bond against Judge Allen's advice is the first sign that Walker had compromising material against her old guardian, or even that he abetted her plans. At multiple points in her dealings with Orcutt, Walker convinced him to act against his instincts through a force of persuasion that was never explained, and that Orcutt himself was in no hurry to disclose. Walker having kompromat on Orcutt would explain, in part, why he submitted three times to a ruse recognizable even in 1875 as an established confidence trick.[21] The three incidents incorporate elements of a classic con: the imminent windfall; the villain in the way; the guarantee by a stranger; the mysteriously disappearing cash. Whatever his reasons, Orcutt borrowed the $1,400 Walker requested from a bank in Ware and turned it over to Walker after their meeting in Palmer with Judge Allen.[22] The $3,000 from James Snow never turned up, and Orcutt was forced to mortgage his farm to pay off the bank.[23]

~

Walker's turn to fraud looks at first like another sensational act—a mark of her uniqueness. How many of the people around her, especially women, were committing financial crimes in the early 1870s? The answer turns out to be plenty. The decade between 1865 and 1875 was the incubator of modern American fraud, providing the economic and political conditions for scandals that shook the nation's faith in its leaders.[24] It also set the stage for smaller-scale swindles that coincided with the golden age of the con. At this second level, many of the innovators of the confidence game were women.

If the 1810s and 1820s in America had been the Era of Good Feelings, then the post–Civil War years (circa 1865–1877) ushered in what has been called the Era of Good Stealings.[25] Buoyed by a thriving economy (at least until the Panic of 1873), the nation's politicians, bankers, and speculators busied themselves with the work of an industrializing state: building railroads, lending money, collecting taxes, trading stocks, and playing the gold market.[26] Each of these activities presented opportunities for fraud, and increasingly, people took them. In 1869, railroad developers Jay Gould and Jim Fisk carried out a scheme to corner the gold market with the help of Abel Corbin, a brother-in-law of President Ulysses S. Grant. When Grant caught on, he released enough US government gold to deflate its artificially high price and avert a depression. The influx of supply, however, spooked investors, and the gold market collapsed on September 24—what became known as Black Friday.[27] A congressional hearing followed that revealed the scheme's tawdry details to the public. The relatively light consequences for Gould and Fisk suggested that in the new con-or-be-conned economy, clever people could commit fraud and get away with it.

The early 1870s reinforced that perception. In 1872, the *New York Sun* broke the Crédit Mobilier scandal, showing how Union Pacific Railroad executives had overcharged the federal government for construction loans, pocketed most of the excess, and funneled the rest into bribes for regulators. Raids in 1875 revealed a scam to match Gould's: the Whiskey Ring, through which distillers had conspired with Grant appointees in the US Treasury since 1871 to secure lower taxes on goods (and kickbacks for politicians). Concurrent scandals uncovered between 1872 and 1876 implicated the US Navy, the US Post Office, the Department of War, the Department of the Interior, and the Bureau of Internal Revenue. To the public, it seemed like the entire administration was a scam.

Democrats, meanwhile, were making headlines of their own. It was the heyday of William M. Tweed, the sometime Gould crony and state senator whose control of New York City politics extended from City Hall—Tammany Hall—into elections, the courts, and public works.[28] Evidence delivered to the *New York Times* in 1871 revealed that Tweed had rigged elections, embezzled city money, and, like the Union Pacific, masterminded overcharging by contractors. The newspaper's reporting set in motion five years of trials, indictments, a jailbreak, and the convictions of Tweed and his circle. Americans followed the scandal through the *Harper's Weekly* cartoons of Thomas Nast, which dramatized Tweed's crimes in a visual language accessible to all.[29] The message was clear: the nation's biggest city was run by men unafraid to lie (or at least fib) to enrich themselves, and who valued the accumulation of wealth above all else.[30] A Gilded Age had begun, and the gilding was paid for by theft.[31]

Young people of Addie Walker's generation watched these scandals unfold as they came of age. Walker was sixteen when Congress investigated the Gold Ring, and eighteen during the first trial of Boss Tweed. The news dominated Massachusetts newspapers of all sizes, from the *Boston Globe* to the *Springfield Republican* and the *Palmer Journal.*[32] This broad coverage familiarized working-class Americans, including Walker, not just with the prevalence of fraud in the new wealth-obsessed culture,[33] but with its methods.[34] If financiers could forge documents, fudge accounts, and exploit the modern banking system, then those below them on the social ladder could, too, at a smaller scale. The information asymmetry fueling Gilded Age business invited deceit at every level.[35] When amateurs like Walker accepted that invitation, they perfected an American art form that had been in development since the 1700s: the confidence game.

Slick operators have been separating fools from their money for as long as there have been fools and money, but the con game that developed in the mid-nineteenth-century United States relied on a stranger's plea for another to trust him. William Thompson, the first person to be called a "confidence man," approached people on the streets of New York City in the 1840s and asked if they had enough confidence in his honesty to let him borrow a pocket watch. Occasionally, someone complied, and Thompson left with the watch and never returned. After his arrest in 1849, a reporter for the *New York Herald* referred to Thompson as "the confidence man," and the name stuck.[36] Con men operated schemes similar to Thompson's in other cities throughout the 1850s, and by the 1860s, after a boost from Herman Melville's 1857 novel *The Confidence-Man,* they were icons of American public life.[37] Cons became so commonplace that city guide books taught travelers how to evade them. In New York City, 10 percent of prosecuted crimes involved confidence tricks.[38] The *Palmer Journal* of Palmer, Massachusetts, a village of only a few hundred people next to West Warren, complained wearily as early as 1870 that "confidence men are things of every day. The city column of every daily paper tells us of their tricks, and informs us of the manner in which they succeed in duping the unwary."[39] The story's unidentified author went on to describe the prevalence of women con artists in New York City in particular:

> The depredations and the ingenious contrivances of the Diddlers in petticoats, are either unknown to the mass of the

> community, or their numerous wickednesses, passed over as amiable weaknesses, or trivial peccadilloes. But Broadway swarms with these harpies. . . . They commit their depredations right and left, levy black mail upon innocent people, hold terrible threats of exposure over the heads of said "rich old cocks," destroy the peace of families, and in nine hundred and ninety-nine times out of a thousand go unwhipped of justice.[40]

A 99 percent success rate: these were tempting odds. A young woman from central Massachusetts with few prospects could do worse than to try her luck. New York City was a train ride away, and rail travel offered opportunities for chatting up strangers—and then escaping before they realized the con.[41] At about the same time that Addie Walker was quitting the carding room at the Warren Cotton Mill, a woman from the neighboring village of Ludlow named Olive Dutton (active 1865–1875) was earning a reputation throughout New England as a "female confidence man."[42] Having started out cashing bad checks in Springfield, she'd moved on to selling phony book subscriptions and forging the signatures of US Treasury officials. In July of 1867 she told a stable manager in Springfield that she needed a horse to get to her sick sister, then rode to Hartford with no intention of coming back.[43] A later article reported that she pretended to be a nun who had escaped from a convent; another that she put off paying a bill of sixty-five dollars in Chicopee by promising that her (nonexistent) husband would arrive and settle it.[44]

In the mid-1870s, while Walker was serially duping Orcutt, women con artists were experimenting with the form that came to be known as a signature of modern confidence crime: the Ponzi scheme. Although the trick of paying off investors with the deposits of new ones has absorbed the name of Charles Ponzi, an Italian immigrant active in the 1910s,[45] its first documented, large-scale practitioner was the German actress Adele Spitzeder. As early as 1869, Spitzeder accepted money from lenders after promising them returns as high as 30 percent.[46] She attracted so many depositors over the next three years that she opened her own "bank," which processed millions of guilders. Behind the scenes, meanwhile, she was racing to funnel money from new customers into the accounts of old ones. Closer to Walker, a woman named Sarah Howe brought Spitzeder's methods to Massachusetts in the form of the Ladies' Deposit Company of Boston, which claimed by 1879 not just to guarantee its women investors reliably high returns, but to operate as a charitable organization. A suspicious reporter at the *Boston Daily Advertiser* investigated the group in a series of articles that led to the company's collapse, and three years in prison for Howe.[47]

The coast-to-coast publicity that flowed out of the Howe case did not deter other American women from starting confidence careers of their own before the end of the decade. Some, like Ann O'Delia Diss Debar and Cassie Chadwick, used spiritualist scams (séances, spirit painting, fortune telling) as a launching pad for financial ones.[48] Others, including Bertha Heyman and Fanny Jordan, got their start in the 1870s before moving on to new frauds and swankier locations—Heyman to New York City via Prussia and Jordan from Ohio to the court of King Ludwig II of Bavaria. Reports of their crimes made their way via wire services to Massachusetts outlets, including the *Springfield Republican* and the *Palmer Journal*.[49] And for every Chadwick, Jordan, and Diss Debar defrauding on a grand scale, there were dozens of women executing smaller frauds—particularly check and bond forgeries like Addie Walker's.[50] Between 1867 and 1874, the *Republican* ran items on thirteen different confidence women working in New York, some of whom were also active in Boston. It covered figures like Dutton and Jordan but also less conspicuous operators: Jane Effie Coolidge, a crooked detective; Anna Gibson, arrested in Rochester; Annie Kley, who posed as a wealthy matron; Jane Pratt (aka Harper), jailed for passing a bad check in Springfield; and Mary C. Miller, who conned a mother-daughter trio out of their clothes and jewels.[51]

Walker's swindling of Columbus Orcutt between 1873 and 1875 reflects, rather than deviates from, this history of confidence crime in America. It also aligns with its development by women.[52] It emerges from the historical context of the Era of Good Stealings and its sibling, the golden age of the con, in which women's participation belied the Victorian stereotype of women as inept at business, and certainly incapable of financial chiseling.[53] Walker's resolve to make money out of nothing using the technology of modern banking (checks, bonds, advances) mirrors the scheming spirit of the early Gilded Age, evident in the regional ambitions of Dutton and Howe as much as the national gambits of Tweed and Gould. When Walker channeled that spirit into her frauds with Orcutt, she demonstrated not a sensational ingenuity but an awareness of a newly flexible social reality—one that allowed her to test the limits of the norms of her time, if not to transcend them.

~

The news that Addie Walker had coaxed more than $3,000 out of Columbus Orcutt since 1873 didn't break open the bank robbery investigation. It did, however, supply a pretext for investigating Walker's activities in January 1875. The detectives jumped at it. On March 7, they went to Hiram Day's house in Northampton,[54] found Walker, and announced they were arresting her on suspicion of fraud. For Walker, it was a repeat of Ernest Ellwood's experience in Chicago: the sudden appearance of police; the request to leave; the pressure to follow, or risk uncertain consequences. Walker complied, as Ellwood had, without resistance. She allowed the police to escort her out of the house and into a carriage that was waiting to take her to Palmer, where lawyers were already planning her arraignment.

The motors of the law whirred speedily, and Walker's arraignment proceeded the next morning before Associate Justice George Robinson of the Eastern Hampden District Court.[55] Since the state of Massachusetts was pursuing the case rather than Orcutt, it proceeded to appoint a prosecutor (Charles L. Gardner)[56] and, on Walker's behalf, a defense attorney (Stephen Swift Taft).[57] Walker then entered a plea of "not guilty" to the charge of "obtaining money under false pretenses." Judge Robinson set her bail at $5,000: the rough total of the amount she stood accused of taking from Orcutt since 1873. Unable to pay, she was remanded to jail in Springfield to await trial.

Judge Robinson used the second week of March to conduct a preliminary investigation of Walker's case. Even in this early phase, before the trial had begun, observers gathered to see the accused in her first public "appearance" since the arrest. "The court-room was jammed from 9 a.m. till after 6 in the evening," a *Springfield Republican* reporter noted, to see "the local attraction for eastern Hampden [County] and the Warren people."[58] When Walker appeared she wore a veil over her head, as if she had anticipated the scrutiny.[59] She offered no testimony herself, but the judge interviewed Orcutt and his wife, Mildred. The latter offered an outsider's perspective of the alleged fraud as well as an inkling that Walker and Orcutt had been business partners as much as adversaries:

> Mrs. Orcutt was very anxious to tell the truth. Addie came to their house when she was twelve years old, and staid [*sic*] for two months; then she came at sixteen, and worked through the summer for $1.50 a week. She had never been fooled by Addie, and had always objected to being called "Mother" by her. She had once written a promissory note at her request, which the girl criticised and burned. She had signed her name to some paper once, in which Addie and the old man were interested, but couldn't tell now what it was. She saw, some two years ago, a forged note Addie brought to the house with her name and her husband's attached. Mr. Orcutt never told her much about his dealings with the girl.[60]

When Judge Robinson interviewed Orcutt, the farmer described incidents that revealed Walker's state of mind during the alleged frauds, including one moment of despair. As a *Springfield Republican* reporter told it:

> Perhaps the most striking feature was his account of a letter received from one E. E. Elwood [*sic*], asking him to come to Palmer to a Mr. Wood's and sell his horses. This Elwood proved to be Addie, in men's clothes, short hair and a delicate mustache. She had developed a scrape in Westfield and this city, and must have money, which was paid her on the street, here in Springfield. Her handing the old man a pistol and begging him to shoot her, during one of her visits to his house, was also graphically described.[61]

Walker had not, it turned out, given up transing gender after the 1873 arrest in Chicago. She had continued to assert a male identity—at least on this one documented occasion in Palmer. The decision to return to living as Ernest Ellwood even temporarily after police interrogation suggests its lasting appeal for Walker. Walker's short hair and mustache, moreover, point to a more than casual level of commitment. If the mustache was "delicate," as the reporter recorded, it may have been the result of a concerted effort by Walker to grow facial hair rather than to use a less convincing set of fake whiskers.

Once Mr. and Mrs. Orcutt had spoken, lawyer Stephen S. Taft introduced an ingenious line of argument for the defense.[62] The charge against his client was "obtaining money under false pretenses." To validate that charge, he pointed out, the court first needed to agree on what the pretenses were. Had Walker obtained money from Orcutt on the strength of the bond from James Snow? Or had she obtained it through a pledge made during their private conversation outside Judge Allen's office? Taft argued that it was the private conversation that had done it. And if that was true, the authenticity of the bond from Snow was irrelevant to the case.[63] Since Orcutt refused to divulge what had passed between him and Walker outside the office, her "pretenses" in obtaining the money were impossible to verify. The pretense of a separate payout (the money allegedly willed to Walker by her late husband) stood equally untested. No one had proved that the husband had left her a fortune, but no one had proved that he hadn't. The premise of "false pretenses" collapsed without proof of the "false" part.

Charles Gardner, for the prosecution, responded to Taft by saying that the Snow bond was indeed the crux of Walker's pretense and that the private conversation made no difference.[64] By this point, however, the inconsistencies surrounding Orcutt's dealings with Walker had multiplied, and spectators were left with "the lurking suspicion that the half had not been told."[65] Judge Robinson weighed his options and decided to send the case to the upcoming spring session of the Hampden County Superior Court in Springfield, which was overseen by a grand jury.[66]

Since the superior court's spring session didn't begin until May 17, Walker—still without $5,000 dollars to make bail—waited out the next two months in a cell of the Hampton County Jail and House of Corrections. When she emerged she appeared seriously ill and showed signs of hemorrhage of the lungs, a symptom of tuberculosis.[67] She nevertheless arrived at the courthouse on the morning of the grand jury's first meeting and sat with her lawyer to watch the proceedings.[68]

What followed repeated much of what had transpired in March. Columbus Orcutt testified, as did Mildred Orcutt.[69] The two lawyers repeated their arguments about the proper definition of Walker's "pretenses" in obtaining Orcutt's money. And as it had before, the mystery of Orcutt's true business with Walker deepened as the farmer failed to convince the jury that he was as innocent of Walker's deals as he had claimed. "The more the case is investigated," marveled the *Republican,* "the more peculiar it appears, the more theories become plausible, and the result becomes more uncertain."[70] The same writer observed in a separate report that "there is some unexplained connection between the two on which the counsel on both sides seem to be totally ignorant. Orcutt is a horny-handed granger, and his answers are excellent displays of shrewd simplicity, of which it is impossible to tell how much is feigned."[71]

The grand jury was equally puzzled. It adjourned after three days of testimony, on May 26, and attempted to hash out a verdict overnight.[72] It failed. On the following day, the jurors announced that they were deadlocked, and the case was therefore over. The court would have to try Walker again with a different jury in its next term.[73] This nondecision denied Walker the resolution she'd been promised, even if, as the *Republican* claimed, a hung jury was the best outcome she could realistically expect.[74] Whatever her reaction, Walker had plenty of time to dwell on it. The Superior Court did not meet again until December. She had to spend the next six months in jail.

~

Between 1867 and 1876, Addie Walker had led a remarkably mobile life. She had traveled across New England and the Midwest, moving between Boston and New York and Chicago at the speed of the latest railroads. She had lived in West Warren, Palmer, Florence, Springfield, and Northampton, and changed her home when it suited her. That period of freedom ended when she returned to her cell in the Hampden County Jail and House of Corrections. It was a cubicle four and a half feet wide, eight feet long, and eight feet high,[75] more closet than room, with a lock clamped on an iron slab of a door.[76] In this confined space she spent most of her daily life for the next six months. Between her reimprisonment after the first trial on May 27 and her retrial on December 11, Walker never left the jail's narrow footprint.[77]

Although no written record of Walker's experiences during this period survives, it's possible to sketch the outlines of her daily routine. She woke up every morning on a tick mattress—stuffed with straw and rarely washed—that took up most of her cell's floor space.[78] One of her few tasks was to collect the bucket she used as a chamber pot and empty it down the hallway. A visitor to the jail in 1886 described the scene:

> The prisoners march down the hall each morning to the closet with soil-buckets in hand. These are emptied into a funnel connecting directly with the sewer and though the iron doors are closed the stench is fearful; the more so as it is added to the foulness of the air that results from overcrowded sleeping apartments.[79]

Six out of seven days of the week, the schedule that followed was identical, with Walker receiving breakfast, dinner, and supper through a slot in her cell door.[80] (In 1875, the food at Springfield was bad enough to inspire complaints to the Massachusetts Board of Prison Commissioners.)[81] Between meals, prisoners convicted of crimes were required to spend ten hours out of every day making carpet slippers in the workshop behind the men's cell block.[82] For their labor, they earned three cents per day.[83] People like Walker, awaiting trial, had no obligation to work but sometimes did it to relieve their boredom, though they earned nothing.[84] If Walker opted to participate, the repetitive menial labor would have been grimly familiar—a return to her ten-hour shift at the Warren cotton mill. Only Sundays offered a change: no work and a chaplain-led worship service at 9:00 a.m.[85] Once a week, Walker had the chance to take a bath, though she had to use the dirty water of the previous bather if she failed to claim one of the two tubs first.[86]

As it had done since she was a child, Walker's gender determined many of the conditions of her life, this time in jail. It raised expectations of her good behavior, since 1870s ideals of femininity expected stricter obedience from women than from men.[87] At the same time, jail and prison administrators saw the transgressions of women prisoners as more serious than men's, and punished them more severely.[88] Gender determined even the layout of the jail itself. An 1874 renovation had created an enclosed yard ninety feet long and thirty-two feet wide in the men's ward. To the women's ward, meanwhile, it added only one outdoor space about six feet by fifteen feet and another closer to ten by four.[89] The disparity reflected the assumption that strengthening one's body was natural for men but unnecessary for women.[90]

Gender segregation also influenced Walker's experience in jail by determining the location of her cell. The windowless women's block at Springfield, particularly the lower floor, was dank and stuffy, with no relief from outside air. As early as 1848, the Boston-based Prison Discipline Society reported to the Massachusetts House of Representatives that "better accommodations for females are wanted at Springfield."[91] Their call went unanswered for the next twenty-eight years.[92] The Massachusetts Board of Prison Commissioners, the society's successor, wrote in their annual report for the year 1871 that "the cells for women are partially underground and wholly unfit, being damp and unwholesome. This is also true to a degree of the lower tier of cells for men, though these, being on the south side, are sweetened by direct sunlight."[93] The disparity was no accident. In the same report on 1871, the prison commissioners admitted that throughout the state, "as a general rule, the poorest and most unfavorable quarters are assigned to women."[94]

In one way, however, the prison's gender segregation system worked in Walker's favor: it shielded her from the overcrowding crisis developing in the men's ward.[95] On September 30, 1876, a statewide prisons census counted four women (one of them Walker) assigned to the Springfield jail, and eleven to the house of corrections. On the same day, it counted thirty-one men in the jail, and ninety in the house of corrections.[96] While thirty cells were available for women, there were only 116 for men, creating a shortage. Increasingly, the prison master sent men without cells to sleep in the hospital, where the mixing of prisoners hastened the spread of disease.[97] An outbreak of diarrhea and cholera in the summer of 1877 sickened between fifty and seventy-five people.[98] The surge in population, meanwhile, strained the prison's infrastructure:

> For the seventy-five men at work in the principal shop to-day, there is but a single closet. This is provided with plumbing and water, but has no upward ventilation, so that the odor extends into the main room. Request was left that the attention of the county commissioners be called to the insufficiency of the accommodations, and the importance of providing for an upward current of air.[99]

Walker faced a grim choice. She could spend her days alone in her damp cell, or she could agree to work, for free, in the germ-ridden and overcrowded shop.[100] If she chose the former, there was a consolation: the prison library. Springfield had maintained a collection of publications for inmates to read since at least 1848, when the prison keeper referred to "a small library, which the men have access to, daily."[101] By 1876, when Walker arrived, it had at least five hundred volumes, including magazines and books on history, biography, and travel.[102] Through them, a curious reader like Walker could temporarily escape from the monotony of life in jail, imagining places far away from her cell. She also may have kept up, here and there, with current events, as the season changed outside her cell wall from spring to summer, and from summer to fall. The tide of American history was rolling on without her. In March, on the other side of Massachusetts, Alexander Graham Bell had made the world's first telephone call. In June, as Walker was facing the prospect of another six months in jail, the first Transcontinental Express Train arrived in San Francisco after a nearly eighty-four-hour journey from New York. Wild Bill Hickok was murdered in Deadwood in August; the Younger brothers survived the Northfield bank raid in September; and Rutherford B. Hayes was elected president in November.

We can't know how much of this news reached Walker, or what she was thinking as she sat in her cell day after day, waiting for her retrial date in December. But it's possible to imagine what she heard, and even what she smelled, over those thousands of hours. The bell in the tower of St. Michael's Roman Catholic Cathedral across State Street would have tolled as she was waking in the morning, as did the bell in the Church of the Unity on her other side. At the high school next door, students tramped into their building on their way to class.[103] At 259 State Street, meanwhile, the address directly across from the women's cell block, a merchant was operating a soap factory.[104] Nineteenth-century soapmaking was a notoriously smelly business involving large amounts of lye and rendered animal fat. These two ingredients are pungent on their own; when they combine, their chemical reaction releases a powerful odor.[105] Even closer to Walker were the smells wafting up from the open sewer below the cells, into which the prisoners' latrines opened. But more symbolic of imprisonment than any of these smells and sounds were the audible reminders of the freedom to move that Walker had lost. A noisy city streetcar line ran along State Street, a few dozen feet from her cell.[106] Six blocks away, to the southwest, trains whistled down a track beside the Connecticut River as they approached the depots on either side of Main Street. Walker, who had heard these whistles before as a passenger, now heard them as a person with no hope of getting to a station.

~

In December 1876, at the twilight of the year and in the depth of winter darkness, a hope for Walker to get out of jail flared up with a weak flame. The Hampden County Superior Criminal Court, having convened for its second annual term, summoned her to appear for the retrial of her case. Walker finally stepped outside of the jail compound and onto State Street—if only to go the handful of blocks to the courthouse. Once she arrived, lawyers Gardner and Taft reprised their roles as prosecution and defense, and the proceedings seemed poised to go on much as they had in May and June. Taft, however, had an ace up his sleeve. In a move that stunned the gallery, he produced never-before-seen evidence: a note signed by Orcutt on March 18, 1873, swearing that the $5,000 the farmer was preparing to pay to his ward on that day was not his own money. It was Walker's, the note attested, gifted to her by a relative named "Uncle Alfred" via a deposit left at a bank in Ware. Orcutt was merely withdrawing said deposit for her.[107] Bewilderingly, Orcutt admitted in court that the signature was his, and that the note's claim was true. But he demurred from explaining why he had helped prosecute Walker for obtaining money from him if the money had really been hers all along. He had never mentioned that fact in his testimony.

The revelation of the note from 1873 "took the wind out of the sails of the prosecution," as the *Springfield Republican* put it.[108] Lawyer Gardner withdrew the charge against Walker. At that point, the court had no option but to release her from custody, and did so. She was free. With a bang of the judge's gavel, the width of her world expanded from a four-and-a-half-foot-wide cell to the limits of her imagination.

Newspapers did not finagle a post-release interview with Walker or speculate on her reaction to the news, though the *Palmer Journal* noted that she maintained the "modest silence" she had displayed throughout the trial. "Now if Addie would only write her autobiography," it continued, "revealing the true inwardness of certain mysterious transactions, it would sell like 'hot cakes.'"[109] The *Republican* announced, "She is now discharged, and the general conclusion will be that there was a great deal of deception on both sides, and that Addie Walker, alias Stanley, alias St. Clair, is an uncommonly smart girl, not likely to be again caught in the meshes of the law."[110]

The *Republican*'s prediction turned out to be wrong. Less than a year later Walker was again caught in the meshes of the law—though not before she tried to enmesh her former guardian first. In May 1877, having found a new home for herself in Northampton, she sued Orcutt for a whopping $10,000, claiming that he owed her that amount.[111] When the suit never went anywhere (or at least anywhere noticed by the newspapers), Walker needed a new source of money to pay for her lodging in the city's Welch End neighborhood.[112] How she managed this in the short term is unclear. Then, on November 3, police arrested her for stealing twenty-five dollars and a gold watch from a man identified only by his hometown (Turners Falls) with whom she'd spent a day out carriage riding.[113] Policemen searched Walker and found nothing, but at the man's urging the case went to trial on November 9. The accuser, however, lost his nerve, much as Orcutt had done, and he failed to appear in court on the appointed date. When he failed to appear again the next day, the court adjourned, and the judge dismissed Walker from custody.

The incident with the man from Turners Falls was a fitting coda to the Orcutt case. It echoed its peculiarities: the plea for restitution; the last-minute withdrawal; the ambiguous relationship between accuser and accused. Like Orcutt, the Turners Falls man had realized too late that proving his claim required him to tell more than he was willing to divulge. The *Hampshire Gazette* dropped the faintest of hints that Walker's business with him had been sexual, underlining the number of hours they had spent alone in her house (three) and calling his behavior "exceedingly disgraceful."[114] But in the end, the nature of their transaction remained a mystery, as did Walker's with Orcutt.

Walker closed out 1877 with little in Massachusetts to hold her there. She remained under indictment in Hampshire County.[115] She was unmarried; her birth parents and two siblings had died. Newspaper coverage of her arrests had saddled her with a reputation (deserved or not) as a con artist and a cheat. Increasingly, she planted her hopes for the future outside her birth state, and outside of New England altogether. As she had done after leaving the Warren Cotton Mill in 1867, she rejected conventional options and imagined something more for herself. She imagined herself, this time, in the West.

Part II

Leon A. Belmont

4.

The Rancher, 1878–1879

> *Report comes from the range, that a woman is doing that country in male attire. She represents herself to be the nephew of August Belmont, and the son of one of the largest cattle dealers in Texas. She is said to be a good talker.... California and Missouri have been giving their reports of females doing their States in male attire, and we are glad to see Kansas toe the mark while such things are all the go.*
>
> —[Untitled], *Kinsley Graphic,* January 25, 1879

At a jewelry shop in Paris in 1877, Baroness Charlotte de Rothschild bought a tiara. It was an aigrette—a headpiece usually worn with the plumage of the bird of the same name, but in this case hung with jewels to mimic the crest of a heron.[1] She told the *bijoutier* not to deliver the ornament to her home but to send it, by steamship, on a solo voyage across the Atlantic Ocean. It arrived in Newport, Rhode Island, via New York weeks later in time to appear as a gift at the wedding of Samuel Shaw Howland[2] to Frederica Belmont, a daughter of the New York City financier August Belmont. The Belmonts and the Rothschilds were distantly related by marriage; Baroness Charlotte's husband, Lionel, and his brothers had also employed August as their American agent in the 1830s. The two families had remained friendly in the decades that followed, especially as Belmont's fortune grew to rival his European cousins'.

By sending the aigrette, the baroness acknowledged not only her affection for August and his children, but also the weight of the

Howland–Belmont union, which brought together the biggest names in American banking, politics, and the military. The groom's best man was James Roosevelt Roosevelt; the bride's grandfather was Commodore Matthew C. Perry. General Ambrose Burnside attended, as did Mrs. John Jacob Astor III. Baroness Charlotte's gift was only one in an array of tributes: a silver bracelet from Peter Marié; silver spoons from Rebecca Howland Roosevelt; Japanese lacquer boxes from Richard Morris Hunt; and a pile of rubies, diamonds, lace, and china.[3] The publicity-savvy Belmonts telegraphed a press release to the *New York Times* and its rivals describing the ceremony, reception, music, decorations—even the total value of the gifts ($50,000) and the bride's gown ($20,000). Newspapers were happy to pass on details of "the event of the season" to their readers.[4] By September 20, people across the United States who had never set foot in Newport knew as well as actual wedding guests that the organist had played Mendelssohn's wedding march; that fronds of smilax had hung above the altar; and that the bride had worn a single orange blossom in her hair. The *New York Herald* (whose editor, James Gordon Bennett Jr., had attended in person) devoted nearly two full columns to the story.

The attention paid to Frederica Belmont's wedding shows the prominent place her family occupied in the American public's imagination in the fall of 1877. August Belmont in particular had emerged since the 1850s as a financial magician capable of conjuring millions of dollars out of junk commodities on Wall Street, profiting even in the lean years following the Panics of 1857 and 1873.[5] By 1874 he had amassed a net worth between $8 and $9 million dollars;[6] by 1882 he was as much an icon of industry as Jay Gould and Cornelius Vanderbilt.[7] But more than Gould and Vanderbilt, Belmont enjoyed a reputation as a cultural tastemaker of the Gilded Age. Once he amassed his fortune, he spent as much time collecting art, furnishing his mansion, and hosting parties as he did following the New York Stock Exchange.[8] Coming of age in Europe in the 1830s, he had absorbed the manners of the most elite families in Germany, England, and France, including the Rothschilds; in his adopted home, his savoir-vivre set him apart from even the richest Knickerbocker aesthetes. In 1867, he funded the annual thoroughbred horse race (the Belmont Stakes) that came to carry his name, and by the 1870s, his stature was secure. Americans of all classes recognized him as an arbiter of fashion and a symbol of good taste, thanks to profiles in major newspapers. In the *New York Sun* in 1877, John Collins offered this assessment:

> He taught New Yorkers how to eat, how to drink, how to dress, how to drive four-in-hands, how to furnish their houses, how to live generally according to the rules of the possibly effete, but unquestionably refined, society of the Old World. It is not exaggeration to say that on the whole of this continent there is not another house of which the appointments are as perfect as those of Mr. Belmont. He is not a mere gastronome, a collector of works of art, or a blind adept of fashion. He is an artist in his household. From the livery of his coachman to the menu of his daily breakfast and the disposition of knickknacks on the mantelpiece of a spare room of his countryhouse, everything is to him an object of sincere artistic solicitude. When he gives a party, the smallest detail of the entertainment does not escape his attention.[9]

Under the surface of this public image flashed a hint of the transgressive. Belmont's cerebral aestheticism could read as unmanly in an American context, as underlined by Collins's word "effete." Then there was his religion. Like his cousins the Rothschilds, Belmont was Jewish, from an unassimilated Sephardic family with roots in the Rhenish town of Alzey. His great-uncle had built Alzey's synagogue, and his father was its president.[10] He had attended the Philanthropin, a progressive Jewish school founded by Mayer Amschel Rothschild. Once in America he kept quiet about this background, choosing to marry his wife (the eminently Gentile Caroline Perry, daughter of the commodore) in an Episcopal ceremony and to baptize his six children.[11] But the fact of his "Jewish extraction," as one magazine put it in 1872, remained an open secret—exotic enough to spice up his image, but not so egregious that New Yorkers felt compelled to snub him.[12] Anthony Trollope noticed this tension in Belmont's persona and fictionalized him as the shady banker Augustus Melmotte in his novel *The*

August Belmont in New York, circa 1883. Photograph by William Kurtz, Getty Museum, http://www.getty.edu:art:collection:object:107GN3. Digital image courtesy of Getty's Open Content Program.

Way We Live Now (1875). In *The Age of Innocence,* which takes place in the 1870s, Edith Wharton offered a more sympathetic portrayal in the form of Julius Beaufort, the Belmont cipher who pursues Countess Ellen Olenska.[13] Both writers recognized the Belmont-esque appeal of the insider who is secretly an outsider, a character whose difference is sensed and fetishized but never entirely defined.

Between reports of his millions, his notoriety, and his daughter's wedding, August Belmont was hard to avoid in 1877. One of the people who noticed him was Addie Walker, still living in Northampton, Massachusetts, after her release from detention on suspicion of theft. Records of Walker's activities during this period do not survive, so the timeline of her annus mirabilis is unclear. But at some point during that year, whether quickly or after months of preparation, Walker used August

Belmont as an inspiration to galvanize her life: first, by committing to a long-term identity as a man, and second, by claiming a relationship to the Belmont family. Ready by now to leave behind Ernest Ellwood, Walker took a new last name; dropped her first; and masculinized her middle name, Liona, with the help of a different vowel and a single space.

Addie Liona Walker became Leon A. Belmont. Like August, Leon would be a gentleman's gentleman—an aesthete, an intellectual, a lover of horses, and a creator rather than a follower of fashion. Also like August, he would guard the secret of his difference even as he relied on it to burnish his appeal.

Leon filled in the details of his history carefully. A few years earlier he had lived through the publicized downfalls of two high-society identity frauds whose examples served as cautionary tales. In 1874, a man claiming to be a Scottish nobleman named Lord Gordon Gordon had committed suicide in Canada after investigators linked his crimes in the United States (embezzlement, grand larceny) to jewelry thefts he'd committed in London.[14] In the same year, a London jury had determined that the claimant of the baronetcy of Sir Roger Tichborne was an impostor and sentenced him to ten years in prison.[15] An 1875 case, in which police arrested Olive E. Dutton for impersonating the wife of US Army Colonel Wesley Merritt, received less international attention but attracted notice in central Massachusetts; Dutton was from Ludlow (Hampshire County), near Belmont's hometown of West Warren.[16] Perhaps with these exposures in mind, Leon aimed lower than his predecessors, presenting himself not as a direct Belmont heir, but as a child of August Belmont's brother. As a nephew of Belmont, rather than a son, he could benefit from the family connection while avoiding the risks of a more intimate claim. He could further protect himself by claiming that he had never known his father, and that his mother had died when he was a young man. If he appeared smaller and more feminine than the typical American man, he could explain that his mother came from an aristocratic English dynasty, and he had inherited her family's fine features.[17]

In sketching out this family tree for himself, Leon gambled on the probability that August Belmont had had an adult brother. He lost. August's only brother, Joseph, had died as a baby in 1821.[18] But Leon had no way of knowing this in 1878, and neither did most of the people he came across in his travels—so long as he stayed away from August's real family and acquaintances in New York.[19] In the end, leaving behind Massachusetts, New York, and all of New England was the best way to safeguard his identity. As he planned a new existence outside of his known part of the world, he was drawn not so much to a specific location as to an idea: the mythical American West.[20] Sometime in 1878 he made the most monumental decision of his life, mapping out a plan to migrate 1,600 miles away from his birth state to an imagined future home in the Great Plains.

~

As he did at other pivotal moments in his life, Belmont responded to the trends developing around him. Mainstream popular culture of the 1870s teemed with visions of a wild wonderland across the Mississippi River, and of the adventurers who dared to remake themselves by journeying there from the timid East. It was the era of the advice "Go West, young man!" with its warning that the youth who did not try his luck in the free-for-all of westward expansion was missing the chance of a lifetime. "Go West, Young Man, Go West!" provided the title for a song with sheet music published in 1872; journalist Horace Greeley adopted it as a kind of personal motto.[21] "O, deceive not yourselves thus, young men!" Greeley cried out in *Wood's Household Magazine,* also in 1872. "Fly, scatter throughout the country—go to the Great West."[22] Travel books described the attractions of the land itself: rushing rivers, scenic vistas, and megafauna like bison and elk.[23] Sensational magazines like the *Illustrated Police News* (based in Boston) chimed in by selling the West as a violent but lucrative playground for miners, hunters, cattle thieves, train robbers, and other flavors of the emerging American icon known as the desperado. It was a place where, so people said, you could as easily get shot as strike it rich. But no matter the outcome, an adventure was guaranteed. If newspapers condemned "guerillas and highwaymen" for their crimes, they also made them into antiheroes for unconventional Easterners, like Belmont, to emulate.[24]

Of all the writers advertising the West in the 1870s, dime novel authors seized on the setting with special gusto.[25] Irish novelist Mayne Reid established the trope of the brave young man adventuring west of the Mississippi in titles like *The Rifle Rangers* (1850), *The Scalp Hunters* (1851), and *The Boy Hunters* (1853). The latter was a genre-setting smash that inspired readers, including a young Theodore Roosevelt, to imagine themselves in a fantasy version of Texas that was wild but still conquerable by sufficiently butch (and white) teenagers.[26] Reid chased that success for the next twenty years with variations on *Boy Hunters'* theme, including *The Yellow Chief: A Romance of the Rocky Mountains* (1869) and *The Lone Ranche: A Tale of the Staked Plain* (1871).

In the 1870s, Horatio Alger updated his moralistic coming-of-age tales to depict New York City boys who made their fortunes in increasingly Western locales: Ohio, and then Wisconsin, and then California by way of epic journeys across the plains.[27] He entertained new readers with *Julius: or, the Street Boy Out West*; *The Western Boy; or, The Road to Success*; and *The Young Adventurer; or, Tom's Trip Across the Plains.* William T. Adams, a Massachusetts native, offered books named *Going West* and *Out West,* though his hero never made it farther west than Michigan.[28] The formula was clear: an ambitious youth must leave behind his Eastern birthplace to claim his destiny as a man in the West, however vaguely defined, and prove himself through feats of bravery.[29]

One of the biggest promoters of the mythical West in the 1870s was not a dime novelist, travel writer, or journalist but General George Armstrong Custer, whose 1874 book *My Life on the Plains, Or, Personal Experiences with Indians* described his campaigns against Native nations in Kansas, Colorado, and Indian Territory. Custer spared no details about the brutality he was directing—violence was a main attraction for readers—but he also lapsed into quasi-religious reveries inspired by the plains' natural beauty. In one passage, he evoked the Wichita Mountains as a feast for the senses in language that outdid even the most effusive travelogue:

> The air is pure and fragrant, and as exhilarating as the purest of wine; the climate entrancingly mild; the sky clear, and blue as the most beautiful sapphire, with here and there clouds of rarest loveliness, presenting to the eye the richest commingling of bright and varied colors; delightful odors are

constantly being wafted by; while the forests, filled with the mocking bird, the colibri, the humming bird, and the thrush, constantly put forth a joyful chorus, and all combine to fill the soul with visions of delight and enhance the perfection and glory of the creation.[30]

Custer referenced creation to drive home his quasi-religious point: the plains were a "new" Eden. And who wouldn't want to live in a new Eden, even if it meant moving across the country? In digressions like these, the promotional Western nonfiction of the 1870s bled into its fiction, and achieved the same result: convincing Easterners that excitement, beauty, and even revelation awaited them if they dared to migrate.

To Belmont, migration to the mythical West offered a promise beyond good fortune. It offered him a way to claim his manhood. By the 1870s, the American standard of manliness had shifted away from the enlightened gentleman-farmer of the Jeffersonian era, the heroic nation-builder of the Jacksonian period, and even the brave citizen-soldier of the Civil War.[31] The new ideal man was rough, brawny, ruthless—violent not by necessity but by nature.[32] He defined himself against others, proving his manhood by exposing (or engineering) the failure of his neighbor.[33] He was a cowboy, a rancher, a hunter, and a brawler, most at home as far away as possible from the feminizing influence of Eastern cities, with their cramped apartments, parlors, bathrooms, offices, and other domestic interiors.[34] For an Easterner to achieve the new manhood, it followed that he must migrate West (whether briefly or permanently) in a symbolic rejection of the effeminate East.

Increasingly, this is what a new generation of American men did. The destination itself was not important; in the minds of hopeful travelers, the diversity of the trans-Mississippi West collapsed into a convenient singularity. Idaho was the same as New Mexico, which was the same as California, Dakota Territory, and Kansas. All represented the mythical West, so all offered a proving ground for masculinity.[35] When Horatio Alger traveled by train from New York to the Pacific Ocean in 1877, the vistas of prairies, mountains, and valleys he saw on his journey spurred him to devote the next years of his writing life to fantasies of masculine maturation.[36] In *The Young Miner; or, Tom Nelson in California* (1879) and *Ben's Nugget* (1882), Alger's adolescent heroes use California mining camps as a setting for realizing their emerging manhood.[37] On the frontier, boys become men, extracting masculine strength from the landscape like ore and growing from teenagers into muscular adults.[38]

The current of inspiration ran in the opposite direction, too, flowing from Western fiction into real life as well as from Western life into fiction. In the early 1880s, before he established himself as a politician, Theodore Roosevelt was a junior state assemblyman from New York struggling to make a career for himself. His older peers in the Republican Party taunted him for being insufficiently masculine. He was a squirt, a weakling, "Punkin-Lily," "Jane-Dandy," and even "Oscar Wilde."[39] Speaker of the House Tom Alvord singled him out for ridicule by joking that the New York assembly had sixty and one-half members, with the half being Roosevelt.[40] A Tammany Democrat, meanwhile, humiliated him in public by calling him a mama's boy.[41] The *New York Times* dismissed him as anemic.[42] In 1883, at the age of twenty-five, he found himself at a turning point in his life—much as Belmont did in 1878 at the same age. Casting about for a way to reinvent himself, he remembered *The Boy Hunter,* the dime novel by Mayne Reid that he had loved as a boy in the 1860s. What better way to prove his manliness than to travel to the West, as the book's heroes had done, and assert his dominance over the land, wild animals, and other men? Intent on thus regendering himself, he moved to Dakota Territory, hunted bison, bought one cattle ranch and then another, and threw himself into a life of strenuous but studied masculinity.[43] The playacting worked. Roosevelt restored his lost confidence, and when he returned East the newspapers pronounced him rugged, bronzed, sturdy, and firm—a Punkin-Lily no more.[44]

A young man named Moreton Frewen arrived at an impasse similar to Roosevelt's in 1879. Frewen, who was so Eastern that he lived in England, was the fifth son of an Anglo-Irish landowner and MP. He planned to marry Clara Jerome, the rich daughter of the American millionaire (and August Belmont associate) Leonard Jerome, but she and her family had expressed doubts about his ability to support her.

To prove himself to them as a financial provider, he rejected London society, bought a cattle ranch in Wyoming, and dedicated himself to becoming a new man.[45] The transformation required displays of masculine prowess as much as business sense. He hunted, camped, rode horses, ate elk ribs, and traveled hundreds of miles on foot. He reveled in his increased strength and marveled at his fitness in letters to his brother.[46] The ranch ultimately failed, especially after the bitter winter of 1886–1887, but Frewen's quest to reinvent himself succeeded: he married Clara Jerome and found new confidence in his more masculine Western persona.[47]

Frewen's and Roosevelt's examples show that fleeing the East to forge your masculinity in the West was a cultural prompt for men living in the late 1870s and early 1880s. Belmont didn't create this prompt; he followed it. The association of western movement with masculinization was so strong that a would-be cowboy could imagine himself growing into his manhood just by moving through space. In an early chapter of *The Scalp Hunters,* Mayne Reid presents his main character experiencing a transformation while preparing to cross the Arkansas River in southern Kansas:

> The dreams of home began to die within me; and with these the illusory ideas of many a young and foolish ambition. Died away, too, dead out of my heart, the allurements of the great city, the memory of soft eyes and silken tresses, the impress of amorous emotions, foes to human happiness; all died away, as if they had never been or I had never felt them! My strength increased, both physically and intellectually. I experienced a buoyancy of spirits and a vigor of body I had never known before. I felt a pleasure in action. My blood seemed to rush warmer and swifter through my veins, and I fancied that my eyes reached to a more distant vision. I could look boldly upon the sun without quivering in my glance. . . . The prairie fever! I feel it now! Whilst I am penning these memories, my fingers twitch to grasp the reins, my knees quiver to press the sides of my noble horse, and wildly wander over the verdant billows of the prairie sea![48]

Recalling his "prairie fever" in the present, Reid's hero relives an experience that sounds like an orgasm, with twitching fingers, quivering knees, and rushing blood. In that moment in Kansas, he remembers, he rejected his feminine preoccupations (cities, emotions, romance, women), and in doing so, rejected the feminine within himself. The landscape, meanwhile, provided him with a kind of fast-acting testosterone boost that endowed him with superhuman powers of sight and strength.[49]

The fantasy of masculinization advertised in novels and lived out by real people like Frewen and Roosevelt caught the attention of those who, like Belmont, migrated from one gender to another as well as from East to West. Some of them were men assigned a female sex at birth making new lives for themselves in their chosen identities; others were women and people we might today call nonbinary, eager to explore their masculine sides.[50] For all three groups, the stakes of transitioning were higher, and the rewards more profound, than they were for men like Moreton Frewen. When Frewen's Wyoming cattle ranch failed, he returned to his life as a gentleman in England relatively unscathed. When Sam Pollard migrated from New York to Nevada in the late 1870s, his wife eventually reported his sex assigned at birth (female) to police, and his life apart from his controlling family was over.[51]

For a brief period in the late nineteenth century, however, a window of opportunity remained open to gender migrants in the American West. So many people ventured through it that in 1878, as Belmont was planning to leave Massachusetts, the *Weekly Register-Call* of Central City, Colorado, reported on a "mania for females to appear in male attire."[52] A year later, a Kansas newspaper called the *Kinsley Graphic* passed on reports of examples in Missouri and California of "females doing their states in male attire," spreading the idea that in Western states, the practice was commonplace.[53] Whether or not it was, young people of Belmont's generation brought this claim closer to the truth. Eastern-born Edward Donovan (ca. 1850–1905) arrived in Montana around 1870 and proceeded to live in his chosen gender for three decades.[54] New Yorker Joe Monahan (ca. 1850–1904) lived similarly in Idaho for more than forty years, making his living as a cattle herder.[55] Both Monahan and Donovan built on an established tradition of Western gender migration dating back to, among others, the stagecoach driver Charley Parkhurst, who came to California from the East Coast during the Gold Rush of 1848 and lived there until his death in 1879.[56]

Monahan and Donovan (and, to a certain extent, Frewen and Roosevelt)[57] were Belmont's peers in westward migration as masculine self-reinvention. The fact that Belmont had peers adds historical context to his leaving Massachusetts in 1878 and moving halfway across the United States. His decision was not sensational or unique, but culturally prompted. It was also underwritten by race. The western-looking strivers lifted up by Reid and Alger were unvaryingly white; Frewen and Roosevelt, too, were from the whitest of white Protestant families. There were practical reasons for this, since men of color could not always presume to travel safely across the United States, or trust that Western communities would embrace them when they arrived. But whiteness was also an inextricable part of the new manliness itself because of its (assumed) guarantee of superiority. However brave, enterprising, and self-reliant a man of color might be, racism insisted that he could never outdo his white neighbor. And outdoing your neighbors was, increasingly, what the new manliness was all about.

~

Once Belmont had committed himself to his Western reinvention, he had to progress from the fantasy of migration to the reality of making it happen. First, he faced the intimidating prospect of choosing a destination. The monolithic West of novels and travel guides was one thing, but it contained over a dozen states and territories. Belmont had no friends or family in them to cushion his arrival in a new home. As he considered his options, he found himself attracted to a state in the precise middle of the country: Kansas.

Kansas seemed to many Americans in 1878 like a radical experiment in personal freedom among the already "wild" republics of the trans-Mississippi West. Only a generation earlier, between 1854 and 1859, the nation had watched the region descend into violence in the ongoing conflict that came to be known as Bleeding Kansas.[58] For those five years, abolitionists had vied with slave-owning settlers from neighboring states to settle the moral (as well as economic) question of whether Kansas would allow the enslavement of African Americans.

Both sides claimed to represent the will of the majority and faced off in a series of contested elections, followed by acts of arson, assault, kidnapping, and intimidation.[59] Assailants murdered an estimated fifty-six people for political reasons.[60] The abolitionists prevailed, aided by the secession of pro-slavery state legislators at the start of the Civil War, and Kansas became a literal Free State. The outcome encouraged the idea of Kansas as a place where liberty could triumph over injustice, and the image held fast to the new state after its admission to the union. It persisted throughout the 1870s, when continued Bleeding Kansas rhetoric encouraged people from diverse backgrounds to migrate there in search of racial and sexual freedom. Some of the most well known are the Exodusters: African American Southerners who came to Kansas in two waves, first in 1874 and again in 1879.[61] Progressive white Kansans relished the symbolism of their state as a beacon of hope; some exaggerated it. Milton W. Reynolds of Parsons rhapsodized in 1879 that "Kansas from the first hour of its birth in tumult and travail of blood, in the first wild, passionate cry of freedom, sent an all-hail and welcome to the oppressed everywhere to come and make these prairies, consecrated in a baptism of fire, the 'homestead of the free.'"[62] This ideal did not always match reality. When a thousand Exodusters prepared to shelter in the city of Wyandotte (later Kansas City) in the spring of 1879, as many residents hurried to turn them away as to welcome them.[63]

Free Thinker Moses Harman, a migrant from Missouri, fared better in the same year when he arrived in the town of Valley Falls. The relatively liberal Kansas atmosphere he found there so inspired him that he started a journal for feminists, anarchists, and sex radicals eventually called *Lucifer, the Light-Bearer*.[64] Looking back on *Lucifer*'s founding five years later, Harman referenced Bleeding Kansas and its (presumed) commitment to freedom as an inspiration:

> *Pioneers and skirmishers* were needed for the outposts of the Free-thought army[;] they have cheerfully given a large portion of their time, energy and means to the task of building up, here in the Great West—here in Kansas, the historic battle ground between Freedom and Despotism—a journal whose

pages should be absolutely free and open to ALL subjects relating to human welfare, no matter how much these subjects may be under the ban of popular creeds and of ignorant and unreasoning prejudices.[65]

Kansas, more than any other Western state, seemed to Harman to offer the sexual freedom he'd been searching for. Equally eager to shake off "unreasoning prejudices" were the women migrants, some of them colleagues of Harman's, who struggled to make gender equality in Kansas a reality. Quiet victories made loud echoes. On January 14, 1876, without recorded protest, legislators in the Kansas House of Representatives chose to allow women and girls to serve as House clerks and pages, respectively.[66] Once elected, they were official members of the state legislature, listed individually in the published proceedings of the House journal.[67] A columnist at the *New York Times* got wind of the situation in 1877 and, no less aggrieved for being a year late to the story, wrote the following:

> Probably the most dissatisfied women now living are the strong-minded women of Kansas. As a rule, the strong-minded woman always is dissatisfied. She is forever scorning the things which she has, and reaching out for the rights and trousers of others. . . . Not many months ago the strong-minded women of Kansas, exasperated at the tyrannical conduct of men who refuse to perform the duties of mothers and housekeepers, and selfishly monopolize occupations from which women are debarred, determined to secure for their sex a share in the legislation of the state.[68]

As the writer's sarcastic tone shows, allowing women to work as legislative clerks or pages in the 1870s was transgressive, and threateningly so. In trying to put Kansas women in their gender-normative place, however, he also spread the news that they were working in a legislature to readers living far outside the Sunflower State. Public comments like his burnished Kansas's national reputation for progressive thinking, and for operating ahead of the social curve.[69]

Apart from the state's association with freedom, radicalism, and gender equality, there were more practical reasons for a young migrant like Belmont to consider transplanting himself from Massachusetts to Kansas. The newspapers were full of them in 1877. "Excellent land can be had anywhere from $3 to $10 per acre," announced the *Boston Globe* under the headline, "Fertile Kansas," continuing, "Any able-bodied man willing to work can have a home of his own in a short time and procure stock and tools by paying for them in labor."[70] The *Palmer Journal* joined the chorus in September with an eye-catching advertisement paid for by J. B. Watkins & Company, based in Lawrence: "The State of Kansas, with her fertile soil, healthful climate, and abundance of pure water, offers advantages to those who wish a change of location, either for health or profit. For those wishing cheap homes, we have a few good grain, stock and fruit farms at very low prices, at just a little more than raw prairie is selling for."[71] When a writer in the *Berkshire County Eagle* set out to answer the question of "Where and How to Live" for residents of Massachusetts in November, he named only one example: Kansas.[72] The journey would have its challenges, he admitted to readers. But would innovations like the railroad, the telegraph, and mail delivery not make it "easier than it was one hundred years ago"?

The timing of this rush of Kansas boosterism in a place as far afield as Massachusetts was no accident. In the late 1870s, white Americans across the country were itching to continue the momentum of Manifest Destiny set in motion by the Kansas–Nebraska Act and the Homestead Act of 1862; by government land grants to the Missouri-Kansas-Texas Railroad in 1863 and the Leavenworth, Lawrence & Galveston Railroad in 1866;[73] and by the admission, between 1858 and 1876, of six new Western states to the Union with a combined total area of more than half a million square miles.[74] Many people stood to make a profit, from Kansas-based companies (like J. B. Watkins) to the New England newspapers (such as the *Palmer Journal*) selling them advertising space. But the bonanza—the lure of millions of acres suddenly available at a cost to no one—was an illusion. The state could offer land and freedom to migrants like Belmont in the 1870s only because it had recently taken them away from Native nations. Kansas after the Civil War was a crucible not of liberty but of the theft of Native land.[75]

In 1865, the United States had shrunk the Osage Nation's reservation, created in strict perpetuity by earlier treaties, by about half (close to 900,000 acres).[76] To persuade Wahzhazhe people to accept this "Diminished Reserve," the government promised to cap the price of the new land it forced them to buy from the Cherokee Nation at fifty cents an acre. It also pledged to secure $776,931.58 in a "Civilization Fund" for both the Wahzhazhe and the Kaw.[77] In 1870, however, the United States allowed the Cherokee to charge seventy cents an acre for a new Wahzhazhe reserve in Indian Territory, breaking the first pledge.[78] It distributed the Civilization Fund, meanwhile, to Native nations other than the Wahzhazhe and Kaw, who received only $189.55 of the total amount.[79] When the Wahzhazhe pointed out the breach of contract, US agents pressured them to forget about the old agreement and make a new one instead,[80] knowing that their desperation for supplies and annuities put them in a poor position to negotiate.[81] In the resulting Drum Creek Treaty (1870), Wahzhazhe leaders reluctantly agreed to leave behind their remaining homeland—eight million acres—and move across the southern Kansas border into a smaller reserve.

If Bleeding Kansas, as Milton W. Reynolds claimed, had issued "a passionate cry of freedom" in the 1850s, in 1870 that sound transmogrified into a howl of grief. "At early dawn on the day after the treaty had been signed," the *Kansas State Record* reported, "the air was filled with the cries of the old people, especially the women, who lamented over the graves of their children, which they were about to leave forever by proceeding to a reservation."[82] Over the following five years, white Kansans made it clear that the state's offer of emancipation did not extend to everyone. It did not apply, for example, to the mixed-race Wahzhazhe people who received government permission to stay on their Kansas farms after the removal act of 1870. In 1872, settler colonists set fire to the houses of some of these Wahzhazhe families, who had recently become US citizens; they dragged Joseph Mosher and his family out of their house and beat them before turning to arson.[83] Wahzhazhe hunters who had moved to the reservation but ventured across the border to find food faced even worse violence.[84] In 1874, in an event that became known as the Medicine Lodge Massacre, settlers killed four Wahzhazhe men passing through Barber County on a hunt and stole their sixty horses.[85] The campaign of intimidation worked. By 1875 no more than a thousand Indigenous people (Wahzhazhe, Bodéwadmi, Kiikaapoa, Thâkîwaki, and Meshkwahkihaki) remained in Kansas.[86] As the state continued to attract white migrants with its "cheap" land and attention to justice in the late 1870s, few of the newcomers appreciated its human cost.[87] Kansas was free in no sense of the word.

~

Once Leon Belmont decided to move from Massachusetts to Kansas in 1878, he faced the task of figuring out how to get there. Though the journey may have been easier than it had been in previous decades (as the *Berkshire County Eagle* claimed), it still required a trek of more than 1,300 miles. Belmont left behind no written record of his trip—the rail lines, coach roads, and steamship lines he used, or his frame of mind while traveling. But one of his peers did. In September 1878, a man in Lowell, Massachusetts, quit his job at a boot factory and set out to find work in Missouri. Though he did not write down his name, this anonymous laborer (AL) kept a diary over the next three months that reveals the challenges of traveling a route similar to Belmont's, without much money, in 1878.

AL started from Lowell in a good position, having received a thirty-five-dollar payout from the boot factory after quitting.[88] He bought an express ticket (first class as far as Pittsburgh) to St. Louis on the Pennsylvania Railroad for $15.50, and a traveling bag for $.50, leaving him around nineteen dollars for the rest of the trip. He spent some of this in getting from Boston to his train's point of departure, New York, via the steamship *Bristol.* In New York he bought undershirts, drawers, a flannel shirt, and a tie (which took another $3.50 out of his savings) and then crossed over into Pennsylvania by train. He enjoyed his stop in Philadelphia, calling it "with the exceptance of Chicago the prettiest city I ever had the pleasure of seeing"—an opinion Belmont might have shared.[89] After a 2:00 a.m. transfer in Pittsburgh and a five-hour delay in Steubenville, Ohio, caused by a flood, he continued overnight through Indiana and arrived in St. Louis the following day at 1:40 p.m. The trip had taken three and a half days. It had made financial sense to move as quickly as possible, since every day spent traveling without working added uncovered expenses; dinners cost ten cents, rooms twenty-five cents, and a bath (a luxury for a working-class traveler like AL) ten more cents.

After St. Louis, AL continued west but opted to save money by walking and hopping freight trains. He found that the rewards for frugality were mud, cold, and sleepless nights:

> We started all on our travels about 10:30 A.M. The roads were very muddy and it was next to impossible to walk on them as there [were] at least 3 or 4 pound of mud stick to each shoe and one also slips back every step of 3 feet about 18 inches, making progress very slow and tiresome. Well, after walking for about 2 miles we took to the railway track, which was not quite so muddy but very hard traveling at night. We had walked between 19 and 20 miles. We then waited from 6 P.M. to 9 P.M. out in the chilly night air waiting to see if we could not get a chance to board a freight. We at last succeeded, got on a cattle car and road about 2 hours, arriving in Pacific [Missouri] about 11:50. [We] about froze to death getting off the train.[90]

Although AL's diary keeps up a positive tone, a sense of exhaustion sticks to some of his entries as he endures the same pains that Belmont might have experienced. A dog bites his traveling companion; the companion loses the revolver he's carrying for protection; mosquitoes plague them while they sleep; a switchman needs a bribe for a reduced fare. AL's mouth aches, forcing him to find a dentist in an unfamiliar town and pay for emergency tooth removal. Belmont's journey, however, involved a stressor that AL did not have to worry about: the possibility that a stranger would confront him about his gender. The episode on the train from Chicago five years earlier would have been fresh in Belmont's mind as he entered each new train carriage, gauging his safety and the potential for conflict. In such situations, changing cars and lines often might have offered an escape from hostile passengers.

AL turned back toward St. Louis after reaching Chamois, but when Belmont traveled a similar path, he continued west across Missouri.

Once he reached Kansas City, routes into the Kansas plains forked out in front of him like the branches of a tree. The Atchison, Topeka & Santa Fe Railroad stretched into Colorado, passing through a station in Dodge City along the way.[91] The Kansas Pacific Railway matched it, taking passengers into the foothills of the Rocky Mountains.[92] With these options in front of him, Belmont chose to go to the heart of the state: the Central Great Plains, home of the Great Bend Sand Prairie, and below them the Southwestern Tablelands, where the elevation rises steadily but imperceptibly as you move from east to west.[93] This was the landscape—flat and open, but with abundant grass—that had nourished migrating bison for thousands of years, and through them, Kaw and Wahzhazhe and other Indigenous people. Settler colonists seized on this area in the 1870s as ideal grazing land for cattle and established it as a leg of the Great Western Cattle Trail (which passed through Dodge) and the Chisholm Trail (which terminated in Chisholm and Abilene).[94]

Like Moreton Frewen in 1879 and Theodore Roosevelt in 1883, when Belmont arrived in his new Western home at the age of twenty-five, he imagined himself as a new icon of settler masculinity: a cattle rancher. Not a cowboy, tasked with the relentless physical labor of moving animals from place to place, but a cowboy's boss, who provided the capital and oversight for the cowboy to do so. The distinction is crucial to understanding Belmont's emerging sense of himself, or at least the way he wanted to be seen. In Kansas, Belmont would be earthy, vigorous, practical, generous with animals and their tenders, but also above them, as one might expect of the nephew of a New York millionaire like August Belmont. Like August Belmont, Frewen, and Roosevelt, Leon Belmont would be a gentleman—ready to get dirty when necessary, but a gentleman nonetheless.

To play his new role, Belmont had to look the part. Ranchers, though superior in status to cowboys, still wore the elements of the cattle-rustling outfits that were already de rigueur: brimmed hats, checked shirts, bandanas, holstered revolvers, heeled boots with spurs, and leg-protecting leather chaparajos, known north of Mexico as chaps.[95] The former proved to be important to Belmont, even when he didn't have the money for them. On January 6, 1879, he found a man in Russell County named Henry Gregory willing to sell him a bridle and two pairs of chaps (one cotton duck, one goatskin and sheepskin) for $21.00. Belmont waved away the issue of payment, telling Gregory he would return with money later. To cover for himself, he gave his name as M. L. Stanley rather than Belmont. Gregory objected, so Belmont reused a move from Addie Walker's 1874 swindling of Columbus Orcutt: he produced a check made out to him by the First National Bank of Leavenworth in the amount of $9,800. He was on his way to the bank that day to cash the check, he said, and would return to Russell County to repay Gregory for the chaps and bridle afterward. As it had done in 1874, distracting from a risky, small lie by introducing a wilder one with no consequences paid off; $21.00 was chump change to a man with $9,800 coming to him. Gregory accepted Belmont's promise, and Belmont left.[96]

When more than a week passed with no sign of Belmont, Gregory got suspicious. Then he got angry. He went to Russell County Justice of the Peace J. C. Burnett and gave a sworn statement claiming that Belmont (as Stanley) had defrauded him of the $21.00, "unlawfully and feloniously."[97] Burnett, acting quickly, issued a warrant for Belmont's arrest at 4:00 p.m.[98] He then enlisted the help of Russell County Sheriff James G. Weakley, who sent a telegram to sheriffs across Kansas warning them that Belmont was at large.[99] Belmont, meanwhile, went about his business making deals, unaware of the manhunt underway. He arranged to deliver three thousand head of cattle to a dealer on Soldier Creek—probably before the animals were his to sell.[100] On the strength of this proposition he raised six hundred dollars in Russell, ran out of investors, and went to the town of Larned in Pawnee County for more.[101] Finding no takers there, he set his sights to the northwest, on a cattle town in Ford County called Dodge.

If Belmont had moved from Massachusetts to Kansas in search of the mythical Wild West, Dodge City in January 1879 must have seemed as likely a place as any to reveal it. Wyatt Earp was back in town as assistant US marshal after chasing train robbers through Texas the previous year. Bat Masterson was one year into his tenure as Ford County sheriff and working alongside his brother James, another marshal. A cowboy had shot and killed a third Masterson brother, Ed, outside a

Dodge City saloon in 1878, and the town's reputation for lawlessness remained strong.[102] But Belmont's visit was probably peaceful. The Dodge City police docket recorded no arrests in January 1879, and the arrests made by Earp, the Mastersons, and others in the surrounding months involved nonviolent crimes.[103]

In spite of the exaggeration of local newspapers, which called Dodge "the rendezvous of all the unemployed scallawagism in seven states,"[104] the city's business was not crime but cattle.[105] Overgrazing earlier in the 1870s had wiped out local competitors (Abilene, Ellsworth, Wichita), giving Dodge a near monopoly on the Kansas cattle trade, and an advantage nationally.[106] Belmont seems to have intuited this when he chose Dodge City as a place to raise money for his cattle deal after he had exhausted Russell and Larned. Once he arrived, he introduced himself not just as August Belmont's nephew, but as "the son of one of the largest cattle dealers in Texas."[107] The *Russell Independent,* reporting on Leon a couple of weeks after the fact, claimed that he'd been "figuring conspicuously among the cow boys of Dodge."[108]

By the beginning of February, Belmont was on the road again, this time in Harper County, on the border between Indian Territory and Kansas. Contrary to the idiom, he may have wanted to get the hell back to Dodge. Having received Weakley's telegram on January 16, Harper County Sheriff Charles D. Bickford was watching for a stranger passing through his jurisdiction who fit Belmont's profile, and when one appeared, he made his move. On the pretext that he suspected Belmont had stolen a horse, Bickford arrested Belmont on February 2 and committed him to the Harper County jail in Anthony.[109] Nearly three years after Addie Walker's arrest in Northampton, Belmont was in police custody. At a subsequent hearing, however, he posted the required two hundred dollars' bail money and awaited his trial outside a cell.[110]

The case of *State vs. Leon Belmont* was decided before Justice of the Peace George A. Zacharias in Anthony on February 23, 1879. From the start, the prosecutor's case was weak. He charged Belmont with horse theft, as well as the kidnapping of a seventeen-year-old boy who'd been traveling with him.[111] The lawyer failed, however, to produce evidence or eyewitness testimony related to the horse,[112] or proof that the boy had been transported without his consent. Thus, for a while, Belmont's luck seemed to hold. The judge acquitted the accused, the court dismissed Belmont, and the aspiring cattle rancher walked out of the Harper County courthouse a free man.[113]

He was not free for long. Belmont felt the cold outside air for only a moment before he noticed someone waiting for him at the courthouse door. It was Sheriff Weakley, standing ready to execute the Russell County warrant for Belmont's other alleged crime: the theft of Henry Gregory's chaps and bridle.[114] Belmont's luck had run out.

5.

The Outlaw, 1879–1880

Alas, Poor Weakley, weakly indeed you have acted.

—"Brevities," *Russell Independent,* June 7, 1879, quoted in B. J. Alderman, "Weakley Family Black Sheep: Why James Geddes Weakley Was Disowned," *Cumberland County History*

James Geddes (J. G.) Weakley was an upstanding citizen of the city of Russell when Leon Belmont came into his life on February 23, 1879. A Civil War veteran and a survivor of the Battle of Gettysburg, Weakley had moved to Russell County from Pennsylvania to administer land sales for the Kansas Pacific Railroad in 1871, then called for his wife and children to join him a year later. After the voters of Russell County elected him to be their sheriff in 1875, he earned respect as a lawman by stabbing and capturing the horse thief Dutch Henry Borne.[1] Weakley proved so popular that Russell City residents made him their marshal in 1878, but he juggled the two offices for only a brief period before turning his attention to his original job as Russell County sheriff.[2] His approach to catching offenders was persistent. To find Belmont, for example, he had traveled to Larned and back (120 miles) on a tip, missed him, and then dashed to Anthony (150 miles).[3] After re-arresting Belmont at the Harper County Courthouse, he escorted his new prisoner back to Russell to ensure that he appeared for his court date.

At 1 p.m. on February 26, Belmont obeyed two subpoenas by testifying in Russell County Court about his alleged theft of the chaps and bridle from Henry Gregory.[4] The judge scheduled his case to be tried in the upcoming term of federal district court (April) and set bail at $200. Having paid the same sum to free himself from jail in Harper County only a few weeks earlier, Belmont was out of money, so he had no choice but to sit in Sheriff Weakley's jail, waiting for his trial.[5]

Or so it seemed.

After putting a distance of seven states between himself and his past, Belmont had fallen back into the cycle of arrests, hearings, trials, and re-arrests that had constrained his last years in Massachusetts. A cell in the "free" land of Kansas was still a cell. The jail in which he now found himself, however, had advantages compared to the one he'd known in Springfield. The sheriff's wife, Kate, cooked and served the prisoners' meals. She kept their spaces tidy and saw to their needs as an unofficial matron, even when she was pregnant.[6] As a rural jail in a city of 1,100 people, too, the Russell County lockup had nothing approaching Springfield's overcrowding problem.[7] For days at a time, or even for his entire time in jail, Belmont may have been the only prisoner in a cell.

In the relative privacy of this arrangement, Belmont started his first documented, long-term romantic relationship. It was with an unlikely person: his jailor. He and Sheriff Weakley had already spent a night together, alone, in a town called Odell, on the way from Anthony back to Russell.[8] There was nothing suggestive about this in itself; as Belmont's escort, Weakley had to keep an eye on his prisoner to make sure he didn't escape, just as Detective Simonds had done with Ernest Ellwood on the train trip from Chicago to West Warren in 1873. In 1879, however, the romance between captor and captured was real rather than imagined. The best evidence of this is a letter Weakley sent to Belmont a year and a half later, when Belmont was embroiled in a different crisis in Minneapolis (see chapter 6). Although the reporter who shared the message in a newspaper write-up at the time did not quote Weakley's words, his summary shows the lawman's feelings for Belmont:

> The writing was in a gentleman's hand, and the signature was simply, "James." The writer addressed the prisoner as "Mr. Leon Belmont" [on the] envelope, and in the letter spoke of her as a female and used many endearing terms. . . . The writer spoke also of the lonesome hours since the separation, and

> stated that he longed for the time when he could again hold her in his arms, and feel her soft, white hands in his. He also expressed the hope that he would soon be able to consummate a marriage with her, so that they could live surrounded by the comforts, if not the luxuries of life.[9]

Filtered through the newspaper article, the gender implications of Weakley's message are murky, especially since it's unclear whether the reporter was paraphrasing the letter or editorializing. Did Weakley choose to emphasize Belmont's femininity, or did the reporter invent it? Responding to an incentive to entertain his readers with a conventional romance, he may have used creative license to imagine Belmont's softness and whiteness. Did the couple's actual relationship reflect this gender dynamic, with Weakley the active admirer and Belmont his pliable wife-to-be? Or was there something more complicated going on? Addie Walker's track record of negotiating power in personal relationships suggests the latter. With Columbus Orcutt and the man who accused her of stealing his watch, Walker had consistently manipulated men's expectations to gain the upper hand. In flirtations with women in Massachusetts (and, later, Dakota Territory and Minnesota), Walker/Belmont also operated as the dominant partner, dictating the terms, dimensions, and outcome of the pursuit. As he did in many of his romances, Belmont benefited from his involvement with James Weakley, and from controlling the progression of their relationship. Weakley, meanwhile, even if he thought of Belmont as a woman, is unlikely to have seen him in any gender mode other than his chaps-wearing cattle-rancher persona. This transmasculine version of Belmont was the one Weakley fell in love with—a fact that shows the sheriff appreciated gender ambiguity, if not gender role reversal.

Weakley's infatuation with his prisoner intensified as March wore on, and by the middle of the month, he resolved to do something about it. The plan he devised changed the course of his life for the next forty years. On March 18, he withdrew a cache of money paid to him as a representative of Russell County: delinquent taxes and federal district court fines. He told his wife he was heading south to apprehend an outlaw, as was common for him, and rented a spring wagon. He packed his belongings, including plenty of guns; collected the family's Newfoundland dog; and stopped by the jail on his way out of town. Then he freed Belmont from his cell and drove off with him in the wagon.[10]

Because Weakley had announced that he was pursuing official sheriff's business, weeks passed before the residents of Russell County suspected that something was amiss. He and Belmont hurried due south, toward the state line. By March 22 they were in Sun City, and by March 23 in Medicine Lodge.[11] Being strangers in these towns, they attracted attention, and those who cared to ask heard a story that matched the one Weakley had rehearsed in Russell: he was on the way to Indian Territory to arrest a wanted criminal, assisted by a Pinkerton detective (Belmont).[12] The townspeople were relatively welcoming, and in Medicine Lodge Weakley and Belmont even chatted with members of the local Odd Fellows Society.[13] They accepted Belmont as a man—or if they didn't, they kept quiet about it. "Considerable suspicion was entertained here by some of the genuine character of these fellows," noted the Medicine Lodge newspaper after the fact, "But generally speaking the people were badly duped."[14] In the first week of April someone spotted Belmont stopping overnight in Anthony: "It is reported that 'Belmont,' the mysterious, was in town one night last week—cause of appearance, mysterious."[15] Then the sightings dried up.

Keeping a low profile in May and early June was a wise move for Belmont and Weakley. Kansas Governor John St. John was riding southwest from Topeka with an entourage of staff bound for Dodge City; a posse of patrol guards was marching north through Clark County to meet him.[16] Catching the renegade sheriff and the freed outlaw ranked high on the governor's list of priorities, dominated though it was by the pending trial of seven Ôhmésêhese (Northern Cheyenne) men accused of murder.[17] Belmont's escape from jail was a serious problem for Russell County, and by extension, for St. John, who had lost not only a prisoner awaiting trial but also a sheriff and a cache of public funds. Until the County Board of Commissioners declared Weakley's position vacant, Russell County had no leader of law enforcement, and could appoint no one to replace him. Anxiety crept into the pages of the *Russell Independent,* which regularly mentioned Weakley's disappearance without accusing him of anything in particular.[18] "No word yet from the absent SHERIFF," a writer opined on May 17, "nor any clue obtained to his whereabouts."[19] When a Harper County official joked that if Russell County wanted its sheriff, it could have him, the *Independent* responded glumly, "Yes, it wants him."[20]

Governor St. John kept Weakley and Belmont on his mind during his visit to the southwest, and on June 1, he found what seemed like a clue among some talkative cowboys. He wrote to a Russell County commissioner to share the news, promised to appoint a new sheriff, and then left it up to him to proceed:

> I do not know whether it is of any interest to you to know the present whereabouts of James Weakley. If it is however, I am inclined to the opinion that a search for him in the southern portion of Comanche County would result in finding him. I had heard of his leaving your county together with the circumstances therewith, and while in Comanche County the first of this month, I inadvertently mentioned the matter to some "cowboys" who said that they had seen Weakley, that he was down there and had a woman with him. I think they also stated he had a span of horses and spring wagon.[21]

The "woman" with him was Belmont. Kansas authorities never found Belmont and Weakley in Comanche County, or in any other county. They remained at large through the summer of 1879, enjoying their money and freedom.

The lack of extant written records covering the months that followed draws a veil over the couple's activities through the spring of 1880. In an interview given later in that year, Belmont claimed to have visited Leavenworth, Kansas, as well as Leadville and Camp Carlin (Colorado), with Weakley during this period.[22] But in the same interview he stated that he'd been born in England (Northamptonshire) and lived there until 1876, so these statements may be just as fanciful. Belmont and Weakley appear to have stayed in cattle country at least through February 1880, when the *Anthony Republican* announced that a cowboy had spotted Belmont (Weakley is not mentioned) living in the Texas panhandle.[23] The Texas trip seems to have fizzled out, and it was around this time that they met, befriended, and formed a traveling party with two young men from Boston: Frank Miller and Morris Clifford.[24] Together, they decided to seek their fortunes in a dramatic new setting: the gold mines of Dakota Territory's Black Hills.

~

For a handful of outsiders to strike it rich in the Black Hills in 1880 was a long shot indeed. Wyatt Earp, whose trail Belmont was again shadowing after visiting Dodge, had left Kansas for Deadwood in 1876, at the height of the Black Hills Gold Rush.[25] By 1880, when Belmont was eyeing Dakota Territory, opportunities for individual miners (as opposed to capital-rich companies) had narrowed. Five years of placer mining since the gold rush's start in 1874 had exhausted the easy-to-reach gold deposits in creek beds. What remained was hard rock that couldn't be panned or sluiced. It needed large-scale industrial extraction, which required equipment, mass labor, and steady investment.[26] Belmont and his friends could supply none of these things. There were other prizes in the Black Hills, however, at least in rumor and theory: silver, tin, quartz, and the money of the people filling up the new mining towns who needed goods and services. An entrepreneur could move to a town like Deadwood, Hill City, or Custer; sell food, guns, and alcohol to the miners; and turn a profit while his customers chased their own fortunes. There were less legal opportunities, too, that involved swindling rather than supplying the same people. Most alluring of all, the Black Hills offered a destination to would-be Wild Bill Hickoks and Calamity Janes (both associated with the Hills) hoping to make names for themselves in Western legend. "The rising young genius who wants to achieve fame in literature at one yellow cover, will please take the first train for the Hills," urged the *Cheyenne Daily Sun* in 1878.[27]

These were Belmont's prospects when he and his party traveled from Kansas to Dakota Territory in the spring of 1880. It was a long road as well as a hard one—270 miles by horse and foot after Cheyenne, beyond which no railroad passed on the route north.[28] Ezra B. Taylor, one of Belmont's Massachusetts neighbors, attempted the journey in 1876 and sent a letter home to his father while on the way. He wrote from Chug Springs on February 12:

> Our Worcester party arrived at Cheyenne last Sunday, after many vexatious delays (for we did not travel by the express train) and on Thurday [*sic*] noon following, we left for the Hills, and we are now 70 miles from Cheyenne. I am lame as the Old Harry, but not so bad as I have been. My big boots are not big enough, they hurt my feet, and I can not march worth a cent. Besides I have an unnatural cold, my nose is running like a mill stream, and my handkerchiefs are blacker than the Black Hills. This is a hard road to travel. Two of our boys left us yesterday morning, and another one this morning, and they are going home East.[29]

If Belmont experienced any of these hardships, he found the stamina in himself to continue. When he and his party arrived in the Hills, they set up their tents (Belmont and Weakley opted to share one) on a hill overlooking the town of Lead, about three miles southwest of Deadwood.[30] Lead was famous for the Homestake Mine, a giant operation on its way to becoming the biggest and deepest gold mine in North America, and to earning a net profit of nearly $2 million between May 1, 1878, and August 31, 1880.[31] As he had done when he'd arrived in Kansas, however, Belmont established himself among the community not as a laborer but as a middle-class gentleman—albeit one living in a tent. He dressed sharply, in the latest fashion, appearing in different suits throughout the week. He befriended the minister of the local church and his wife, squiring the latter through the streets of Lead. Unmarried young women responded enthusiastically to his flirtations and accepted him as their escort to parties and dances.[32]

As Belmont attracted attention around Lead, his new neighbors questioned his gender but declined to make it an issue. "During her residence here she was suspected by many with whom she was acquainted of being a female," wrote a Deadwood resident in a letter to the *Minneapolis Evening Journal* later in the year.[33] Why was Belmont allowed to pass? Part of the answer lies in the frontier context of Dakota Territory in the early 1880s, which allowed for a degree of gender diversity.[34] Female-assigned people who presented themselves as men, or masculine, did so for a variety of reasons that may have overlapped:

to express a personal gender preference; to pursue women as romantic partners; to travel alone without fear of predation; to pursue jobs and experiences reserved for men. All of them, no matter their motives, benefited from the fact that their choice to trans gender aligned with the progress narrative of the American West.[35] Residents of new towns like Lead saw themselves as the vanguard of a project to advance the nation. The gold they mined, the fields they plowed, the timber they felled, and the tracks they laid built up the country's wealth, propelling it into a new era of global influence. If people seen as women had to cut their hair and wear pants in order to assist this nationalist project, was it not their duty to do so? If they swaggered and spit while they did it, this, too, could be chalked up to the boldness of frontier progress.

When people like Belmont transed gender in the West, they could cover the cost of their transgression by participating, visibly and enthusiastically, in settler colonialism.[36] Belmont seems to have intuited this when he arrived in Kansas and passed himself off as a cattle rancher, eager to transform Wahzhazhe grassland into "productive" capital. There were others like him. A man named Sammy Williams made a living as a cook for ranch hands in Dakota Territory in the 1880s before continuing on to Montana. At Williams's death, in 1908, an undertaker determined that the lumberjack had been assigned a female sex at birth.[37] In 1885, a "weak-looking fellow" named Daniel Furness built a homestead in Towner County (also Dakota Territory) and defended it from claim jumpers.[38] Furness's subsequent murder led a friend to learn he'd been assigned female at birth; his killers, however, had targeted him in order to steal his property rather than to punish him for transing gender.

A more famous icon of gender variance in the Dakotas, Martha Jane Canary (Calamity Jane), made a name for herself as a Wild West icon by riding into Deadwood in 1876 dressed in a buckskin suit as part of Wild Bill Hickok's wagon train, en route from Fort Laramie.[39] She made the Black Hills her home for the next five years.[40] The newspapers that celebrated (and exaggerated) her exploits added to her reputation as a woman who explored masculinity.[41] At the same time, however, they took pains to stress her settler colonist bona fides: scouting for the US Army, accompanying expeditions into Native land,

and fighting in battles against Native people, even when the truth of these claims was dubious.[42]

As Canary's example suggests, the leading index of belonging in Dakota Territory in 1880 was not gender but settler colonist commitment.[43] The most important question was not "Are you a man or a woman?" but "Are you a settler?"[44] Gender migrants like Belmont, Williams, Furness, and Canary could answer yes, planting themselves on the side of the United States opposite Native nations. This was the stance that mattered most after the climax of a conflict in which settlers had taken the land from its original inhabitants, and by dishonest means. In 1868, Lakȟóta leaders had signed a treaty at Fort Laramie that protected the Ȟe Sápa (Black Hills) from a settler land grab.[45] The area was, and remains today, a crucial part of Lakȟóta spiritual identity, and Lakȟóta leaders were anxious to preserve the sacred land for future generations.[46] The Fort Laramie Treaty reflected this, setting aside a territory that included the Ȟe Sápa "for the absolute undisturbed use and occupation of the Indians herein named."[47] The treaty also pledged to punish settlers who squatted on Lakȟóta land—something they were already doing, amid rumors of gold in the Hills—and to consider future treaties invalid if they did not meet the approval of at least three-fourths of all adult male Lakȟóta.

Having made these promises in 1868, the US government broke each of them. Prospectors, adventurers, and settlers (Belmont's forerunners) continued to trespass on the Ȟe Sápa without consequences throughout the early 1870s. In 1874, after an expedition led by George A. Custer confirmed the presence of gold, thousands of settlers converged on the land that had been declared sacrosanct six years earlier, and government officials allowed it. The Manypenny Agreement of 1876 (ratified as the Great Sioux Agreement of 1877) further violated the Fort Laramie treaty by stripping the Ȟe Sápa out of the Lakȟóta reservation and incorporating the land into Dakota Territory.[48] Only 10 percent of adult Lakȟóta men signed it.[49]

In Lead, as in the towns across Dakota Territory, non-Native newcomers belonged when they performed their status as settler colonists, and Belmont did this with flair. When he and Weakley pitched their tent on the hill above Lead, Belmont demonstrated his entitlement to stolen Lakȟóta land. When he participated in the town's economy, depending as it did on the extraction of resources from that land, he confirmed his membership in the settler colonist class. And when he appeared in public alongside the symbols of the town's legitimacy (e.g., the minister and his wife), he assured the community that he wanted to support its emerging settler structure rather than challenge it.

Acting as a settler colonist did not override Belmont's gender variance, but it did mitigate it. Lead was only four years old in 1880, its legitimacy still in doubt and its survival uncertain. The Great Sioux Agreement of 1877 was so recent that local miners worried the authorities would nullify the claims they'd filed before that year.[50] In a town with no history, moreover, everyone is from somewhere else—an outsider. Once origin is eliminated as a common denominator, points of connection along other identity lines are far from guaranteed. In a Black Hills mining town representing diverse classes, ethnicities, races, trades, and ages, all that settlers could be sure they had in common was a belief in their entitlement to Native land. It was by cleaving to this shared trait and tolerating their differences that Lead's citizens built their communal identity.[51] The nationalist need to unify against the Lakȟóta opened up a space—albeit a small, fragile one—for tolerance of gender variance in people assigned a female sex at birth.[52]

~

During his time in Lead in that spring of 1880, Belmont continued to weave himself into the social fabric of the town. One day he met a man named Charles L. Watts, a Maine native who had worked as a teamster in California before moving to Minneapolis.[53] Now he was in Dakota Territory and, like Belmont, trying to wring money out of the Black Hills. When Belmont inquired if Watts had any books he'd be willing to lend him, the older man said he would—as soon as his wife and children arrived from Minneapolis with more of the family's belongings.[54]

A few days later, Belmont walked to a well in town to draw water for himself and noticed two women standing there. They turned out to be Charles Watts's wife, Clarinda, and their oldest daughter, Furnella Grace, known as Grace (or Nellie). They had already heard about Belmont from Charles and greeted him cordially, with Mrs. Watts mentioning that her husband had told them about their meeting. She suggested a book exchange, in which she would lend Belmont her reading material in return for the few titles he had in his tent, and they agreed to meet again.[55]

Belmont grew closer to the Watts women over the following weeks. At the same time, he began to withdraw from Weakley, who had accepted work as a laborer attached to a mining camp.[56] Weakley sensed that Belmont's feelings for him were cooling off, and when he confronted him about it, they quarreled. Weakley wanted to sell their horses to restore their shrinking pile of money; Belmont refused to let him, then threatened to reveal the sheriff's identity to the people of Lead if he persisted in his plan. When Weakley urged him to leave Lead with him, Belmont said he could not. He admitted that he had "become much attached" to Miss Watts, finding her to be "true and womanly and noble."[57] Then, the final news: Belmont was going to marry her.

After this revelation, Belmont and Weakley split up.[58] Belmont moved out of their tent and into the Watts family's house in town, where his bond with the mother and her daughter intensified. When he got sick, Mrs. Watts nursed him back to health.[59] Belmont and Miss Watts formalized their engagement and planned to marry months later in Minneapolis, after the young fiancé had established himself in the family's home city. The Watts women, it turned out, had already had enough of Dakota Territory. They intended to take a train back to the Twin Cities, and to bring Belmont with them. Mr. Watts, whose friendliness to Belmont had cooled off as the young man grew closer to his wife and daughter, made no move to stop their plans.[60]

By separating from Weakley and engaging himself to Grace Watts, Belmont had entered into his first documented long-term relationship with a woman. He had expressed romantic interest in women before, in Warren and Palmer and (potentially) on the train to Chicago. But this was his first step toward something as serious as marriage, with any partner. In the account he gave months later in a Minneapolis courtroom full of spectators, Belmont portrayed himself as a victim of fate, too polite to stop the cascading effects of what had started out as an innocent friendship. Of one romantic interest he stated, "[She] of course believed me a man, and she met me so cordially and lovingly that I continued to float along in the current I was in. I could not undeceive her."[61] This may have been true, and useful for Belmont to emphasize during the hearing. His pattern of behavior, however, shows that he was moving into a phase of his life in which he was more interested in having relationships with women than with men. Throughout 1880 and into 1881, Belmont pursued two more women on trajectories that pointed to serious interest. The third relationship ended in a wedding and a legal union that lasted for twenty years (see chapter 7). While it's believable that Belmont drifted passively into his first engagement, his subsequent relationships throughout the year make more sense as strategic pursuits than they do as serial accidents. By that point, if Belmont was floating along in a current, it was one he had powered himself.

At around the same time Belmont and Grace Watts announced their engagement, Grace received good news in a letter from Minneapolis: the principal of the Marcy School in that city had offered her a position as a teacher and was summoning her to work. To seize the opportunity she went quickly, leaving her mother and Belmont behind in Lead with the understanding that they'd follow her afterward.[62] And follow they did—once Belmont put together enough money for a train ticket. For this, he returned to Weakley and appealed to what was left of the goodwill between them. He prevailed, and Weakley magnanimously raised $480 (eighty dollars of which had to be lent by Mr. Watts) to send him on his way.[63]

With money in hand and a fiancée waiting for him in Minneapolis, Belmont seemed ready to retire his cattle rancher/outlaw persona for something more domestic. It was now May 1880, and he had been away from the East Coast for two years. Minnesota was undeniably Western compared to Massachusetts, but it offered a milder flavor of frontier culture than he had tasted in Kansas and Dakota Territory. Perhaps in the crowds of Minneapolis he could continue to express his masculinity while escaping the attention he'd sometimes attracted in his other homes.

This turned out not to be the case. As Belmont rode with Mrs. Watts aboard an eastbound train out of the Black Hills, he was speeding into an episode of his life that would expose him to more public scrutiny than he had experienced in Springfield, Northampton, and

Chicago. The shape of things to come revealed itself before Belmont had even left the train. He had dressed up for the ride, adding this time the flourish of a gold watch and chain, and was chatting with Mrs. Watts about the upcoming wedding. He called her "Mother." Then, while the train was between Bismarck and Fargo, a group of men—an increase over the one individual who had confronted him on the way to Chicago—made comments loud enough for Belmont, Mrs. Watts, and the other passengers to hear.[64]

Belmont was not a man, they insisted. And they would not stop talking about it.

6.

The Celebrity, 1880–1881

"I just wish the public would let me alone. I have stood about all I am going to stand."

—Leon A. Belmont, quoted in "The Belmont Mystery," *Minneapolis Tribune,* November 12, 1880

On a Friday evening in November 1880, a newspaper reporter called at a house at the intersection of Sixth Street and Second Avenue North in Minneapolis. The young man who opened the front door carried a candle that flickered in the chilly air, illuminating his overcoat and the slouch hat perched on his head. When the reporter asked about his recent detention by police, the man demurred, saying he was a private citizen under no obligation to talk to "nasty people who have no right to bother me, and I won't be bothered, so there." The reporter refused to leave. He demanded to hear the details of the man's release, leading to this exchange (as reported in the *Minneapolis Tribune*):

Reporter: Why did Judge Cooley discharge you?

Man: Because he had a right to. He said that I was foolish to plead guilty to the charge of being a woman, when I was first brought up for trial.

Reporter: But didn't Doctor Putnam swear you were a woman?

Man: He took my statement for it. He merely hammered on my chest and said I had a boy's chest. . . .

Reporter: I infer from that that you are one of those beings who have a right to wear the clothing of either sex?

Man: There you are wrong, and I want you to know that I have a right to be in this town; I have a right to wear what clothing I want to, and I am going to exercise that right. I am not going to say anything to hurt anybody, and if Miss Brackett wouldn't prefer charges against me, I am not going to say anything against her. I have friends in this town who will take care of me. I have been trouble enough to them already, and as I am free from the law it's nobody's business.[1]

The reporter, convinced that his source would say no more, retreated into the dark to write up his scoop. He had achieved no small feat: a face-to-face interview with the most gossiped about, speculated on, and sought-after personality in Minneapolis. The text appeared in the next day's paper under a splashy headline that announced the young man's intention to stay in the city and wear men's clothing to his heart's content.

The young man was Leon Belmont.

The interview had unfolded at the height of the Belmont sensation—a multiweek media frenzy in which the *Minneapolis Tribune* and its local competitors (the *Evening Journal* in Minneapolis and the *Pioneer Press* and *Daily Globe* in St. Paul) raced to outdo each other with coverage of the adventurer from out of town. Between October 30 and November 25, the papers published more than sixty items on Belmont, some of them thousands of words long. In them, reporters wrestled with how to respond to a person they assumed to be a woman seducing other women and dressing in clothes they associated with men. Their conclusions shifted as the sensation went on, with some writers celebrating Belmont as seductive and others condemning him for his claim to "masculine privilege." On October 30, the *Minneapolis Tribune* highlighted him as a "curious and romantic sensation," pointing to two responses to the case: curiosity, which sometimes curdled into revulsion; and romantic attraction, bordering on desire. Rather

Leon A. Belmont.

(Se stycket "En Minneapolis-sensation" i Minneapolisafdelningen.)

Leon Belmont, 1880. From *Minnesota Stats Tidning,* November 4, 1880, 3.

than cancel each other out, these feelings reinforced each other and created the kind of modern celebrity only recently encouraged by the rise of wire services.[2]

For Belmont, the transition from Black Hills grifter to Twin Cities heartthrob had been abrupt. Having survived his run-in with hecklers on the train, who eventually left him alone, he had arrived safely at the depot in downtown Minneapolis with Clarinda Watts. When he stepped onto the station platform, he found himself in a dense urban landscape a world away from Lead, Russell City, and even Springfield in the mid-1870s.[3] Minneapolis in 1880 was, like Nelson Algren's Chicago, a city on the make. Eight years earlier, in 1872, it had annexed St. Anthony—a windfall that brought with it some 5,000 citizens. It had also won the prize of St. Anthony Falls, and with it the lucrative water-powered milling industries that it supported. In 1880, the baby metropolis had more than 46,000 citizens. The Minneapolis Street Railway, which offered streetcar service throughout downtown, was in its fifth year of operation; James J. Hill's new St. Paul, Minneapolis and Manitoba Railway whisked away Twin Cities residents to points north and west and back again in a matter of days. Architect LeRoy Buffington was building a massive flour mill for Charles Pillsbury at 116 Third Avenue Southeast that stood half completed along the Mississippi River.[4]

On that May day at the depot, Grace was waiting to greet her mother and fiancé and welcome them into the Watts house, which she had prepared for their arrival.[5] The family owned two properties. One stood at 1234 Chestnut Avenue, at the edge of downtown, three blocks northeast of Hennepin Avenue. The other was at 610 Fifth Avenue South, closer to the city's core, and Belmont moved into this building.[6] A US census taker visited the household by the end of the month and noted six inhabitants: Belmont; Clarinda Watts; Grace Watts; her siblings, Edgar (thirteen) and Carrie (ten); and Sarah Brackett, a family friend who had been Belmont's pen pal in Lead.

Belmont spent the summer exploring his new home and availing himself of its amenities. His location set him up within walking distance (or a streetcar ride) of all that Minneapolis had to offer, from theaters and bookshops to shopping arcades and stables. He acquired suits of fashionable clothes and entered society as an apparent gentleman of means, attending plays, lectures, and services at an Episcopal church. At the recommendation of an acquaintance of Mrs. Watts, he found a respectable position as a kind of student assistant in the office of Dr. Calvin Goodrich—a role that allowed him to learn on the job and achieve some degree of medical competency.[7]

Even after the train incident en route to Minneapolis, Belmont asserted himself in public space. In Minneapolis, as in Kansas and Dakota Territory, fear of "discovery" did not hold him back. During one summer excursion to Lake Minnetonka, for example, he befriended a young man and agreed to share a bed with him overnight. He kept on his long underwear while sleeping, he said, to protect against mosquitoes. Later, when the youth invited him to go swimming in the nude, Belmont agreed enthusiastically and took off with him to the beach, only to feel a chill coming on at the last moment and demur.[8] In June, he indulged his love of horses by buying a team at Smith Brothers on short-term credit. The price tag was $300. After returning home, in an echo of one of Addie Walker's cons on Columbus Orcutt, he announced that he had been robbed of exactly that amount. When police came to 610 Fifth Avenue to investigate, they accused Belmont of both fraud and stealing money from Sarah Brackett, who had also reported a robbery that day. They suggested he was "a woman in disguise." Brackett, Clarinda Watts, and her daughter dismissed the idea as ridiculous, proclaimed their faith in Belmont's character, and pushed the police out the door.[9] For the time being, the officers left him alone.

At the same time Belmont was going about his summer adventures, his interest in Grace Watts was cooling off. Whether this was the natural end of a genuine attachment or the conclusion of a ploy to trick the Watts women into boarding him is impossible to know. Increasingly, he spent his time with Sarah Brackett, Grace's twenty-three-year-old friend, fellow schoolteacher, and housemate, as well as Belmont's. Between June and August, Belmont courted Sarah, even as he continued to refer to Grace as his fiancée. It became easier for the new couple to see each other away from Watts family eyes once Brackett moved out of the Fifth Avenue house and into rooms half a mile away, at 721 Hennepin Avenue.[10] As a token of his love, Belmont gave Sarah a piano he claimed to have bought with money from his rich New York uncle. It later turned out to be a rental.[11]

As summer turned into fall, the two-timing with Sarah became impossible for Grace Watts to ignore, and by the middle of September she had ended her and Belmont's engagement.[12] But in a testament to Belmont's inexhaustible goodwill with the Watts family, neither Mrs. Watts nor her daughter kicked him out of the Fifth Avenue house, and he continued to board there rent free. He might have stayed on indefinitely if he hadn't dragged his feet in repaying Sarah fifty dollars she had lent him. On October 29, she and Miranda Wardwell (the principal of the Jefferson School, and Brackett's boss) reported him to Minneapolis Police Chief Albert S. Munger. Brackett claimed that her lover had finagled the money from her under false pretenses—that is, by presenting himself to her as a man. An 1867 city ordinance had outlawed cross-dressing in Minneapolis, making it possible for Belmont to be charged with a crime.[13] Munger therefore went promptly to the Fifth Avenue house and arrested him. He then called in local doctor Charles W. Putnam, who carried out an examination and concluded that Brackett's debtor was a woman.[14]

Local newspapers got wind of the situation, and the Belmont sensation exploded on October 30, 1880. The *Minneapolis Tribune* broke a story titled "In Disguise" with the subheadings "Woman Who Lived in Male Attire for a Year and a Half" and "Exercis[ed] the Masculine Prerogative of Making Love to Two Women at Once." On the same morning, the *St. Paul Pioneer Press* published "A Woman in Pantaloons Who Makes Love and Pilfers with Masculine Coolness and Success." The backstory Belmont fed to reporters matched the one he'd given the Watts family back in Lead City: birth in Tennessee, aristocratic English relations, a millionaire American uncle, two dead parents, a spa treatment in Germany, a sojourn in Kansas—only in this version he had a humped back removed via surgery. His mother's fortune was as good as his so long as he claimed it after his twenty-first birthday, which he said was just around the corner, in June 1881.[15]

The *Minneapolis Tribune,* the *Minneapolis Journal,* and the *St. Paul Pioneer Press* had got the jump on the Belmont saga, and the *St. Paul Daily Globe* scrambled to catch up. All four papers sent reporters to cover Belmont's arraignment in municipal court on October 31, but the *Globe* spared no detail:

> At 9 o'clock the news had spread far and wide, and the courthouse was crowded to its utmost capacity to see this distinguished individual. She came in shortly after 10. She removed her felt hat and ran her hands through her curly hair as if she were as high toned as any other society gentleman. She was dressed in a dark business suit, heavy overcoat, and boots, with a slouch hat just removed from her blonde curly head, on which the hair waved very prettily and was nicely parted on one side. . . . The masculine make-up was perfect, even to the gold button and necktie. Seated in the court room the woman evinced not a particle of distress or fear, and unless informed

> to the contrary, a person would naturally have taken her for a disinterested spectator.[16]

During the interrogation that followed, Belmont "confessed." Sort of. Confined by the language of the city ordinance, which outlined the crime of wearing "dress not belonging to his or her sex," Judge DeWitt Clinton Cooley did not ask Belmont if he was a woman. Instead, he asked if the charge was true, and Belmont replied, "It is." Cooley then ordered him to pay a fifty-dollar fine or serve a sixty-day sentence in jail. When Belmont refused to pay, police brought him to the house of Sheriff Nathaniel R. Thompson rather than to a cell.

~

Over the course of the next week, Belmont emerged as a bona fide celebrity. Local photographer Alonzo H. Beal took a picture of him during the arraignment and displayed it to the public at his Minneapolis gallery on Fourth Avenue. The *Minneapolis Tribune* got hold of an engraving of the same image and published it on November 1. Yet another version, hung in the window of a bookstore, attracted crowds of people. Belmont, for his part, avoided speaking to the press but received fans and supporters in Sheriff Thompson's parlor. One particularly dedicated group raised money to pay his fifty-dollar fine and release him from custody.[17]

Portrayals of Belmont in these early days of the sensation were positive. The *St. Paul Daily Globe*'s October 31 article took an approving stance, calling him "distinguished," "high toned," "a gentleman," and "perfect," worthy of the admiration of men and women alike. The *Minneapolis Tribune*'s concurrent article, even while calling Belmont a "monstrosity" and speculating that he was a prostitute or a criminal, admitted that he "speaks with fluency, uses excellent language, and is to all appearances a remarkably shrewd individual."[18] In a later feature it went further, promoting him as a sensitive aesthete:

> Belmont evidently had a winning way that completely captivated the hearts of the women. She was a person of considerable refinement of tastes and of a good deal of artistic

> appreciation. She would see beauties in a poem or a picture that others would pass by, and had the faculty of pointing them out so that others might enjoy them.[19]

What person of either sex, the *Tribune* seemed to ask, could resist? And what reader could fail to buy the next day's paper to keep up with the story?

Unfortunately for the *Minneapolis Tribune,* as Belmont remained in custody throughout the week of November 1, new details were hard to come by. "She still lingers in durance vile," the newspaper informed readers on Tuesday, using the language of a melodramatic poem and casting Belmont as its hero(ine) in peril. On Wednesday, the paper merely stated that it had nothing new to report.[20]

On Thursday, the *St. Paul Daily Globe* stepped in to fill the lull with a dramatic revision of its stance on Belmont in particular, and the sensation in general. Under the subhead "Some people look upon her as a goddess," an unnamed reporter set out to put an end to the hero worship, lambasting his colleagues for creating "a superior individual, a person of dramatic interest, out of a mass of shame and disgrace." This writer saw Belmont not as an idol but as an "abominable character," a "hypocritical and detestable being," a "traitor to womanhood," and "a creature to be looked on with contempt."[21] The impassioned editorial, a kind of anti-Belmont manifesto, spilled over into the next day's paper:

> Enough has been made known to establish Belmont as the most despicable creature that ever breathed the air of Minnesota. The lowest woman of the street is respectable by the side of this mass of abomination. The ladies who have chatted and almost sympathized with this creature, enjoying the best apartment in Sheriff Thompson's mansion, will, after thinking the matter over, feel proud of their performances. The woman who shows to the world her true character, be it ever so bad, is a princess by the side of this Belmont, who has betrayed her womanhood and misled two as respectable young ladies as

> there are in the community, in the most delicate of all matters, which is nothing more nor less than love.[22]

It's tempting to read this passage as a reaction to Belmont's perceived sexual deviance. The word "abomination" did imply religious condemnation of same-sex activity in the 1880s, as it does today.[23] But the main objection is rooted elsewhere. The *St. Paul Daily Globe* writer criticized Belmont not for being a woman who had seduced other women but for being a liar who had misled the community that welcomed him. In other words, his crime was not same-sex desire but perceived dishonesty. The writer did not seem to have considered that Belmont might have pursued Watts and Brackett out of genuine sexual attraction, or even that such an attraction was possible. Instead, the writer implied, the motive must have been financial. Belmont had "betrayed . . . womanhood" through gender variance, but here again the implied fault was not so much cross-dressing itself as it was the perceived deception that it creates.[24] Belmont, the writer suggested, had broken the social contract that requires members of a community to represent themselves accurately to one another. By pursuing Watts and Brackett, he misrepresented himself as a legitimate romantic prospect, causing them to invest in a courtship that could never lead to marriage. In other words, he wasted their time, and it was this abomination of trust—not an abomination of nature—that the *Globe* writer deemed a "tragedy."

Belmont remained in custody at Sheriff Thompson's house until November 11, when Judge Cooley summoned him to appear in Hennepin County Municipal Court. The *Minneapolis Tribune* had predicted on the previous day that Belmont would pay his fifty-dollar fine for cross-dressing and then face immediate re-arrest for obtaining money under false pretenses from Sarah Brackett. The actual outcome surprised everyone, probably including Belmont. He did pay his fine, but after consulting privately with Brackett, Minneapolis City Attorney Reuben C. Benton withdrew the new charge. There was nothing more for Judge Cooley to do than release Belmont on the condition that he wear "appropriate" clothing in the future.[25]

With that, the heartthrob was free. The *Minneapolis Tribune* responded with three concurrent items, including a gossip column that mentioned the case four times. "It is again at large," the paper announced, before asking, "Is it a hero or a heroine?" It was at this moment that Belmont's star appeal reached its apex, elevated by *Tribune* comments like "Belmont will now receive innumerable epistles from romantic swains" and "Eligible young men or young ladies desiring to become engaged may apply to Leon A. Belmont." Even the *St. Paul Daily Globe* returned to the Belmont beat with a relatively positive tone, reporting, "Belmont is free at last."[26]

It's unclear where Belmont lived immediately after his release. On the evening of November 11, he was at the Watts family's Fifth Avenue house, where the *Minneapolis Tribune* reporter found him and conducted the candlelit interview. He insisted not just that he would stay in Minneapolis and continue to wear men's clothes, but that he had the right to do both. At the same time, he pleaded for privacy and vowed to stop talking to the press:

> I just wish the public would let me alone. I have stood about all I am going to stand. There is no use in you or any other reporter asking me any questions, because I won't answer one. I am not going to say a word to anybody again.[27]

Belmont kept his promise. For the remainder of his time in Minnesota—which was far from over—he granted no interviews and issued no public comments.

~

The so-called Belmont sensation arrived in Minneapolis at a transitional moment in the history of sex and gender in the United States.[28] American laypeople had not yet, in 1880, come to think of sex and gender variance as a kind of disease, as they would over the following three decades. Nor did they see it as evidence of a fixed identity. During the first two weeks of their coverage, none of the Twin Cities newspapers labeled Belmont as a "kind" of person (e.g., a lesbian or an invert), whether for his relationships with women or for his presentation of himself as a man. Concepts of sexual orientation and gender identity as we know them today did not exist in the Minneapolis of 1880, or in any other US city of the period. Modern sexology—the scientific study of human sexual behavior—was only beginning to gather steam as a legitimate field, primarily among doctors in Europe. As a result, "homosexual," "lesbian," and "transgender" (as well as "heterosexual" and "cisgender") were not categories that reporters would have used to understand Belmont, or that Belmont would have used to understand himself.[29]

The Twin Cities media attempted to label Belmont as someone outside the norms of sex or gender only once, and not until November 13. On that day, the *Minneapolis Tribune* floated the possibility that he was a "hermaphrodite."[30] This identity category, unlike those named above, was well established in 1880.[31] Although "hermaphrodite" overlaps with the twenty-first-century definition of intersex, nineteenth-century doctors (lacking the technology to detect chromosomes or measure hormones) labeled people hermaphrodites when they failed to read as unambiguously male or female during physical examinations.[32] Laypeople, meanwhile, used the word less precisely to describe a range of androgynous traits, and for this reason people labeled as hermaphrodites have been legible in American culture since colonization. Indigenous American cultures recognized, and in many cases honored, gender variance long before then.[33] In the early nineteenth century, however, Americans of European heritage shifted from thinking that hermaphrodites were monsters worthy of disgust to believing that they were impostors in need of unmasking.[34] The Belmont sensation played out in a transitional period, after the impostor concept had taken hold but before gender ambiguity became tied to the new "disease" of homosexuality. The newspapers' treatment of Belmont reflects this in-between state. With the important exception of the November 13 article in the *Minneapolis Tribune,* the press focused on exposing Belmont as a liar, not on classifying him as a hermaphrodite or a homosexual. To the question "What is it?" most reporters accepted only two possible answers: a man, or a woman pretending to be a man. The likelihood of fraud, not of sexual deviance, was the axis around which the Belmont drama turned.

In these social, legal, and sexual contexts Minneapolis was not unique among American cities in 1880. Nor was the Belmont sensation an isolated case. Newspapers across the United States ran exposés on gender-variant people throughout the late nineteenth century, showing not just that there was a widespread appetite for such stories, but also that gender variance itself was relatively common. The *Minneapolis Tribune* and *St. Paul Daily Globe* reported on four such local cases in addition to Belmont's in the 1880s alone—two of them related to white people and two of them to Black people.[35] But the individuals who attracted the most and longest-lasting coverage were usually, like Belmont, white.[36] More than any other trait, Belmont's race dictated the packaging of his story, leading reporters to celebrate (to an extent) his performance of white masculinity. His whiteness shielded him from the abuse that might have followed a person of color in his situation and relegated him to a single paragraph—a one-off curiosity rather than a heroic individual. It also softened his treatment by police, giving him the special treatment (custody in a private home rather than a jail) he was perceived to deserve as someone who was "really" a white woman.

While sexual orientation and gender identity were works in progress in 1880, the infrastructure of modern celebrity, as of racial hierarchy, was well developed.[37] A national and even transatlantic star-making system was already humming, powered by technology like the telegraph, the railroad, and the mass-circulation press. Before the early nineteenth century, in classical Rome and Renaissance Italy and Enlightenment France, for example, society had bestowed renown on "great" men (and they were usually men).[38] These figures had deserved fame because of their accomplishments: high office, victory in war, scientific discovery, feats of speed and strength and innovation. The Romantic Era broke that mold, lifting up rebellious artist types, like Lord Byron, who earned fame for their panache, eccentricity, and nonconformity as much as for their deeds in art or politics.[39] A new celebrity system thus emerged that rewarded sexy outsiders who defied the status quo with hero worship as well as condemnation. Being famous increasingly meant being different, and insisting on that difference publicly, with shamelessness and flair, began to pay off as a self-promotional strategy as the nineteenth century went on.[40]

Indifference to norms, blatant defiance, matchless audacity—these were the pillars of the Belmont persona erected by his chroniclers at the *Globe*, the *Journal*, and the *Tribune*. It makes sense that reporters would seize on these qualities.[41] In deciding whom to cover, they looked to the recent moneymakers, and to the celebrity types of the times: the showman (e.g., P. T. Barnum), the diva (e.g., Sarah Bernhardt), and the dandy (e.g., James McNeill Whistler).[42] The *Minneapolis Tribune* promoted Belmont as a Barnum-Bernhardt-Whistler hybrid, highlighting his deceptions, his theatricality, and his aestheticism at different moments in the sensation. In doing so it manufactured a celebrity triple threat uniquely positioned to fascinate readers and whip up a sensation with weeks-long staying power—and sales.

Staying power for newspaper sales and staying power for Belmont were two different things. The shamelessness that made him a star also threatened his safety in Minneapolis, and even after his release from police detention, it was unclear to what extent the city would tolerate him if he continued to dress in men's clothes. No one following the story at the time predicted the turn of events that was to give him, for a moment, the upper hand.

~

After the police released Belmont from custody on November 11, rumors flew that some unnamed but authoritative person behind the scenes had decided that Belmont had been a man all along. On November 12, the *St. Paul Daily Globe* announced that a second medical investigation had taken place, this one observed by "a distinguished benevolent lady." Said lady and the examining doctor, the *Globe* reported, had verified Belmont's male sex. Not to be outdone, a *Minneapolis Tribune* reporter rushed "to discover some one who was ready to declare that Belmont has the right to wear male attire," but his efforts failed. He did identify the *Globe*'s distinguished lady as sixty-one-year-old society matron Charlotte Van Cleve, and claim that her testimony had swayed Judge Cooley to release Belmont.

Charlotte Ouisconsin Clark Van Cleve was an unlikely second-act character in the Belmont drama. A widow well known as one of the first settler colonists in Minnesota (she'd been born west of the Mississippi in 1819), Van Cleve was by 1880 a pillar of Twin Cities society.[43]

Her father, Lieutenant Nathan Clark, had served at Fort Snelling; her husband, Lieutenant Horatio P. Van Cleve, had fought in the Civil War with the Second Minnesota Volunteer Infantry. She further enhanced her reputation in 1879 by incorporating Bethany Home for unwed mothers in Minneapolis. Van Cleve's involvement in the Belmont case probably arose out of her interest in helping women who, in the eyes of the community, had "fallen." As a presumed single woman, Belmont was endangering himself and his virtue by leading a scandalous public life without the protection of a male relative. Van Cleve's social standing added weight to her opinion on Belmont, investing it with the authority of settler colonial renown.

Van Cleve responded to the *Globe* immediately to set the record straight, saying via a letter to the editor that she was far from convinced the young swain was a man. Instead, she "supposed, with others, that [Belmont] is a woman in man's attire, and [had] consulted with her and others with regard to the preparation of clothing suitable to her sex."[44] She may have visited Belmont during his confinement at Sheriff Thompson's house as early as November 1. Less than two weeks later, the *St. Paul Daily Globe* and the *Minneapolis Tribune* were alternately starting and disproving rumors that Van Cleve had participated in a second medical examination. The *St. Paul Pioneer Press* seized the opportunity for a bombshell on November 14, when it published an interview with Alonzo A. "Doc" Ames, a physician as well as a former mayor of Minneapolis. Dr. Ames had examined Belmont and, contrary to Van Cleve's declaration, found him to be a man.[45]

The Ames verdict forced reporters to rewrite their sensation. The *Minneapolis Tribune* posited that, weeks earlier, Belmont—a man—had told Dr. Putnam he was a woman to escape his engagements to Watts and Brackett. If Belmont fooled his girlfriends into thinking he had actually been a woman the whole time, this theory went, they could hardly demand that he honor his promises. This would enable him to walk away from the mess he'd made without being denounced as a cad.[46]

This version of the story created a problem for the press. A few days earlier, the *Minneapolis Tribune* had turned up an affectionate letter addressed to Belmont from James Weakley, alias James Taylor. The sheriff-turned-outlaw was working for the railroad in Sioux City,

Drawings of Leon Belmont and Sarah Brackett in the *Illustrated Police News,* November 20, 1880, 5.

Iowa, and remembering happier times. He missed Belmont, he wrote, longed to embrace him again, and looked forward to marrying him. The letter therefore created a scenario in which a man was in love with another man, and this was evidently beyond belief for the newspaper. "Men are not in the habit of desiring to fold one another in each other's arms, and all that," the *Tribune* pointed out. So it hedged its bets, asking, "Can Dr. Ames have been victimized, or what? Belmont is still a perpetual conundrum."[47]

Dr. Putnam was having none of it. Aware that Dr. Ames's verdict made him look incompetent, he confronted Belmont in person and demanded that he admit he was a woman. The *St. Paul Daily Globe* reported the following scene:

> The publication of [Dr. Ames's examination of Belmont] placed Dr. Putnam in a bad position, as it appeared he couldn't tell a woman from a man, and he proceeded to seek an interview with Belmont. He found her at the jail with Mrs. Thompson and another lady. He spoke of the false impression that had been erected against him, and proposed to have the matter set right. He pointed his finger at Belmont's face and

> told her that she was a woman, and she knew it. Belmont demurred. She said she was a man, and [had] lied to the doctor when he, she or it [had] told him at the Security [B]ank that he, she or it was a woman.[48]

In spite of Belmont's avowal of his manhood, Putnam got him to agree to a third examination in his office on November 15. The day came and went, and Belmont never appeared.[49] And so with the *Minneapolis Tribune* at a loss for words, Belmont reversing his story, and the two most prominent doctors in Minneapolis contradicting each other, the sensation reached its frenzied height. Charlotte Van Cleve threw fuel on the fire by writing a second letter to the *Tribune*—this one in the heartthrob's defense. After further conversation she had changed her mind. "Leon A. Belmont is unequivocally masculine," she proclaimed, "and hence entitled to wear the garments he now wears." She urged sympathy for the "homeless and unfriended boy, who, under circumstances of extreme perplexity, took a false and foolish step for which he has been abundantly punished and of which I believe he has sincerely repented."[50]

As the debate raged, the "homeless and unfriended boy" was doing well for himself; the papers even announced that Dr. Ames had invited him to study medicine at his office.[51] This last development was a step too far for the *Minneapolis Tribune,* which, for the first time, condemned Belmont in *Globe*-like terms and called for an end to the same sensation it had helped create.[52] Van Cleve's verdict softened that reaction, and the paper recanted on the following day:

> As to just what are the antecedents of Mr. Belmont, this is not the public's business so long as he behaves himself in this community—which The Tribune trusts he will carefully do hereafter. This is the end of the Belmont affair.[53]

It wasn't.

~

The disagreement between Ames and Putnam raises the possibility that Belmont had traits we would today consider intersex. If he had characteristics associated with both dyadic sexes, it would make sense for one doctor to interpret him as male and another as female within the span of two weeks. Several intersex conditions are associated with the coexistence of male- and female-typed reproductive organs. Androgen insensitivity syndrome (AIS), for example, can lead to undescended testes in place of a uterus in a phenotypically female person. The condition known as 5-alpha-reductase 2 deficiency (5α-r2D), meanwhile, can produce fused labia and a "macroclitoris" or "micropenis." The classic form of congenital adrenal hyperplasia (CAH) results in similar "gender-ambiguous" genitalia and is one of the most common intersex conditions.[54] Although doctors in the late 1800s lacked the technology to detect AIS, 5α-r2D, and CAH, they wrote about contemporaries of Belmont with similar traits. And like Ames and Putnam, they often disagreed. A doctor in Winchester, Virginia, who examined a female-assigned patient called A. B. in 1884, observed that in place of a vagina and uterus she had two testicles and a penis less than an inch long.[55] Feeling that these organs outweighed the evidence of her otherwise "feminine features," he declared her a man; he even recommended surgery to adjust the placement of her urethra so she could urinate while standing up. A second doctor read about the case in a medical journal and objected, saying that his colleague had mistaken a "hypertrophied" clitoris for a penis, and atypical ovaries for testes.

Another case comparable to Belmont's unfolded between 1869 and 1873, when multiple French judges disagreed on the right of a court in Alès to nullify the marriage of landowner Antoine-Etienne Darbousse to his wife, Justine Jumas. Even after a family doctor examined Jumas and pronounced her female, Darbousse insisted that Jumas was a man, and that the couple's marriage was therefore void. He appealed to the Cour suprême, where legal experts testified that Jumas's lack of internal sexual organs trumped all other factors.[56] A woman without a vagina, they said, was not a woman, even if she had a clitoris, a mons veneris, and labia, and acted as a woman in her community.

The rationale of the Jumas "experts" reveals a rift in the European understanding of nondyadic sex (intersex) that was only just starting to open in the 1870s. As mentioned in chapter 1, doctors were leaving behind the idea of nondyadic people as monsters to be managed (prevalent since the 1600s) and identifying them instead as impostors to be unmasked, examined, and forced to signify as either male or female.[57] But the late nineteenth century was also a period in which the logic of sex itself changed, and it was this shift that demanded the repeated examinations of people like Belmont, A. B., and Jumas.[58] If the essence of sex lay no longer in social roles (e.g., a man was someone who was a husband, uncle, blacksmith, mayor, etc.) but in the body (e.g., a man was someone who had a penis, testes, etc.), then the proper method of sex determination was not talking to patients and interviewing their families but examining their bodies. Patients could lie, but bodies, doctors now believed, told the truth. That the truth they told varied depending on who was doing the listening failed to shake them from their emerging dogma.

Regardless of whether Belmont, like his contemporaries A. B. and Jumas, fits the modern definition of intersex, his experience in Minneapolis illuminates 1800s intersex history. It hinges on a defining trauma of 1800s intersex experience: the coerced medical examination to determine "true" sex. Doctors used the exam to "enact" and then read the sex of nondyadic people in the nineteenth century, but they enlisted a range of techniques to do so.[59] Here, too, the Belmont sensation sits at a moment of historic change. Before about 1860, the standard exam to determine sex involved looking at, but not touching, a patient's external genitals.[60] Beginning in the 1860s, as the locus of "true" sex moved inside the body, physicians adopted more hands-on procedures: palpating the pelvis, penetrating orifices, listening to abdominal sounds, and masturbating the genitals.[61] The exam of a nondyadic French patient named Marie Raab in 1883 even involved collecting ejaculate.[62] Belmont's first exam, by Dr. Putnam on October 30, seems to have been conservative, and may not have involved even a viewing of genitalia. As Belmont reported, Putnam had "merely hammered on my chest and said I had a boy's chest."[63] It was the second examination, conducted by Dr. Ames on November 14, that might have used the more invasive medical practices used after 1860. The postexamination interview captured by the *St. Paul Pioneer Press* is suggestive:

Reporter: Well, doctor, have you seen it?

Dr. Ames: It? What?

Reporter: Why, the mystery in pantaloons—the Belmont.

Dr. Ames: Certainly. I have just spent two hours with it.

Reporter: Has it a sex?

Dr. Ames: It has, most decidedly—of the male persuasion.

Reporter: No! Why, how can that be, when Dr. Putnam recently certified, as a medical man, that it was a full-blown woman?

Dr. Ames: Well, Dr. Putnam's glasses were out of order, perhaps. At any rate he didn't get at the bottom facts in the case.

Reporter: It is a positive fact, then, that Belmont is a genuine man?

Dr. Ames: Belmont certainly is a man by a large majority; a man with no deviation whatever from the established formula.[64]

Both Ames and the reporter rely on innuendo to make their point: Putnam never looked at Belmont's genitals, and Ames has. Ames has seen "it"; he has uncovered the "bottom facts" and found them to be convincingly "large." The two-hour length of the exam, moreover, would have given Ames time to measure, palpate, and stimulate Belmont according to the emerging sexual science. If Ames chose to conduct a pelvic exam through a sheet, as was still common practice with female-assigned patients for reasons of modesty, he could have interpreted an erect "macroclitoris" as proof of a male sex.[65]

Whatever Ames's justification for his verdict, Belmont received it only by suffering through a second examination. Just as exams and other medical procedures are often traumatic experiences for intersex people in the twenty-first century,[66] they were equally harrowing in the nineteenth, before the routines of modern medicine encouraged patients to separate their selves from their physical bodies.[67] As they do today, intersex people in the 1800s resisted their objectification. Justine Jumas refused to submit to a court-arranged examination in 1869 and again in 1872, even after a court ordered her to reply (she was accused of "formal disobedience" in 1873).[68] Belmont, too, exerted agency by ducking his appointment with Dr. Putnam on November 15.

Ames's and Putnam's disagreement on Belmont's sex is not an anomaly but a historical trend—a reflection of changes in Western medicine's definition of sex in 1880, and of the instability of sex itself. Even in its most dramatic moments, Belmont's experience in Minneapolis was not so much sensational as it was typical.

~

By mid-November 1880, the Belmont sensation had become a national story. Via wire services, it ran through the month and into December on the front pages of the *Boston Daily Globe* and the *Washington Evening Star,* as well as in papers in New York, California, Dakota Territory, Vermont, Kansas, Alabama, and Kentucky. One item showed up in a Connecticut newspaper and caught the attention of a reader who recognized the Minneapolis celebrity as someone he had known years earlier in Northampton, Massachusetts.

That was all it took. Addie Walker had caught up with Leon Belmont.

The reader wrote a letter to a friend in Minneapolis saying that he believed Belmont was a woman named Mrs. Leon A. Stanley. Her unmarried name had been Addie Walker, he explained, and she had been indicted in 1876 for "obtaining a large sum of money under false pretenses" in Springfield, after which she had spent five months in jail. In 1878 she had moved to Kansas, just as Belmont claimed to have done.[69] The friend informed the *Minneapolis Tribune,* which attempted to connect the dots for the first time on November 15. The *Boston Globe* eventually verified Walker's indictment and other details, and the *Tribune* confirmed on February 21 that Belmont had been born not in England in the 1860s but in Warren, Massachusetts, in 1853. He was the heir not of August Belmont, the horse-breeding millionaire, but of

Albert Walker, an impoverished shoemaker. And he'd been assigned a female sex at birth.[70]

As dramatic as the *Minneapolis Tribune*'s revelations were, they posed no immediate threat to Belmont. Detectives showed no interest in reopening his case, even as he continued to appear on the street in men's clothes. The Massachusetts authorities, moreover, made no moves to intervene in what had become a Minnesota story. So the heartthrob did what he had claimed as his right in his November 12 *Tribune* interview: he stayed in Minneapolis and went about his business.

At some point later in the same month, Belmont moved out of the Watts home and into 1000 Fourth Street South, where he became the boarder of a couple named George and Melvina Campbell.[71] George Campbell was a second-generation British immigrant who worked in a lumberyard; his wife, Melvina, looked after their five-year-old daughter and managed a house that included Eugene (her adult son from a previous marriage) and two adult nephews.[72] Her sister Miranda Wardwell was the principal of Jefferson School and therefore the boss of Sarah Brackett, and it's likely that Belmont found his place in her home through this personal connection. Wardwell had helped Brackett call the police on Belmont back on October 30, but the arrest and ensuing scandal did not deter the Campbells from taking him in. In the case of Melvina Campbell, his hounding by the newspapers may have burnished his appeal as a vulnerable youth in need of an older woman's care, as it had for Clarinda Watts and Charlotte Van Cleve. That he was also handsome did not hurt his case, and over the course of a few weeks, Belmont's and Campbell's tenant–boarder relationship grew into a friendship, and then into a romance.

Melvina Campbell was receptive to Belmont's charms in December and January 1880–1881. For one thing, the weather was dismal. Historically dismal. In what came to be called the Snow Winter (Laura Ingalls Wilder made it famous in *The Long Winter*), frigid temperatures and relentless blizzards shut down cities across the Great Plains.[73] Melvina was stuck indoors with a five-year-old and little chance of getting time for herself, let alone going out. More seriously, George Campbell threatened her with verbal and physical abuse—a pattern he had established early in their relationship. Melvina later testified in court that "soon after the marriage her husband began to be cross, peevish and hateful, and within two years after marriage [1871] and ever since he has treated her in a cruel and inhuman manner, such as to make her life one of continued and almost unbroken and unbearable hardship and misery."[74] As recently as September 1880 he had choked and beaten her in an attack witnessed by her son, Eugene.[75]

When Belmont arrived, he was George's opposite: loving, sensitive, and affectionate. He had (or so he said) only twenty-one years to George's forty-eight.[76] He told Melvina the same origin story he had given to the Watts family, Sarah Brackett, and the newspapers, with its promises of noble relations, a millionaire uncle, an imminent fortune, and a family estate. Any one of these held out a potential lifeline to Melvina. Together, they offered not just an escape from an abusive relationship but a renovation of her life.

When Melvina confessed to her husband that she had feelings for Belmont, George ordered her to throw him out. Melvina agreed but stalled, leading to more orders, more agreements, and more delays, so Belmont remained in the house through January. He and Melvina went out together on sleigh rides and for walks, sometimes leaving at night and not coming home until close to midnight.[77] The neighbors noticed (and told reporters). Miranda Wardwell intervened, warning her sister that her suitor was untrustworthy, but by then the flirtation had deepened into something more serious. Near the end of the month, George and Melvina separated, and on February 8, Melvina sued him for divorce.[78]

What were Belmont's feelings for Melvina Campbell? Since he held fast to his media blackout through the spring of 1881, no interviews survive from this period that capture his feelings in his own words, or at least a reporter's paraphrase of them. Equally crucial is the question of how Melvina really felt about Belmont. Both parties stood to gain from the relationship, whether it was feigned or genuine. The *Minneapolis Tribune* dismissed the affair as a one-way swindle, a con perpetrated on a naive housewife. But in 1881 Melvina Campbell was, if not a woman of the world, then at least a person with life experience. She'd been married to two different men, and had a child with each of them. The Civil War had widowed her at eighteen and compelled her to move with her brother to a city halfway across the country from her home state of Maine, sight unseen.[79] (For details, see chapter 8.) Nine years of spousal abuse had shown her the worst of the power imbalance between men and women, and the danger of taking a partner at face value. If Belmont was bilking Melvina, Melvina may have known it, and calculated that it was worth it to play along and bilk him in return.

At the same time, it's a disservice to Melvina to assume that she *couldn't* have been genuinely attracted to Belmont, and in particular to his gender expression. Journalists had thwarted their own ability to understand Belmont's relationships with Watts and Brackett by writing off both same-sex attraction and the transing of gender as impossible. They had failed, as well, to consider the sexual appeal of a person we might today call butch or transmasculine. Doing justice to Melvina today, as to Weakley, Watts, and Brackett, requires staying open to multiple possibilities: that she saw Belmont as a masculine woman and was attracted to him for that reason; that she saw Belmont as a kind of man she hadn't seen before and was attracted to him for *that* reason; that she admired gender fluidity and in-between-ness; and that she simply wanted a life away from George Campbell and didn't give much thought to Belmont's gender identity. It seems likely, in fact, that she pursued a relationship with him, and he with her, for a mixture of all of these reasons: practical and sentimental, sexual and platonic, deceitful and sincere. This is the messy truth of all romantic relationships—not just ones involving gender variance.

In the absence of their own words, the surviving evidence of what was really going on with Belmont and Melvina lies in their actions: what they chose to do, and how, and on what timeline. They moved quickly with the divorce suit against George Campbell, with Melvina testifying in court on February 8 that "cruel and inhuman treatment" warranted the separation.[80] Neither Campbell nor a lawyer representing him appeared on that day, so Melvina won the suit by default. Belmont then set out to find a new place for them to live by visiting a local real estate agency. With the divorce only a few weeks away, he was already representing himself as Melvina's husband—a fact noticed by the realtors, who turned the encounter into an opportunity for advertising by placing an item in the *Tribune* on February 27:

> This notorious individual called at the office of Messrs. Moffitt & Nind, real estate agents, a short time since to rent a house, and said a small house would answer his purpose as he only wanted it for HIMSELF AND WIFE! Houses for rent being scarce, however, he could not be suited; but if Leon A. Belmont, Addie Walker, Mrs. Stanley, or August Belmont himself or any other man or woman wants to *buy* a small house, large house, residence lots, business lots, farms, lands, or any class of real estate, they can be suited by calling on MOFFITT & NIND, 224 Hennepin Avenue.[81]

In spite of the ongoing attention, Belmont and Melvina were committed to getting married, and quickly. The divorce settlement had not been finalized, so Belmont had no guarantee that the wedding would enrich him beyond Melvina's personal savings. But whether out of genuine affection or commitment to a scheme, Belmont's mind was made up. In early April he and Melvina traveled more than forty miles north of the Twin Cities to Spencer Brook—a tiny community insulated from the effects of Belmontmania. It was also the home of Melvina's brother, Fred Lowell, and his wife, Mary. The Isanti County clerk installed there issued the couple a marriage license, and Fred and Mary consented to appear as witnesses. At a subsequent ceremony on April 6, presumably without knowing it, Justice of the Peace W. A. Smith legally married two people who had been assigned a female sex at birth.[82] Belmont was a husband, and Melvina added to her name: Melvina A. Lowell Barry Campbell Belmont.

After he returned to Minneapolis, Belmont did not act like a man counting on an easy windfall, but like a husband arranging to provide for his new family. The Minneapolis City Council was ready to elect a new slate of officers, and when it met on April 12, Belmont presented himself as a candidate for the office of city physician. His challengers included John De Laittre, a former mayor. In a series of ballot revisions, Belmont appeared to receive at least one vote—perhaps by accident:

> No result was obtained until the thirtieth ballot. The candidates were Drs. Salisbury, Spaulding, Evans, Cockburn, Foster, Pratt, John DeLaittre and Belmont. On the fifteenth ballot the vote was slightly changed, probably by the aldermen who had voted for John DeLaittre and Leon Mary Belmont. . . . On the thirtieth ballot Dr. A. H. Salisbury received 10, Spalding 6 and Foster 1. Dr. Salisbury was declared the physician with a sigh of relief from each of the tellers and reporters.[83]

Just two days after the election, however, there was good news: George Campbell had settled half his property on Melvina.[84] If Belmont had been gambling, his bet had paid off.

The newlyweds settled into their new life together and found a place to board with a man named George Fleet, close to Melvina's old house. Melvina's daughter, Josie, may have gone with her.[85] In May, Belmont passed the one-year anniversary of his arrival in Minneapolis. But the new domestic arrangement did not outlast the summer. At the beginning of August, Fleet abruptly ejected the family from his house, for reasons unspecified in a subsequent *Globe* article.[86] His treatment was so harsh that even George Campbell rallied to his ex-wife's defense, giving the man a beating that Fleet reported to the police as assault and battery. The *Globe* piece was the last of the Twin Cities media's coverage of Belmont, and it marked the last time his name appeared in print in local newspapers.

The Belmont sensation, from its debut in the fall of 1880 through its decline in the spring of 1881, provoked a public reckoning with sex and gender in Minneapolis. It raised questions about the stability of both categories, since Belmont appeared to confound them with ease. Though reporters reacted differently to his transgressions, with some reveling in his gender ambiguity and others condemning it, they all constructed a distinctly modern celebrity—an icon recognized for his showmanship and artistry who was neither a showman nor an artist. A person, that is, who was famous for being famous.

By the fall of 1881, Belmont's time in Minnesota, and Melvina's, had drawn to a close.[87] They decided to move on. Maine and Massachusetts, their birth states, were half a continent away and tied to sad memories: James Barry's death, Addie Walker's childhood struggles and prison time. Dakota Territory had once seemed promising to Belmont, but by 1881 the waning Black Hills Gold Rush offered more promise to tycoons than to regular people. In the end, the couple settled on a place that had brought Belmont happiness and freedom, where his wearing of men's clothing "was not thought strange" and he could immerse himself in his chosen identity.

They moved to Kansas.

7.

The Hustler, 1881–1902

Dr. Belmonts, of Winfield, has established a cattle ranche on Deer Creek, about 12 miles from this place. The Doctor is rather effeminate for a cattle man.

—*Arkansas City Weekly Traveler,* March 8, 1882

South-central Kansas had struggled during Belmont's year and a half in the North. According to the compiler of an 1882 profile of Cowley County, 1880 was "another year of drouth and disaster," on par with the already mythical grasshopper plagues of 1874.[1] No rain fell; corn and wheat withered; some plantings failed entirely. The situation was so dire that nearly two thousand people (10 percent of the county's total population) left their homesteads for good.

By the time Belmont was turning his gaze from Minnesota back to Kansas, things in Cowley County were improving, but barely. "In 1881, the recuperation began," the compiler noted, "but the causes of the drouth were only partially removed, and the crops were below the average." The bad weather did not deter Belmont from considering the Cowley County city of Winfield among his options for a new home, even as he made plans to resurrect his pre-Minnesota plan of becoming a cattle dealer. Nor was he deterred by the fact that Winfield was sixty miles away from Anthony, the city where he'd been arrested in 1879, and a handful of counties away from Russell, where he was still wanted for escaping from jail with Sheriff Weakley. Winfield was close enough to Belmont's old haunts to remind him of the prairie he'd fallen in love with in 1879, but not so close that he risked being rearrested.

Belmont, it turned out, couldn't quit Kansas, and he chose Winfield for the site of his homecoming. He arrived in the town via Minneapolis in 1881 with Melvina and her daughter—now his daughter, six-year-old Josie. In Kansas, the girl's parents dropped her old first name and began to call her Maud.[2] Belmont himself, meanwhile, burnished his own name with a title he had never earned, and introduced himself to his new neighbors as "Dr. Belmont."

The atlas of Cowley County published in 1883 suggests how Winfield might have appeared to the Belmont family when they arrived two years earlier. In comparison with Minneapolis, it was almost rural; fewer than three thousand people lived within the city's borders.[3] Eager to attract new residents, the author of the city's atlas entry noted its "large class of the most intelligent and enterprising business men, who have been keen and wide awake to the interests of their city and county."[4] But the city's achievements to date were modest, and the profile writer struggled to come up with a list of its offerings beyond basic infrastructure: stone quarries, two railroads, two flour mills, three grain elevators, and twelve miles of sidewalks. There were also two banks ("of the soundest character," the writer reassured readers) and two iron bridges—not counting three railroad spans nearby, which the writer also pointed out with pride. The reality revealed between the lines is of a city eager to come into its own as a county seat equal to its larger neighbors, but still scrambling to build a foundation to do it.

Belmont, however, had not moved to Winfield for its urban refinements. He had experienced plenty of those (and the media machine that came with them) in Minneapolis. If Cowley County did not have the theaters and libraries and liveries that Belmont appreciated, it had something more valuable to him in this phase of his life: cheap land. If he was going to make it as a cattle rancher, this was his first and most crucial acquisition. In January 1882 he learned that a man named John R. Cochran was looking to sell an already up-and-running cattle ranch only a couple of miles outside of Winfield. His 160 acres followed a bend in a narrow offshoot of the Walnut River called Deer or Timber Creek, which was itself a tributary of the Arkansas River. The flat, open land was ideal for pasture; the creek supplied a place for watering cattle. Belmont jumped at the chance and bought the ranch from Cochran. The 1882 Cowley County atlas included in its "list of patrons" one "L. A. Belmont, stock raiser and dealer," resident of Winfield, and specified that he'd been born in England.[5]

If Belmont had been play-acting the role of a settler colonist in the past, his purchase of the ranch realized it. The original patent, issued by the Land Office on September 10, 1872, cited the "twelfth section of the act of 15th of July, 1870" as proof of the plot's status as salable land, eligible to buyers like Cochran.[6] This was the Osage Removal Act, the treaty that had ordered the migration of about three thousand Wahzhazhe people from their Kansas homelands to a reservation in Indian Territory.[7] It had dissolved the Osage Diminished Reserve—the last Wahzhazhe territory in Kansas, inside of which the ranchland sat—and added it to an existing Osage Land Trust, through which sales like Cochran's were administered.[8] In September 1872, when Cochran was in the Augusta land office signing paperwork to make the property his, Wahzhazhe families had been exiled from the Timber Creek area (and all of Kansas) for less than a year.[9] Even a decade later, when Belmont arrived, on a historical time scale the ranch had been Wahzhazhe land only a moment earlier. By legacy, right, and spiritual kinship, it still was. Belmont's purchase implicated him in a years-long process of Native land dispossession that stretched from the Osage Treaty of 1825 to the infamous Sturges Osage Treaty of 1868, which was so dishonest that even the US government stopped it from happening.[10] If Belmont's gender variance attracted unwanted attention, and sometimes even compromised his freedom, it did not disqualify him from the entitlements of the settler-colonist class—first among them being stolen Native land.

In 1882 that unwelcome attention returned, though not on the scale Belmont had seen in Minneapolis. Unlike in Dodge in 1879, when he had posed as a rancher but may never have owned any cattle, at Timber Creek in 1882 Belmont appears to have run a legitimate business. At the end of January he placed ads in both the *Winfield Courier* and the *Cowley County Current* in an effort to sell milk cows, telling interested buyers to ask for "Dr. L. A. Belmont."[11] In March the *Arkansas City Traveler* (another Cowley County newspaper) included in its town announcements a reference to his "cattle ranche on Deer Creek."[12] But he seems to have deserved a mention for reasons other than his business. "The Doctor," the writer added with a sniff, "is rather effeminate for a cattle man." Then, in July, Belmont and Melvina took a trip to Sedan, the seat of Chautauqua County, and established themselves at the Lindell Hotel. Their reception there was cool. Belmont's failure to pass led to a write-up in the city's *Weekly Times Star* on July 27:

> On the Lindell Hotel register is the following: "L. A. Belmont & Wife, Winfield." The gentleman claimed to be a son of August Belmont, the great New York banker, but from the fact that he remained here several days to get a $25 check cashed, it is not generally believed. From the effeminate appearance of the individual, some persons even went so far as to surmise that he (or she as the case may be) was a female woman, in disguise. However there was no positive proof furnished us that such was the case.[13]

Even in the aftermath of the Belmont sensation, Leon was sticking to his imagined pedigree, this time upping the ante with a claim that he was not just Belmont Sr.'s nephew, but his son (though it's possible that the reporter simply got this wrong). In Sedan, however, there was no city ordinance against cross-dressing as there had been in Minneapolis, meaning police had no reason to arrest him. Kansans were reacting to Belmont with curiosity, but not with the kind of panic that might have inspired a call to the police. At the Lindell Hotel, at least, Belmont's gender variance did not rise to the level of a crisis demanding action from bystanders. Observers noticed him, judged him, and speculated about him, but they were content to move on afterward.

Belmont moved on, too, with the business of running his ranch. The spring and summer of 1882 brought enough rain to water his cattle at Timber Creek, and to feed them on the thriving prairie. The writer of the Cowley County atlas captured the mood of Belmont's neighbors in a summary of the season's good fortune:

> As we write now, August 1, 1882, Cowley county is "booming." . . . Fruit trees are loaded down with the richest and

> choicest fruits; the prairies are covered heavily with grass; the cattle, sheep and horses on the ranges are fat; the weather is fine and comfortable; there has been sufficient rainfall, and in moderate showers; everything wears the air of wealth and luxury; the farmers are jubilant; every one wears a happy smile; immigrants are arriving; men of capital are securing farms and locating their families in this county, and the statistics to be gathered in the spring of 1883, will show a larger advance than any other year.[14]

Even adjusting for the exaggerations of a writer promoting his home to readers of the atlas (it's hard to believe *everyone* was smiling and jubilant), the description suggests that Cowley County was doing well in the summer of 1882. But Belmont failed to translate these conditions into success on his ranch as the year drew to a close. He was not, after all, trained in the management of livestock, and he had no experience dealing with the challenges of a large-scale business. If the *Winfield Courier* was correct, he had inherited a sizable herd; the paper noted in January that before the sale to Belmont, Cochran "had gathered together quite a bunch of cattle and was fast becoming a bloated bondholder."[15] The head start was not enough for Belmont. By 1883 he had abandoned the ranch and moved his family to a new county. It was the first step of a sequence that was to repeat itself over the next eighteen years: arrive in a new place, attempt a new business, abandon it, and move on. For the rest of the 1880s and through the 1890s, Belmont hustled.

His first hustle after ranching was baking. After staying at the Commercial Hotel in Douglass in March 1883 ("L. A. Belmont wife and child" appeared on the guest register), he found a home for himself, Melvina, and Maud, as well as a storefront in which to open a bakery in town.[16] Recognizing his limited knowledge of the trade this time, he took the step of hiring someone to handle production for him, reserving a more managerial role for himself. He also made sure that the *Douglass Index* knew about his project and ran news items/advertisements in its pages:

> Dr. L. A. Belmont, who has established a bakery in Dr. Knote's old store, has secured the services of the well known baker Frank Hoffman, formerly of Douglass. Dr. Belmont has built a fine oven and has every convenience to prosecute his business successfully. He will also carry a full line of confectionary.[17]

The notice ran twice: first on March 30 and again on April 6. Free samples may have encouraged the publicity. In April, the paper's editor announced, "We are indebted to Dr. Belmont for some very excellent bread and buns from his new bakery made by Frank Hoffman."[18] A June item described him as so successful that he had to work day and night to keep up with demand, and he stayed open at least through October, when the *Douglass Index* ran one final promotion.[19] But by February 1884, less than a year after he had started this second business, he had abandoned it and moved on to his next hustle: medicine.

Although Belmont had passed himself off as a doctor after returning to Kansas from Minnesota, he had so far been a physician in title only. In 1884, he changed that. First, he moved his family again, this time from Douglass to Cherokee Township.[20] Having teamed up with a pediatrician/obstetrician already taking patients at an office in Burden, he offered his medical services—with "surgery a specialty"—to the people of Cowley County.[21] Evidently not content with this alone, he also took extended trips across the state border with Indian Territory, where he sought out patients among both Cherokee people and the African Americans—also Cherokee citizens—living among them twenty-one years after their emancipation.[22]

Of all of Belmont's fibs, cons, lies, and bluffs, his stint as a doctor in the Cherokee Nation stands out as one of the most unethical. Up until that point, he had taken advantage of individuals whose wealth, power, and position surpassed his own: Columbus Orcutt, James Weakley, the man from Turners Falls, Clarinda Watts, Grace Watts, and Sarah Brackett. In 1884 he crossed a line, preying upon a group of comparatively marginalized people whose lack of power made them especially vulnerable to his schemes.

One element of that vulnerability involved health. In the 1880s, there were few practicing doctors in Indian Territory qualified to treat the region's diseases. The Native people who'd been forced to move there from their homelands had brought with them centuries-old medicine traditions tied to local plants, but these were not always available or effective in their new environment. Central Oklahoma, for example, was prone to thunderstorms that attracted swarms of malaria-carrying anopheline mosquitoes.[23] Malarial fever and ague resisted Native medicines, as did measles and dysentery. The most effective treatments were available only from doctors with the necessary supplies and training, and these were hard to find in Indian Territory.[24] But if medical school graduates hesitated to move there, quacks, amateurs, and bogus substitutes were eager to step in to supply the unmet demand.[25] They flooded into places like Guthrie, where in 1889 seventy-five people claimed to be practicing medicine—only two months after the town was founded.[26] The Cherokee Nation had responded in 1881 by requiring would-be doctors to pay a twenty-dollar fee, but the deluge persisted.[27] An 1884 report from the Union Indian Agency in Muscogee, whose jurisdiction included the Cherokee Nation, showed that the influx of untrained, predatory doctors was tied to the larger challenge of controlling the movement of crooked outsiders of all kinds. Indian Agent John Q. Tufts wrote:

> The number of intruders is increasing rapidly, and there being practically no law to punish for intrusion, it is only a question of time when they will control the country. The removal of intruders by the troops is a farce of the first water. When complaint is made by the Indian authorities of the presence of intruders, the military is called upon at once to remove the intruders beyond the limits of this agency. The troops go to the locality, and if the intruder has not stepped into the woods and out of sight for a day or two, they arrest and escort him to the State line, and turn him loose. The intruder takes one or two breaths of State air, and returns to the Territory and the place from whence the troops took him.[28]

The report explains Belmont's ability to infiltrate the reservation; if an authority challenged him, he could simply disappear for a day and then return later. Removal across the state line did not upend a dubious medical practice for good. And Belmont's practice, if not strictly illegal, was morally dubious at best, even if he did intend to perform to the best of his limited ability. Newspapers had reported in 1880 that he'd held a position in Calvin Goodrich's Minneapolis medical office, either as a student or a trainee. Assuming his studies began as soon as he arrived in the city in May and continued through his arrest on October 30, Belmont had received, at most, five months of education.[29] When he arrived in the Cherokee Nation he had no degree and no license—a fact that he admitted to Melvina.[30] He also had no partner, like Dr. Rude in Burden, who might have compensated for his lack of experience. In Indian Territory, he was on his own.

There is no surviving record of Belmont's patients, their conditions, or their treatments, if he provided any. By 1885 he and Melvina were in Goose Neck Bend, a settlement on the Arkansas River outside Fort Gibson and about ten miles southwest of Tahlequah, the capital of the Cherokee Nation. Melvina, however, returned to Kansas ("I could not stay down there," she told a federal examiner in 1922, without explaining the reason), and Belmont continued by himself.[31] His presence added to the continuing issue of Cherokee exploitation by non-Cherokee citizens. In 1886, an Indian agent reported from Muscogee that an estimated 5,000 people living on the reservation (out of a total population of 90,000) were "willful intruders," with an additional 1,500 present as "emigrants, visitors, and pleasure-seekers."[32] He also lamented that "the intruders are numerous and difficult to manage" and described them as "intruding cowmen, farming intruders, coal and timber thieves, tramps, vagrants, refugees from justice, professional thieves, and whisky-peddlers."[33] However many of these labels applied to Belmont, he was part of the problem, and the historical moment it created.

But not for long. By the end of 1885, Belmont was on the move again, leaving behind whatever patients he'd found in Indian Territory, uprooting his family from their home in Cherokee Township, and finding a new one in Independence. He also added a new hustle that could not have been further from medicine: traveling around south-central Kansas selling washing machines. The randomness of this venture suggests that by this point Belmont was, if not desperate for a way to make money, then compelled to take what he could get. In March, the *Oswego Courant* ran an advertisement whose self-promotional tone—probably coming from Belmont himself—recalled the ads for his bakery in the *Douglass Index*:

> L. A. Belmont is in our county convassing for the Marie des Cygne Washing Machine and the Champion Wringer. This is the best machine made. It does its own work thereby saving a large portion of the time usually taken in a family. It uses much less soap than is required by any other method. Clothes wears double the time when washed by Mr. Belmont's machine. It is truly a life, labor and clothes saving washer. Every family should have one. Can be seen at Clover's mill, in Oswego.[34]

Work as a traveling doctor-salesman fit the peripatetic rhythm of Belmont's life in the late 1880s. With Melvina and Maud set up in Independence, Belmont resisted being tied down, and he roamed in search of patients and/or customers. "Usually when he would go away," Melvina recalled of this period decades later, "he would go all around the country everywhere and when he came home he would tell me where he had been."[35] He relied on his charm to get by, but this worked for a limited time, adding to the incentive to keep moving: "He had a very pleasing personality and would easily make friends but could not keep them," Melvina observed.[36] Belmont continued to "pretend," to use Melvina's choice of words, to practice medicine while he developed his trade as a salesman, evidently still drawing income from the enterprise.[37]

For a five-year period starting in 1881, after the resolution of the media sensation in Minneapolis, Belmont had stayed out of legal trouble, or at least kept it out of newspapers. That changed on December 4, 1886, when his name appeared in the *Coffeyville Weekly Journal* as the defendant in a civil lawsuit. The *Journal* never reported the charges involved in *Orin Smith v. L. A. Belmont,* but the case was serious enough to prompt Belmont to hire a couple of attorneys, and sticky enough to drag on for eight months.[38] While that case was still in process, Belmont got in more serious trouble. On June 9, 1887, a policeman arrested him in Independence on the charge of "using language calculated to provoke a disturbance."[39] He refused to plead guilty but was nevertheless convicted and forced to pay $12.50. The incident landed his name in the crime news section of the *Independence Daily Reporter*—only a faint echo of the Minneapolis coverage but a blow to his local reputation nonetheless. This time, however, the issue of his sex did not come up. On August 10, a judge finally dismissed *Orin Smith v. L. A. Belmont* on the condition that Belmont paid his accuser's legal bills.[40] Belmont agreed, and the flare-up of attention dissipated. The Belmont sensation did not repeat itself in Kansas.

~

After 1887, surviving documentation of Belmont's year-by-year activities thins out. While it's possible to reconstruct his moves almost month by month in certain parts of 1879, 1880, and 1881, the late 1880s through 1902 are short on detail. Most of the federal census population schedules of 1890, which would have counted the Belmont family and listed Leon's occupation, were destroyed by fire in 1921.[41] In 1895, when the Belmonts were living in Missouri, that state no longer conducted decennial state censuses, so there is no information representing that year. The 1900 federal census helps, as do a handful of newspaper mentions and Melvina's depositions to the US Bureau of Pensions in the 1920s. From these, broad outlines emerge. Between 1890 and 1891 the family moved from Independence to the town of Joplin, Missouri, where they stayed through 1894. By 1895 they had moved to Webb City, where Belmont sold groceries. After Maud got married in the same year, Belmont and Melvina moved to Carthage, where he was unemployed. They lived out the nineteenth century in the city of Springfield and remained there under their married names until 1902.

Newspaper columnists hungry for stories had presented Belmont as a romantic sensation in 1880. But his uniqueness was a mirage. As the previous chapters have shown, gender variance in the United States at the end of the nineteenth century was far from rare. It inspired a variety of reactions from the gender-normative public, from legislation to indifference, and from distaste to enthusiasm. A person assigned a female sex at birth living as a man was not, in himself, a romantic sensation. During Belmont's decade in Missouri, the real romantic sensation was the revolution in popular thinking about gender and sexuality that reached into, and grew from, his adopted homes in Kansas and Missouri. That revolution produced two radical results: New Womanhood and the emergence of a modern lesbian identity.

The relatively progressive gender ideology known as New Womanhood appeared in the United States in the 1880s but did not attract widespread attention until the 1890s.[42] The term "New Woman" appeared in essays, cartoons, and editorials as both an object of satire—a misogynists' bugbear too busy riding her bicycle to take care of her children—and a feminist ideal out of reach for all but the most tenacious and wealthy.[43] Behind both of them were the real women who identified with the label, including writers,[44] artists,[45] athletes,[46] and reformers.[47] One trait that united them was their independence. Many lived in their own households apart from men as same-sex couples, professional partners, and/or mutually supportive friends. Often, those categories overlapped. They supported themselves financially, taking up space in the public sphere as travelers, performers, and lecturers, and entering professions dominated by men. Their example turned the dial of what was considered "normal" womanhood away from its mid-century Victorian setting toward one that admitted a degree of activity and intellect. In this way New Women rejected the Cult of True Womanhood, the dogma of female passivity that had both defined and enforced acceptable feminine behavior between the 1820s and the 1860s. The shift was seismic: a shake-up of feminine mythology that opened routes for women into the public sphere.[48]

Public debate about New Womanhood reached beyond coastal cities and into Belmont's corner of the Great Plains. In 1890, the Springfield newspaper *Patrick Henry* endorsed the feminist[49] publication *Lucifer, the Light-Bearer,* headquartered across the Kansas border in the small town of Valley Falls.[50] *Lucifer* was one of the most vocal supporters of New Womanhood in the country, and in the 1880s it authorized two Missouri sales points: one in Joplin and another in Carthage (both of them towns in which Belmont lived).[51] In 1895, the

"The New Woman—Wash Day." Stereograph, 1901. Library of Congress, Prints and Photographs Division, LC-DIG-stereo-1s16054. https://www.loc.gov/resource/stereo.1s16054.

paper had published a three-part manifesto calling for free love, divorce reform, and women's economic emancipation from men.[52] Some Springfield women wrote letters to *Lucifer*'s editor; one even bought a personals ad.[53] The Chautauqua circuit's lecture tours, meanwhile, also brought New Womanist ideals into the region. A church in Independence, Kansas, hosted Chautauqua regular Reverend George F. Hall on May 23, 1899, for his lecture "The Model New Woman."[54]

The "woman question" was hardly a settled one by the end of the

1890s. Women who entered male-dominated professions in Kansas and Missouri still faced condescension at best, and condemnation at worst. Public depictions of New Women remained ambivalent. An 1897 item in the *Cherokee County Republican* drew attention to efforts to define the concept, but it also repeated the joke that New Womanhood was "Man's newest and best reason for remaining single."[55] Over time, however, its example had a normalizing effect. Alongside the freethinker radicals showcased in *Lucifer,* women who merely stayed unmarried and worked in gender-normative professions seemed tame by comparison. They seemed relatively benign, too, next to a woman like Carry A. Nation, whose 1901 bottle-smashing campaign in Topeka raised the bar for outrageous feminine behavior.[56] At her home in Medicine Lodge (another former haunt of Belmont's) in 1900, Nation claimed to have knelt by her bed and received instructions from God to achieve her temperance movement goals through radical means.[57] In response, she had taken a brickbat, entered saloons throughout Kiowa, and smashed whatever bottles, mirrors, and windows she found there. Joined by other temperance activists, she took her campaign to Wichita and upgraded her brickbat to a hatchet, inspiring her to call these actions "hatchetations."

Although Nation did not align herself with New Womanhood, her strategic acts of vandalism shook the Cult of True Womanhood to its core.[58] Critics responded in gendered terms, making her into a New Woman even if she didn't identify as one. Some wrote off her disobedience as hysteria—the overexcitement to be expected of a fragile woman asserting herself in public. Others took the opposite tack, calling her "masculinized," "unfemale," and "unwomanly."[59] Whether she was too feminine or not feminine enough, the trouble with Nation had something to do with gender. She had too much of it, or too little; it was perverted, or imbalanced.[60]

Like Carry Nation, the political organizer Mary Elizabeth Lease challenged gender conventions in Kansas without explicitly transing gender. She emerged from socialist and labor-organizing circles in the late 1880s to establish herself, beginning in 1890, as a supporter of the political movement known as Populism. Her stump speeches for Populist candidates like Lorenzo D. Lewelling (governor of Kansas,

1893–1895) pulled no punches as Lease incited listeners to reject Wall Street, overturn wage slavery, support women's suffrage, and fight for their interests as farmers and laborers. As an orator she was loud, uncompromising, and insistent—traits that startled audiences used to more demure women speakers, if they were used to women speakers at all. Although sanding down the edges of her oppositional style might have earned her sympathy, Lease refused to diminish herself in order to reflect the Cult of True Womanhood's dogmatic view of women as quiet helpmeets.[61] Reporters claimed she shouted at Kansas farmers to "raise less corn and more hell"; Lease responded that she had not used those words, but that she agreed with their sentiment nonetheless.[62]

Public reaction to Lease was severe and, as it was with Nation, gendered. Skipping over the content of her political arguments, critics attacked her dress, health, mental state, and relationship with her husband.[63] When she claimed in 1894 to belong to a Kansas chapter of the Masons, an organization that did not admit women, one writer rejoined that though Lease couldn't have been a Mason, she was believable enough as a man (a remark intended to be an insult).[64] The amount of ink spilled in denunciations of Lease points to the effectiveness of her campaign in normalizing women's public protest. Had she been less effective, and therefore less threatening, opponents might have spared themselves the trouble. But Lease was most dangerous because she was part of a broader movement to rethink gender assumptions in the 1890s—a weak but growing willingness to accept women as participants in the public sphere.[65]

Cracks in the facade of True Womanhood were widening in Missouri, too. After returning to her home state after fourteen years in Louisiana, Kate Chopin began to work through her frustration with gender dogma while raising five sons (and a daughter) in St. Louis. By 1899 she had written poems, essays, and three novels, to considerable acclaim.[66] But her final novel, *The Awakening*, attracted more attention than all of her previous work combined. In a forthright realist style, Chopin drew readers into the inner world of Edna Pontellier, a New Orleans wife and mother who realizes during a family vacation that she wants more out of life than domestic conformity. In the wake of that realization, Edna embraces her sensual impulses, nurtures her independent identity, moves out of her husband's house, and (Chopin implies) commits adultery. More than just voicing the desires of women, Chopin was questioning whether marriage and motherhood alone could fulfill them—the foundational assumption of the Cult of True Womanhood.[67]

Public reaction to *The Awakening* was severe. In a surge of negative press, reviewers took Chopin to task not so much for writing a bad book as for stepping outside the domain of subjects that were appropriate for a woman writer. They called the story repellent, morbid, poisonous, and sordid ("sordid" was from Willa Cather).[68] A writer for the *New Orleans Times-Democrat* dismissed it as "gilded dirt . . . promoting unholy imaginations and unclean desires"; the *New Orleans Times-Democrat*'s critic lamented that Chopin had failed to include "a single note of censure of [Edna's] totally unjustifiable conduct."[69] But the denunciations masked a deeper vein of reaction that showed the concept of gender liberation resonating with some readers. Instead of dismissing Edna Pontellier's self-empowerment as unhealthy, a reviewer writing in the *Boston Beacon* portrayed it as the understandable reaction of a woman held back by archaic social norms. In this view, Edna was "a normal woman . . . experiencing a full awakening of the entire human nature."[70] Another went further in the *St. Louis Republican,* presenting Edna as "[a] woman who has been merely quiescent, who has accepted life as it came to her, without analysis and without question, [who] finally awakens to the fact that she has never lived."[71] And when the *New York Times* asked, "Would it have been better had Mrs. Kate Chopin's heroine slept on forever and never had an awakening?," it left room for a negative answer.[72] The tension between these two responses—a reactionary defense of True Womanhood on one hand and an admission of its failings on the other—intensified at the end of the 1890s, when High Victorian gender doctrine had weakened but not yet collapsed.

At the same time these gender sensations were unfolding during Belmont's Missouri years, a quiet revolution in the public understanding of sexuality was underway in the United States, encouraged by a medical science emerging in Europe called sexology. When reporters across the country had written about Belmont in 1880, they had understood his masculinity and relationships with women as behaviors rather than pathologies. If he deserved condemnation, they showed, he deserved it because of the actions he had chosen rather than a disease he had inherited. As explored in chapter 6, the modern concept of sexual orientation—of a world made up of homosexual, bisexual, and heterosexual "types" of people—did not exist as we know it today. By 1902, this had shifted. The sexologists Havelock Ellis and Richard von Krafft-Ebing had published influential studies of so-called sexual inversion, deviance, and homosexuality that challenged the behavior-based sexual schema of the Victorian period by introducing one based on inborn identity.[73] Opportunities to label someone like Belmont multiplied as the sexological terms "invert," "lesbian," and "homosexual" entered popular use. The change was gradual but unmistakable. One era of sexual ideology had ended, and a new one was beginning. Homosexuals had been invented, their deviance a social problem to be studied, named, and treated.[74]

Out of the fertile soil of 1890s sexology a subcategory of homosexual grew that inspired fear in the newly christened heterosexual mainstream: the mannish lesbian. American women had, of course, expressed masculinity earlier in the 1800s. They had also built bonds with other women on a spectrum ranging from sensual to sexual. But by 1900, Americans under the influence of sexology were calling out these same women as sick, pitiable, and even criminal for their relationships, especially when they expressed masculinity.[75] Reporters writing for sensational newspapers devoted attention to stories that combined lesbianism and violent death, leading to the birth of a new genre: lesbian love murder.[76] In 1892, for example, they converged in Memphis to cover the trial of Alice Mitchell, a masculine-of-center nineteen-year-old accused of murdering her lover, Freda Ward (seventeen), by cutting her throat.[77] Some of their stories defended Mitchell; others drew on sexological language to raise the possibility that her love for Ward was "perverted," "insane," and "morbid"—the dangerously "unnatural" delusion of an "erotomaniac."[78] As it did during the publication of *The Awakening*, public reaction skewed sympathetic on one side and condemning on the other, reflecting the in-process status of sexual/gender realignments in the 1890s. During the Mitchell trial, however, so many writers engaged with the specter of the masculine invert driven to murder by her unnatural desires that they brought the stereotype into circulation.[79] Public discussion of Mitchell's character introduced laypeople to a suite of psychomedical concepts that had once been confined to clinics. For this reason it also hastened the transition—underway but not complete—from a Victorian way of thinking about sexuality based on behavior to a modern understanding based on identity.[80]

~

If Belmont's life between 1890 and 1902 absorbed these shocks to the gender/sexual status quo, extant records do not reveal it. Instead, next to Nation's hatchetation, Lease's hell-raising, Chopin's *Awakening,* and Ward's murder, Belmont's documented activities in Missouri appear tame. In June 1895, Belmont's name appeared in the *Galena Times* for the neighborly act of giving a ride to a stranger with a sick baby. As the paper reported it, after a doctor diagnosed the baby with cholera, and the desperate mother "despair[ed] of having no way to reach Oronogo[,] L. A. Belmont took compassion upon her and took her over in his surrey."[81] A few months later, when Belmont hosted his daughter's wedding at his home, another newspaper wrote up the wholesome scene:

> **WARREN–BELMONT.**
> A Union Between Joplin and Webb City Young People.
>
> Webb City *Register*: Mr. Fountain Hansford Warren of Joplin and Miss Maud Campbell Belmont of Webb City were united in marriage at 6 o'clock Sunday evening by Rev. J. T. Neville, pastor of the First Baptist church, at the residence of the parents of the bride, Mr. and Mrs. L. A. Belmont, of west Daugherty street in Webb City. It was a quiet home wedding, there being present only the family of Mr. Belmont, the brother of the groom, ex-Deputy Sheriff W. H. Warren and his wife, and Rev. and Mrs. Geville [*sic*]. After the ceremony they partook of a sumptuous wedding supper. Mr. and Mrs. Warren will be

> at home after November 18th, on Gray avenue, in Joplin. The bride is a charming, pretty blonde and a most estimable little lady, well liked by her circle of friends in this city and Joplin, where she formerly resided with her parents. The groom is a young man of good family, sober and industrious and stands well among his associates.[82]

In the eyes of his community, Belmont was an upstanding citizen by 1895, able to invite a Baptist reverend and a former sheriff to witness his daughter's marriage inside his home. This time, he did not elope with the sheriff. If the event was a "quiet home wedding" rather than the social event of the season, it was also a model of respectability. Fountain Warren and his parents appear not to have guessed that Belmont was transing gender, and that Maud was not his biological daughter. If they did, that inkling did not prevent them from accepting an alliance between the two families. Maud Belmont's success in society also suggests that Leon's assigned sex at birth was either unknown or a nonissue, allowing his daughter to remain eligible for marriage with a "sober and industrious" young man "of good family."

At the time of Maud's wedding in 1895, Leon worked in Webb City in the humble calling of running a grocery, making enough money from the work to afford the house on Daugherty Street and splurges like the wedding supper. This was an achievement during the nadir of the lean years after the Panic of 1893, which had no small impact on Missouri entrepreneurs and the consumers who kept them in business.[83] Within a year of the Webb City wedding, once Belmont and Melvina had moved to Carthage, Belmont was unemployed, and he remained so for about a year. Leon, however, weathered the storm, and by 1896 he had opened a new grocery store in Springfield. He was in legal trouble again in 1898, named as the defendant in a case called *L. Spire v. Leon Belmont,* but a judge dismissed the case when the prosecution failed to materialize.[84]

In general, Belmont's life in Springfield seems to have been low key, less apt to attract attention than his previous decade. In 1900, after nineteen years of marriage, Belmont was forty-seven years old, and Melvina was fifty-eight.[85] The Belmont genealogy remained intact. Leon told the 1900 US census enumerator that he was a grocer; that he'd been born in Tennessee; that his father, as made sense for a brother of August Belmont, had been born in Germany; and that his mother, the heiress, had been born in England.[86] At the turn of the twentieth century, however, this family tree was the only sensational thing about Belmont. And it was a fiction.

The Leon Belmont era ended in 1902, having lasted for twenty-four years. In that time, he'd seen much of the middle of the country, from Kansas to Dakota Territory to Minnesota and back again. He'd touched down in Colorado, Texas, and Indian Territory, and lingered in Missouri. People across the country had harassed him, arrested him, and sensationalized him. But they had also accepted him, praised him, and fallen in love with him. His example shows that it was possible for a person to trans gender at the end of the nineteenth century and live a "typical" life, complete with family milestones (courtship, marriage, parenting), exciting moments (escaping from jail, eloping with a sheriff) and mundane ones (losing a wallet, selling washing machines, being unemployed). He was not, so far as the record shows, the first of anything. He wasn't even the first gender migrant to run a grocery store in Missouri. In that he was preceded by Frank Gray, the Kansas City saloon keeper who also found success as a realtor and a grocer between 1883 and 1885.[87] Nor was Belmont unique in his willingness to take on a variety of noncomplementary jobs. Joseph Cox worked on a farm and in a factory in Aurora, Missouri, in 1889;[88] Tom King combined selling magazines with the Belmont-esque side hustle of cattle ranching (or at least pretending to do so) in Indian Territory in the 1890s.[89] All three had been assigned a female sex at birth.[90]

Though he had his moments of adventure, between 1879 and 1902 Belmont was not a sensation, a hero, or an outlier. He was a person and a product of his time. The strongest proof is a newspaper article published in the *St. Louis Republic* in 1902—a year after the end of the Belmont era. Its dismissive language hides a normalizing admission: that gender migration was a recognized phenomenon in Belmont's time. Even Belmont's legal marriage and fatherhood had precedents:

> Within a year six women have been discovered, in America alone, who have successfully masqueraded as men; have gone through a legal form of marriage and even posed as the fathers of families. Upward of a score of similar cases have come to public attention recently in different parts of the world. There have been forty-three instances of women posing as husbands in the last ten years. One medical authority claims that one woman in every 3,000 is the victim of this particular mania. Two new instances have been added recently to the amazing list of women who have lived and died disguised as men.[91]

Amazing, perhaps. But not sensational. The definition of the word "sensation" is built on public reaction: an outpouring of excitement inspired by an unusual person or event. But while gender migrants like Belmont sometimes inspired media sensations, they were not unusual. When they did produce mass excitement, as Belmont did in 1880, it was a manufactured kind. Just as often, people who transed gender lived among their neighbors without incident.[92] The path of Belmont's life between 1878 and 1902 bears this out, showing that for every interaction that led to harassment, arrest, or tipping off a reporter, there were dozens more encounters that led to nothing at all. Community reaction when Belmont failed to pass as what we would today call cisgender leaned toward curiosity but away from confrontation. It is this social default that explains how he was able to live in Kansas and Missouri for twenty years—if not in harmony, then at least in relative peace.

Part III

A. Nova McClure Carr

8.

The New Woman, 1902–1913

Yes, I knew the person that was supposed to be Miss McClure but the general opinion in the neighborhood was that Miss McClure and Mr. Belmont were one and the same person. No one ever saw Belmont and Miss McClure at the house at the same time.

—Sworn testimony of John Williams, neighbor of Leon and Melvina Belmont, to special examiner T. Quinn Jones, April 19, 1922, US Bureau of Pensions, pension file of Allen E. Barry, 106

It's common for the wives of gender-variant people in the nineteenth century to drop out of the official narratives of their relationships. Although they're equally present, they receive less attention (for better and worse) in the newspaper articles and case files that scrutinize their masculine partners. So it goes, too, with the gender-conforming women who sidestep the status of "wife": girlfriends and fiancées, accomplices and romantic friends, life mates and admirers. The typical "woman who lived as a man" exposé of the late nineteenth and early twentieth century devoted hundreds of words to a debonair "female husband," but spared only a sentence or two for his partner(s).[1]

While exploring Belmont's story, we can fight against femme invisibility in the historical record by giving Melvina her own hearing. Melvina was her own story's protagonist—a dreamer and contriver whose life experience evolved apart from her husband of twenty-one years.[2] So who was this woman who married Belmont and traveled with him across three states? What experiences shaped her before they met? A paper trail left behind by Melvina in the 1910s and 1920s, including eleven letters written in her own words, helps answer these questions. It illuminates her character in the brief but vivid flashes of its own light, away from the glare of Belmont's charisma.

~

Melvina Augusta Lowell was born on September 9, 1841, in the village of Whitneyville, Maine.[3] Her father, Simeon, worked in the local lumber industry, as did many of the laborers attracted to the area by the prospect of a steady job.[4] He and his wife, Mary Ann (also spelled Marian), got in the habit of giving their daughters names beginning with "M," and by 1853 their household included Martha, Miranda, Mary, and Mariah (the sisters of Melvina) as well as her brothers, John, Daniel, and Frederick. Melvina was the second youngest of eight children.[5]

As Melvina grew into a young adult in the 1850s, her life began to mirror her sister Miranda's. Both women married men in their own social circle, Miranda a clergyman named Irving A. Wardwell and Melvina a school teacher named Allen E. Barry. They had their weddings in the same year (1858), when Miranda was twenty-three and Melvina seventeen.[6] Miranda gave birth to her first son, Irving Lee, in 1860, and her second, Edgar Morris, in early 1861.[7] Melvina then had a son of her own on May 25, 1861, and gave him his father's middle name: Eugene.[8] Miranda attended to her sister during the delivery.[9] The Wardwells set up house in Trenton, not far from Bar Harbor, while Melvina and Allen stayed next door to Simeon Lowell's home in Whitneyville.[10] The two young families seemed poised to settle down to their respective lives.

The spring of 1861, however, was not a time in which many Americans could settle down. Citizens of Maine responded enthusiastically to Governor Israel Washburn Jr.'s call for Union Army volunteers to fight the Confederacy after the bombardment of Fort Sumter on April 12 and 13.[11] Irving Wardwell and Allen Barry both eventually enlisted and followed their regiments south.[12] Wardwell died of typhoid at Donaldsonville, Louisiana, in July 1863, after nine months of service.[13] Melvina's husband Allen Barry was gravely wounded while fighting with the

First Maine Heavy Artillery Regiment during the Second Battle of Petersburg, in Virginia, and died hours later on June 19, 1864.[14]

By that summer of 1864, the Lowell family had suffered a double loss. Melvina and Miranda were single mothers with children under the age of five and no immediate way of making a living for themselves beyond their widows' pensions. With their father, Simeon, they imagined a new future for themselves outside Maine, away from its reminders of their planned-for lives with their husbands. Simeon looked for a place where he could continue to work in his trade of lumber milling.

In the mid-1860s, few states offered brighter opportunities for Maine lumbermen than Minnesota. The Maine–Minnesota pathway was so well established, in fact, that a migrant from the Pine Tree State could reasonably expect to get hired onto a St. Anthony lumber crew simply by saying "I'm from Maine."[15] There was a personal connection, too. Simeon's older brother Henry Clay Lowell had moved to Rice County, Minnesota, in 1855 and become a prominent judge.[16] Buoyed by these assurances, Simeon, his wife, one of their sons, and their two youngest daughters decided to transplant themselves to what "Old" New Englanders then saw as a remote corner of the United States.

In 1865, the family made the journey from Whitneyville, with its population of fewer than six hundred people, to Minneapolis and its next-door rival, St. Anthony, with their combined tens of thousands.[17] The Minnesota state census of that year (completed by June 1) counted Simeon Lowell living with Miranda and her two sons in Minneapolis.[18] By 1867, Miranda was working as a teacher, and she seized the opportunity to join the faculty of the Madison School after it opened in 1870.[19] She did so well there that when the Jefferson School needed a principal a few years later, it hired her away from Madison, and she assumed responsibility for the institution.[20]

Melvina took a less professional path. In 1867 she met George A. Campbell, another Maine-born lumberman lured west by Minnesota's white pine, and married him on October 23, 1869.[21] The marriage disqualified both Melvina and her son, Eugene, from future pension payments tied to their relationship to Allen Barry. Perhaps with this in mind, Melvina chose to transfer legal guardianship of Eugene from herself to Miranda. Hennepin County Probate Court granted Miranda legal guardianship of the eight-year-old boy on April 30, 1870, and reinstated his monthly payment of fifteen dollars (with a two-dollar bonus included).[22]

Miranda's adoption of Eugene points to the closeness of the sisters throughout the 1870s. Together they had experienced marriage, motherhood, widowhood, and moving to Minnesota, and these shared experiences appear to have bonded them. The two women visited the pension office together in 1873 to testify to Eugene's date of birth and continue his pension through his sixteenth birthday.[23] By 1875 they had even merged households, with the three Wardwells (Miranda, Irving, and Edgar) living in the same unit as the four Campbells: Melvina, George, Eugene, and the couple's infant daughter, Josie.[24] As Irving and Edgar grew up, they continued to board with the Campbells while attending school, even after Miranda moved into lodgings of her own.[25]

It was through this enduring connection to her sister that Melvina met Leon Belmont in 1880. Without it, they might never have crossed paths. Miranda helped report Belmont to the police on October 29 after one of the teachers she supervised at the Jefferson School, Sarah Brackett, confided that her beau owed her money . . . and might be a woman.[26] The arrest set in motion the Belmont sensation, the event that brought Belmont into Miranda's social orbit, and, by extension, Melvina's.

As mentioned in chapter 6, Melvina had multiple reasons to respond to Belmont's courtship in the waning days of 1880, even as newspapers were exposing his seduction of two other women. George Campbell abused her and had done so for years. The winter was relentlessly snowy and cold. Belmont was charming, handsome, and distracting, and took her on romantic sleigh rides. Given his record with Columbus Orcutt, James Weakley, Sarah Brackett, and the Watts family, it's likely that Belmont painted a rosy picture of his prospects to his new paramour, assuring Melvina that starting a new life with him was a path to happiness. Melvina chose that path, divorced Campbell on March 23, and married Belmont on April 6. She may not have known her new husband's gender identity, but it's possible that she knew it and chose to pursue a relationship with him *because* of his transmasculinity. Doing justice to the complexity of Melvina's story requires us not only to hold open both of those possibilities at the same time, but to consider the distance between "she knew" on one side and "she didn't know" on the other. Like knowledge, ignorance is more often partial and ephemeral than it is total and static.[27] Melvina may have recognized some aspects of Belmont's embodied gender but not others, and those points of recognition may have grown, transformed, and subsided at different moments in the couple's relationship.

When Melvina married Belmont on April 6, 1881, she entered a new phase of her life, one defined by movement and freedom as well as uncertainty and hardship. She relocated more than half a dozen times in twenty years, following Belmont as he cycled through Kansas, Indian Territory, Missouri, and various business ventures, none of which achieved lasting success. By the time Melvina and Belmont arrived in Springfield, Missouri, in 1900, they were no longer the same people who had ventured out together into the frigid Minneapolis winter for sleigh rides. Melvina was fifty-eight years old; Belmont was forty-seven but may have been weakened by the long-term illness or disability he had suffered in Carthage.[28]

In order to understand what Belmont did in 1902, we need to flash forward fourteen years to 1916, the year in which Melvina began writing to the US Bureau of Pensions to restore her status as a pension-eligible Civil War widow. The process dragged on until 1922, with the bureau denying her request for renewal multiple times on account of her marriage to Belmont. As a result, the pension file of Allen E. Barry is more than two hundred pages long and contains not only dozens of letters written by Melvina, but also the depositions that she, her family, and her neighbors gave to one of the bureau's examiners. These records provide insight into Melvina's relationship with Belmont between 1902 and 1913, and in particular to the events of March 17, 1902, when Belmont took on a new identity.

~

On September 8, 1916, the US Congress passed an act increasing the annual pension awarded to the widows of Civil War soldiers from twelve to twenty dollars.[29] At the same time, it offered an equal pension to all widows over seventy years old, regardless of whether they had remarried or divorced (without "fault") since the soldier's death. Melvina, at this point, hadn't received a pension as the widow of Allen Barry since 1869—the year in which she had married George Campbell. She had married Belmont immediately after her divorce from Campbell in 1881, and had therefore remained ineligible for a pension for as long as this third marriage lasted. But as she read over the details of the new act in 1916, Melvina became convinced that it restored her eligibility. She was by now seventy-four and living in Joplin, Missouri, with her daughter and son-in-law. Twenty dollars a year wasn't a fortune, but it promised to pay for things Melvina might have shied away from requesting from the couple who were already giving her so much.

She acted quickly. On September 20, 1916, barely two weeks after the pension bill had passed, Melvina addressed a letter to the US Commissioner of Pensions, noting her first husband's service: "I feel that I am entitled and should receive this allowance, otherwise I should not be writing this letter. . . . I have no husband living. I would appreciate very much if you would give this your earliest attention, and if there is not too much red tape to go through I may be benefited in my declining years. Should I not receive that allowance under the circumstances for the past four years since my seventieth birthday?" She signed as "Mrs. Allen E. Barry, Widow of Lieut. Allen E. Barry."[30]

Melvina had fired the opening salvo of what was to become a seven-year battle—mostly by correspondence—with the federal government. She established herself as a shrewd adversary, emphasizing the circumstances in her favor and leaving out those that threatened her case. She wrote as the widow of Allen E. Barry, entitled to the restoration of her pension, but failed to mention her subsequent marriages, both of which impacted her eligibility. Pensions Commissioner G. M. Saltzgaber responded with a blank application for Melvina but called her out on the subterfuge. "The records of this Bureau," he wrote, "indicate that Melvina A. Barry, the widow of the above named soldier, was married to George C. Campbell on October 23, 1869. If you are that widow, it is not known why you sign your name as Mrs. Allen E. Barry."[31] Melvina fired back on October 11 to say that yes, she had married Campbell in 1869, but the bureau ought to know as much already, since it had her information on file. She then must have judged that the benefit of mentioning Belmont outweighed the cost. She added in the same letter:

> In the year 1882 I was married to Leon A. Belmont at Spencer Brook Minn. That proved not to be his right name and I was rescued by my friend!! and without recourse to law. We separated and I again took my former name Melvina A. Barry. There is no record of such a marriage taking place. I do not know where that person is, if living or dead.[32]

While the only untruth in this report was the wedding year (Melvina married Belmont in 1881), the rest was sleight of hand, fudging, and wishful thinking. She described the marriage as brief, informal, inconsequential—hardly even legal. In fact, it was the opposite: a sworn, witnessed, and certified marriage that lasted for twenty years. The record she claims never existed had been filed in the Isanti County clerk's office after the wedding, as she either knew herself or had conveniently forgotten.[33] In this account of the relationship, moreover, Melvina seems to have married Belmont, separated from him, and changed her name again within a span of weeks or months. This last part was false; the Springfield city directory listed her as "Mrs. Melvina A. Belmont" between 1903 and 1910, and the US census of 1910 counted "Melvina A. Belmont" in Springfield. Melvina herself later testified under oath that "I was known as Mrs. Belmont all of the time I was in Springfield, Mo., and I did not resume the name of Barry until after I was divorced from Mr. Belmont [in 1922]."[34]

The compression of time in Melvina's account makes it impossible to know when the "rescue" she mentioned took place. Did it happen immediately after the wedding? Twenty years later? If the former, Melvina hid her decision to stay with Belmont in spite of his deception; if the latter, she glossed over the two-decade span of their marriage. What, moreover, did the rescue by the friend involve? Melvina never again mentioned the discovery of Belmont's original name in her letters, and the episode with the friend dropped out of her official version of events. (In an affidavit written four years later, she even claimed, "I suppose [Belmont] married me under his leagal [*sic*] name.")[35]

Saltzgaber failed to respond to Melvina's October letter, so she wrote to him again on December 15, 1916: "Do you not think that Santa Claus could assist in the restoration of my claim, which is no. 38058?"[36] He couldn't, and didn't. But Saltzgaber goofed, explaining the delay on January 27 by telling Melvina that he had not yet received her application when he had.[37] She hastened to point this out in yet another letter on January 31, and Saltzgaber lost patience: "In response to your letter of the 31st ultimo you are advised that your above cited claim for remarried widow's pension under the Act of September 8, 1916 is one of about forty thousand claims filed under the second and third sections of said Act."[38]

The reply silenced Melvina—for the time being. The gears of the Bureau of Pensions ground slowly on as February became March, and then April, and then May. Saltzgaber relayed the verdict in a single sentence sent to Melvina on May 2: "Your claim for pension under the act of September 8, 1916, filed October 16, 1916, is rejected on the ground that you have contracted more than one marriage since the soldier's death."[39] Melvina did not accept the news, and wasted no time in protesting it:

> Rejected! Why, that seems an awfully harsh word. I can scarcely believe it. I would spurn an unworthy act, for no complications can make right out of wrong. I made my claim with a clear conscience of right or I should never have made the claim. I am very sorry. I am an old woman past three score years and ten, and I ask the price of blood and am denied! I felt the "barriers had been burned away" by this act of Sept. 8, 1916, and I know I am entitled to my former pension! Will you please think so, too?[40]

She enlisted a chorus of flourishes to amplify her indignation: underlining, archaic language, metaphor, ironic non-apology—even a reference to the melodramatic Christian novel *Barriers Burned Away*.[41] As a writer, she seems to have sensed that she needed to use every tool at her disposal to convince Saltzgaber it was worth his time to continue the exchange. And continue it did, with the commissioner assuring Melvina on May 12 that the decision did not reflect her "honesty or personal worth."[42] Instead, he explained, although the pension act applied to remarried widows who had been widowed a second time, it did not provide for widows who had remarried more than once after the soldier's death.

The bureau's denial of Melvina's plea stems from its rationale for paying pensions in the first place—a gendered logic that dates back to the earliest American pension laws.[43] The bureau never intended to compensate a widow for the trauma of losing a husband; instead, it offered to provide stopgap support until she married again. It tided her over, that is, until she could find another man to provide for her. The appearance of a new husband on the scene ended her perceived need, and with it her eligibility. A widow's greatest presumed trouble was therefore not her grief, which was unending, but her lack of a man, which was seen as temporary.[44]

The bureau further shored up gender roles by enforcing a narrow definition of womanhood. By defining a "deserving" widow as one who remarried no more than once after her husband's death, the government promoted the idea that a good woman was also a chaste one. Multiple marriages implied prolific (hetero)sexual activity, which was next door to promiscuity.[45] Multiple marriages not only nullified widows' rights; they disqualified women from calling themselves widows in the first place. A real widow, the bureau's rules suggested, was one who kept her sexuality in check.[46]

In spite of this pressure, remarried Civil War widows persisted in petitioning the Pension Bureau for support. Some waged multiyear and even multidecade campaigns similar to Melvina's, and in that respect, her saga is not unique. A Black woman named Charlotte Banks Holloway Capehart applied for a widow's pension in North Carolina in 1869 and sent subsequent petitions in 1873, 1890, and 1904, and 1905.[47] Capehart's case was complicated not only by multiple marriages but also by the bureau's reluctance to acknowledge her original marriage to Caesar Banks—a common experience for Civil War widows who married while they were enslaved.[48] Another Black widow from North

Carolina, Fanny Whitney, submitted her first pension claim in 1867 and defended it from doubts of her credibility in person and in writing, from 1873 into the 1890s.[49]

Saltzgaber's May 12 letter was not the end of the road for Melvina. She sat in her daughter's house in Joplin through the summer and fall of 1917 and ruminated on her dependent state.[50] She contacted lawyers, hoping to find a loophole to the more-than-one-remarriage rule. They offered nothing concrete but emboldened Melvina to try again, and she reentered the fray with another dispatch to Saltzgaber on December 17:

> Will you not please reconsider and think what you would do if it was <u>your own mother</u> asking for that which is rightfully hers. I feel like a <u>mendicant begging</u>, but for my rights. My father's family gave five to the Civil War, and not one of them left to ask for a pension but myself. I <u>may die trying</u> but it will be <u>scientifically</u>. I shall certainly try.[51]

At this moment, as Melvina set out to contravene the ruling of a US government agency, her stance was as stubborn as Belmont's had been in Minneapolis in 1880. They were a well-matched pair. As Belmont had done, Melvina refused to bow to a system that singled her out, judged her to be undeserving for superficial reasons, and denied her rights based on that judgment. Like Belmont, she could not be content. Also like Belmont, she resolved to stick to her story, embellishing where it served her purpose. The Lowell family does not appear to have lost five members to the Civil War, as claimed by Melvina. Her own first husband and brother-in-law were casualties, but neither man was a Lowell. And of her remaining brothers, uncles, and cousins, only two passed away while the war was in progress: her uncle Henry Clay Lowell (1863) and her paternal cousin Josiah N. Lowell (1861).[52] Both died as unenlisted civilians.

The December 17 letter, for all its bravado, failed to win over Saltzgaber, who told Melvina that if she disagreed with the bureau's decision she could take it up with the secretary of the interior.[53] Melvina called his bluff and did just that, writing to Woodrow Wilson appointee Franklin Knight Lane and initiating an appeals process that lasted into July 1918.[54] The verdict, when it came, was the same: Melvina did not qualify for a renewal of pension because she had married two men after the death of Allen Barry. The Department of the Interior rejected her appeal and affirmed Saltzgaber's reasoning.[55]

The settlement of the appeal in 1918 marked the closing of a chapter of Melvina's campaign, but it was far from the end. The conclusion of World War I led to a wave of pension reforms that increased dollar amounts and restored eligibility to excluded groups. As Melvina noticed, the Fuller Pension Bill, signed into law by President Wilson on May 1, 1920, authorized pensions for widows who had remarried but then divorced "without fault."[56] If Melvina could provide proof of a no-fault divorce from Belmont, she was now back in the game.[57] By this time, the Bureau of Pensions had a "Widow Division," so it was with that department that Melvina corresponded, after an assist from Saltzgaber. When its commissioner reminded her that the next step was a legal divorce, she responded:

> The prolonged absence of L. A. Belmont since the spring of 1902 has been such a relief to me that I have shrunk from the publicity also the expense of a divorce, but if that should be necessary I can procure one. I am satisfied that he is not living, and it would be like a divorce from a deceased man. I have not heard from him in that length of time in any way, or received any support from him as I have stated under oath.[58]

Melvina's certainty about Belmont's death had evolved. In 1916, she had not known whether he was alive or dead. Now, in 1920, she was satisfied that he was not living. The shift stemmed not from new information about Belmont, but from a change in Melvina's approach to representing what had happened to him. She had upgraded his status from missing to presumed dead . . . though not to *confirmed* dead, as if she knew that proving as much would be impossible. It was as if Belmont had ceased to exist without dying—had expired through some means other than death. Only in these queer circumstances could a divorce from Belmont be "like" a divorce from a deceased man, rather than the real thing.

The case dragged on into 1921, and then into 1922. Saltzgaber left the Bureau of Pensions and was replaced by a man named Washington Gardiner. Melvina wrote to US Congressman I. V. McPherson (her state representative) and persuaded him to check in with Gardiner to keep things moving on her behalf.[59] With this high-profile help, Melvina reached the last hurdle of the pension-renewal process: an in-person interview that would verify her eligibility once and for all.

~

In January 1922, Washington Gardiner handed over Melvina's case to T. Quinn Jones, a ten-year veteran of the Special Examination Division who carried out investigations in the Upper Midwest.[60] In spite of their name, special examinations were a standard procedure used since 1864, when the bureau was inundated with claims related to the Civil War.[61] The assignment Jones received was typical for a traveling pensions agent: determine through a series of interviews whether the claimant (Melvina) was concealing a pre-1922 at-fault divorce from Belmont or had lived with another partner since 1902. To do this, he installed himself near the claimant's home in Joplin, Missouri, to access city directories, leaf through newspapers, and review divorce-court records.[62] His main objective, however, was to arrange the depositions of witnesses and evaluate their testimony.

The depositions raise as many questions about Belmont's life after 1902 as they answer. Viewed together, they give the picture of a man who represented himself differently to each of the people he knew, to the point where one witness's version of Belmont hardly resembles another's. At the same time that the testimonies fragment Belmont's identity, however, they also bring into focus Nova McClure Carr, the woman who lived with Melvina at 926 West Elm between 1902 and 1913.

Jones sat down with Melvina in Joplin to record her first deposition on February 13, 1922. In spite of having lived with Belmont for twenty years, she claimed not to know anything about his family or activities before 1879. After their marriage, he had practiced medicine without a license in Indian Territory and Kansas, and was often out of town. In 1902, he had left their house in Springfield one day, as if to go on a business trip, and never returned. Melvina shot down

Jones's suggestion that a fight had caused their breakup, insisting that although "I did not like the way he acted and he would not support me and I had to work and earn my own living . . . we never quarreled."[63] Much of the remaining testimony was negative: Belmont had no family, belonged to no church or lodge, never served in the military, had no medical office in Springfield, was not a "woman chaser." He was like a charming but unreliable ghost, "a very pleasing personality" who "would easily make friends but not keep them."[64] He was tall (five-foot-eleven), with blue eyes and light-brown hair, and never wore a beard. When Jones pressed Melvina on her motive for divorce, she explained that restoring her pension required her either to declare him dead or to divorce him, "and I could not declare him dead."[65]

On the same day, Jones also sat down with Maude Warren, Melvina's daughter with George Campbell (and Belmont's stepdaughter). Maude's account broadly matched her mother's but left it open to doubt. "I was not there when [Belmont] left," she explained, "and I do not know the exact circumstances under which he left. Mother did not speak of them having any especial trouble. I do not know that Mother assigned any reason for him leaving or for her not looking him up. I think she thought that he would return if nothing happened, but he did not return."[66]

For Jones, this was mysterious but consistent with what he had already heard. He moved next to set up depositions of witnesses outside the family who might offer a contrasting perspective: Jennie M. Gehrett, the Belmonts' next-door neighbor in Springfield; John W. Williams, another Springfield neighbor; and Charles A. Greene, Belmont's business associate since the late 1890s. He met with them separately on April 19, 1922, and in each interview the subject turned to Nova McClure, a supposed cousin of Belmont's who had lived with Melvina between 1902 and 1913. Jennie Gehrett testified:

> I well remember Mr. and Mrs. Belmont who lived next door to me for eight years, anyhow. These people were very mysterious and were the talk of the neighborhood. . . . The general belief was that this cousin who posed as Miss McClure was identical with Mr. Belmont. Miss McClure was of identically

> the same build as Mr. Belmont and the voice was almost identical. I have talked to her a great deal and one of the first things that was noticed was the similarity of voices. Miss McClure posed as a trained nurse and would go off on supposedly nursing trips.[67]

Melvina had shared none of these details with Jones—never mentioned a woman who had arrived after Belmont's disappearance and lived with her for more than a decade. The implication of Gehrett's testimony was clear: Melvina was lying. Belmont had never left 926 West Elm Street on the night of March 17, 1902, but had taken up a new identity the next morning as Nova McClure. In Latin, the word "nova" means new; since it's a singular and feminine form, one of its substantive meanings is "a new woman." Like Belmont, McClure was trained (to some degree) in medicine, and passed off her absences from Springfield as visits to patients. Gehrett ended her interview by noting that when McClure first appeared to her, she wore a veil that covered her face, and afterward a hooded sunbonnet.[68] During the few interactions in which McClure revealed her profile, Gehrett noticed "she had the same shape face as Mr. Belmont."[69]

Jones's next witness, John W. Williams, corroborated Gehrett's claims. He remembered McClure as "a masculine coarse looking woman and medium fleshy and large boned," with "a good deal the same build as the man I knew as Belmont."[70] Williams, too, was surprised to hear that Belmont had been a doctor, and reported talking to him about horses and some unsettled business of Belmont's in Nashville.

When Jones spoke to Charles A. Green about Nova McClure, he heard for the first time that she had presented herself to some people as Belmont's cousin. This twist showed that Belmont had stayed true to his invented genealogy. In 1880, he had claimed to descend on his mother's side from the house of McClure, and to stand to inherit a fortune in England because of it.[71] Nova McClure, presumably, was the imagined daughter of one of his mother's siblings, and one of Belmont's cousins. An explanation for why this British heiress was compelled to take up nursing in America did not follow. As Green explained it:

> Miss McClure was supposed to be a cousin of Belmont. She was supposed to have come from New York, from the Bellevue Hospital, and was a trained nurse. She was supposed to take care of Mrs. Belmont while Mr. Belmont went away to have the estate settled. . . . Belmont went from [Springfield] to New York City and I got a letter from him a few days after he got there. The way he wrote me was that there was $300,000 in cash and this place in Tennessee that was coming to him. I do not know where Belmont Hall is but it is about twenty miles from Nashville and most everyone would know where the place is . . . Dr. Belmont was a short, heavy set man. I should say, by guess, that he was about 65 years old when left here. He was not very strong physically. He just seemed down and out.[72]

Green's report contradicted Melvina's deposition even more than Gehrett's and Williams's had done. Suddenly, Belmont had not only a living family member, but one whom he had brought to Springfield to live with his wife. He had left town not for a routine business trip that turned indefinite, but for the purpose of claiming his Tennessee estate.[73] Even the two accounts' most basic facts about Belmont failed to line up.[74] Melvina had said he was five-foot-eleven, and Green now said he was short. Green seemed to anticipate this mismatch and raised the possibility that seventy-nine-year-old Melvina was senile—her mind "not exactly right." Whether this belief was genuine or not, it offered to Jones a convenient explanation for the discrepancies to come. If Melvina was misremembering something as fundamental as her ex-husband's height, who could count on her to recall the dynamics of their relationship in 1902?

Full of new questions, Jones arranged for a follow-up interview with Melvina to be held two days later, on April 21, 1922. Melvina agreed, and they sat down together in the Warrens' Joplin house for a second time. Both interviewer and interviewee were testy this time around. Their unease comes through in the transcript of their conversation, as Jones tried to push through Melvina's wall of denials:

Jones: Was Miss McClure and Mr. Belmont one and the same person?

Melvina: They were not the same person. She never represented to me that she was a cousin to Belmont. No, they were not the same person. Miss McClure was much larger and stouter tha[n] Mr. Belmont . . . No, sir, if my life depended on it, he never said that he was going to look after any estate. He left in the morning and never said where he was going. No, sir, Miss McClure never represented to me that she was a cousin of Belmont. She may have told Green that. I know she went out with Green one night and she told me that he tried to insult her. *I could not swear that Miss McClure was a woman any more than I could swear any other woman was a woman.* Mr. Belmont was crooked in his deals and would never keep his word. He never did anything to get in jail for or to get arrested for.[75] Miss McClure was never in any trouble that I know of. She was always liked as a nurse and had plenty of work. . . . Miss McClure and I lived together seven or eight years and Kenneth was the only child there.[76]

Melvina ceded no ground. Even when confronted with the testimony of Gehrett, Williams, and Green, she stood by her earlier statements.[77]

Multiple possibilities follow from incomplete facts. In one scenario, Melvina recognized Belmont's identity as a man assigned a female sex at birth early on in their relationship. As mentioned already in this chapter, she may have been attracted to him *because* he transed gender. In that case, she moved through their married life as someone who knew about and supported Belmont's gender identity but hid it from others for his protection.[78] In a second scenario, Melvina did not learn that Belmont had been assigned a female sex at birth until 1902. He decided to go through a gender transition in that year, but this time he explained his history to Melvina before following through, or she discovered it afterward.

A third scenario strains belief but deserves consideration: that

Melvina told to Quinn T. Jones and the Bureau of Pensions what was, for her, the truth. Belmont really did disappear in 1902 with no explanation, an unrelated lodger named Nova McClure arrived afterward, and the two women lived together before parting ways in 1913.

In both of the two latter scenarios, Melvina lived as Belmont's wife for twenty years without knowing that he'd been assigned a female sex at birth. History cautions us to stay open to this possibility. In 1906, when a Chicago coroner reported that a deceased man named Nicolai De Raylan had been assigned a female sex at birth, De Raylan's wife not only denied knowing about it but insisted that the coroner had got it wrong.[79] "I think I ought to know as much as the doctors about it," Anna De Raylan told a newspaper reporter, "and I say he was a man."[80] Irishwoman Martha Coulter was married to her husband, John, for close to three decades, and declined to agree that he had been female at an inquest held after his death in 1884.[81] And when farmhand William C. Howard died, in New York State, in 1902, and a coroner pronounced him female, his wife, Edith, wrote out a sworn statement affirming his identity as her husband and referring to him as "he."[82]

Melvina's alternative understanding of her partner's sex and gender is as possible as Anna De Raylan's, Martha Coulter's, and Edith Howard's. It's easy, from the perspective of a twenty-first-century reader, to dismiss their perceived ignorance as feigned, naive, or delusional. It's easy to ask the question, "How could they not have known?" But that response raises the questioner to the level of an omniscient observer, privy to "the truth" about a historical figure's identity that his partner could not reach. Melvina may have had sexual contact with Belmont of many kinds, or none at all, and still believed that he was a man because it felt true—*was* true—in the context of their relationship. Ruling out the possibilities of that lived experience narrows the spectrum of the couple's dynamic, which, prism-like, seems to have reflected multiple truths over the decades.[83]

Why might Belmont have committed himself to the second gender transition of his life at the time he did? He had lived as Addie Walker for twenty-five years, from 1853 into 1878. In 1902, he was approaching the same quarter-century milestone as Leon Belmont. It's possible that his relationship to his gender had shifted as he moved into middle age, and that by 1902, the Belmont persona no longer aligned with his identity, prompting him to adopt a new one. If this is an accurate description of his experience, it fits within the modern definition of gender fluidity—the inclination to move through multiple gender identities and expressions over a lifetime.[84] Although gender fluidity is a modern term, it's recognizable in Belmont's historical precedents. About a hundred years before Addie Walker grew up in West Warren, another baby was born in Massachusetts, assigned a female sex, and raised in a working-class family before going through multiple gender transitions. The child lived from 1760 until 1782 as Deborah Sampson before becoming Robert Shurtliff and enlisting in the Continental Army. Shurtliff fought in the American Revolution for three years, retained a man's identity after mustering out, and then eventually resumed a woman's identity as Deborah Gannett, the wife of farmer Benjamin Gannett.[85] This second transition seems not to have been coerced, but to have reflected Shurtliff's evolving gender identification.[86] It's possible that Belmont, like Shurtliff, followed his evolving gender identity where it led.

While the reasons for Belmont's transition are unknowable, its likely effects are not. The United States was a different place in 1902 than it had been in the 1870s, when Belmont had first articulated his identity as a man on the plains of Kansas and "was not thought strange."[87] Scrutiny of gender-variant people in the United States was intensifying.[88] The wave of cross-dressing ordinances that had triggered the 1880 Belmont sensation in Minneapolis was cresting.[89] By 1902, several of the cities in Belmont's ambit—Cedar Falls, Iowa, as well as St. Louis, Kansas City, and Columbia, Missouri; Denver, Colorado; and Lincoln and Omaha, Nebraska—were arresting perceived offenders.[90] This era of public surveillance coincided with a turn toward studying, stigmatizing, and pathologizing gender variance. In their studies of the patients they labeled "inverts" (according to the new language of sexual science), European sexologists led American doctors and psychiatrists to understand people who transed gender as the sufferers of a disease. But icons of New Womanhood (as discussed in chapter 7) were also stretching the limits of what was considered gender-appropriate behavior for women.[91] Because of these shifts, it was easier for Belmont to live the life he wanted—to travel alone, to earn a living—as a woman in 1902 than it had been in the 1870s. As a woman, he now had more breathing room; as a transmasculine person, he faced more threats.

Becoming Nova McClure protected Belmont from arrest, abuse, and scrutiny. Even if he evaded "exposure" during his lifetime, Melvina might face a sensational inquest after his death. William C. Howard's inquest played out in New York State on March 22, 1902, just days after Belmont began living as Nova McClure in Missouri.[92] In the same month, the death of a man named George Green in Virginia led to a flurry of newspaper coverage when loved ones preparing his body for burial judged it to be female. Reporters interviewed Mary Green, his widow, in spite of the fact that she was "almost overcome with grief" and "no sorrow more profound or deeper was ever seen."[93] Belmont's transformation into Nova McClure ensured that a publicity circus like the one that surrounded George Green's family wouldn't overshadow his own death. It also prevented a sequel to the Belmont sensation—the invasion of privacy that had disrupted his life in 1880.

This was the social and personal context of Belmont's second gender transition. Its effects reverberated across time, reaching into Melvina's home in 1922, and from there into the US Bureau of Pensions. When T. Quinn Jones finished his second interview with Melvina on April 21, his examination was complete. He found himself in the unenviable position of having to condense the messy, contradictory notes he had collected into a report for his boss back at the bureau. He gave himself a day to rest, gathered his thoughts, and wrote the following on April 22:

> The neighbors are all of the honest belief that there was never such a persona as Miss McClure, but that Belmont remained in Springfield with claimant for many years after Belmont was supposed to leave. That during this time he masqueraded as Miss McClure, a trained nurse.
>
> In the pension case this is irrelevant except that if it were proven that Belmont and Miss McClure were identical it would account for many years of the whereabouts of Belmont

> that we know nothing about now. . . . Belmont owed money and it [is] not impossible that he would have attempted such a thing, but it hardly seems probable that he could have carried through such a program for so many years without detection.[94]

Having laid out the evidence, Jones wrapped things up. Four months into his investigation, he was ready to call it quits. He had no way to locate Belmont, and without him, "There is not enough testimony obtainable in this district upon which to base an intelligent recommendation for further special examination. It is therefore recommended that the case be referred to the Board of Review."[95] If the Bureau of Pensions wanted to pursue Belmont, it would have to call in a new agent.

The Bureau of Pensions did not want to pursue Belmont. After reviewing Jones's report, it granted Melvina a pension at a rate of thirty dollars a month on May 24, 1922.[96] At long last, she had secured what she believed was entitled to her. Any satisfaction she felt from that victory, however, was short lived. On September 14, 1922, seven months after Jones had interviewed her, Melvina's daughter, Maude, died of breast cancer, at the age of forty-seven. She had known she was sick since at least 1919, when she had a related surgery, but the cancer had persisted. When one of Maude's sisters-in-law helped the coroner fill out the death certificate, she specified that Maude's father was "Dr. A. Belmont," and that there was no record of his place of birth.[97]

Melvina continued to live in Joplin with her son-in-law until her own death, on August 20, 1931. The cause of death was arteriosclerosis, but the coroner noted "senility" as a contributing factor.[98] It was the end of a distinctly American life, marked by migration, self-reinvention, and the pursuit of a perceived entitlement. A life not unlike Belmont's. Since her 1840s childhood in Maine, Melvina had witnessed some of the most dramatic shifts in US history, from the Civil War and the Industrial Revolution to the stock market crash of 1929. She had given birth to two children, fostered a third, and been married to three men. Her relationship with Belmont and then with Nova McClure had encompassed thirty-three of her eighty-eight years, and had turned out to be among the most lasting of her life. But outside that influence she had been the agent of her own life, piloting its course until the end.

9.

The Mother, 1913–1927

Q: Who was Kenneth, the boy?

A: A little boy that was abandoned on the train. He went as Kenneth McClure. The last I heard of him he was in Carthage, Mo., nine years ago [1913] living with a nurse named Nova McClure.

—Deposition of Melvina A. Barry, April 21, 1922,
US Bureau of Pensions, pension file of Allen E. Barry, 14

At the same time that Nova McClure's relationship with Melvina was evolving in the first decade of the 1900s, a new relationship entered Nova's life and eclipsed it. Leon Belmont had been a stepfather to Melvina's daughter, Maude, since 1881, and hosted Maude's wedding to Fountain Warren in 1895. When he left behind his gender identity in 1902 to become Nova, he also left behind his identity as a parent. Nova McClure could not see Maude in person without risking being recognized as Belmont. Nova McClure had no children.

At first.

In 1913, a train pulled into a station in Springfield, Missouri, carrying a young and lonely passenger. He was a boy, less than ten years old, without parents or caregivers, far from home and evidently abandoned. A Springfield resident named Mrs. Blood gave him a place to stay temporarily, but he needed something permanent. Nova McClure heard about the situation, took the boy home to 926 West Elm, and made him her adopted son.[1] She even gave him a new name that implied he had been hers all along: Kenneth McClure. It was a kind gesture, one that headed off questions from strangers about how the woman and the young boy were related. The shared name made it known that they were family of one kind or another. Kenneth had plenty of time to appreciate this symbol of Nova's commitment; he lived with her as his mother for the next decade and a half.

Nova McClure's adoption of Kenneth shows a generous side of her character that's hard to make out during her years as Addie Walker, Ernest Ellwood, and Leon Belmont. If it was already there, it was latent—obscured by the self-interested questing, hustling, and romancing of youth. Belmont had accepted fatherhood in 1881 when he married Melvina, but it came with the enticement of his bride's money. When Nova adopted Kenneth in the 1910s, parenting offered no reward other than an emotional bond with a vulnerable child who needed help. It's unclear if Nova expected Melvina to share the cost of raising Kenneth when she brought him home; if she didn't, she chose for herself the expenses and stresses of working-class single parenthood. While Nova's desires are rarely visible in this decade, this one shines through. In middle age, she wanted to be a mother.

Whether Nova planned to raise Kenneth by herself or found herself in that situation through unforeseen circumstances, Kenneth's arrival overlapped with a turning point in her intimacy with Melvina. The entries for their home at 926 West Elm in the Springfield city directory between 1902 and 1913 show the fluidity of their household in these years. In 1902, Melvina gave out her name as "Marion" and boarded a clerk named Harry Stephens for extra income. Belmont appears in 1903, but in 1904 and 1905 he's replaced by Ada/Addie L. McClure, whose profession is "traveling sales"; in this way McClure experimented with bringing back her old first name before settling on a new one. By 1906, she had compromised by shrinking "Addie" into a leading initial before "Nova" to make a name that tied her childhood to her new (*nova*) womanhood: "A. Nova McClure."

The entry for 1905 is hard to interpret, since both Leon A. Belmont and Addie L. McClure appear together, with no mention of Melvina. Did McClure live in two different identities, one male and one female, in this single year? And did Melvina move out, or did McClure merely fail to mention her when asked to contribute to the Spring-

Year	Residents of 926 West Elm Street, Springfield
1902	Marion A. Belmont; Harry Stephens, clerk (boarder)
1903	Mrs. Mell A. Belmont; Leon A. Belmont
1904	Mrs. Mell A. Belmont; Ada L. McClure (traveling sales)
1905	Leon A. Belmont; Addie L. McClure (traveling sales)
1906	Mrs. Mell A. Belmont; A. Nova McClure (traveling sales)
1907	Mrs. Mell Belmont
1908	Mrs. Mell Belmont
1909	Mrs. Melvina A. Belmont
1910	Mrs. Melvina A. Belmont
1911	Mrs. Melvina A. Belmont
1912	Mrs. Melvina A. Belmont
1913	Melvina McClure and Nova McClure

Springfield city directory entries, 1902–1913.

field directory? Records from this period offer no answers, but they do reveal someone trying on different names in an attempt to find ones that fit. Between 1907 and 1912, Addie/Nova McClure may not have lived at the Springfield house, which would account for her absence from the 1910 census. In that year, Melvina appears alone.[2] In 1913, however, Nova was back in the directory as a coresident of the West Elm house with "Melvina McClure." Two McClures. The entry is the only instance of Melvina using a last name other than her own.

The reunion in 1913 did not last. By that year, Nova had Kenneth with her, and they were both gone from the Springfield house by 1914. So was Melvina, who moved in with Maud and Fountain Warren. "I continued to reside at 926 Elm Street," Melvina wrote in a 1920 affidavit, "until 1913 I came to my daughter's 214 Gray Ave Joplin where I have since resided."[3] Nova passed with Kenneth through Ava and Carthage, Missouri, before turning west to the state that always drew her back: Kansas.[4] With the moves came one final surname change, from McClure to Carr. Nova and Melvina both told neighbors that the new name came from a recent marriage to a military veteran named Mr. Carr,[5] but the man never appeared in person—just as Addie Walker's professed husband, Mr. Stanley, had failed to materialize in 1875. In both situations, Walker/McClure said she had married a man whom no one ever saw, the idea of whose existence made her "respectable." In both cases, too, claiming marriage allowed her to solve a crisis. After declaring the unseen Stanley dead in 1875, Addie used the prospect of a windfall from his will to get loans from Columbus Orcutt that lifted her out of of debt. McClure in 1913 was starting life as the mother of a son at a time when introducing yourself to strangers as an unwed mother (even an adoptive one) risked inviting gossip at best, and ostracism at worst.[6] If Miss McClure made herself a Mrs., in name if not in reality, she removed an obstacle from Kenneth's already steep climb to acceptance in his new home.

Legally or not, Nova McClure was using the name Nova Carr by 1915 and living with Kenneth in Parsons, Kansas. He was twelve years old. As Belmont, McClure had rejected assumptions about who counted as "real" relatives and chose her own family—one rooted in emotional kinship rather than bloodline.[7] Belmont's family had appeared conventional from the outside, but it transgressed overlapping norms of gender and parenting below the surface: Leon was both a stepparent and a father who'd been assigned a female sex at birth. McClure's chosen family was more openly queer, consisting as it did of a middle-aged woman without a male partner raising a son who was not her blood relative.

Nova became a mother during a time of raised expectations for women caring for children. It was a transitional period in which the Victorian vision of mothers as all-knowing saints (motherhood as religion) ceded ground to an ideal that required guidance from doctors, now seen as the "real" experts on how to raise a child (motherhood as science).[8] Earlier generations of caregivers had counted on their maternal instincts. By the 1910s, a woman like Nova McClure aiming to be a good mother needed to read childcare manuals, keep up with medical research, and consult pediatricians.[9] Magazine ads, increasingly hard to avoid during the rise of mass-consumer culture, signaled that a mother's wrong choice would set her child on the path to "maladjustment" as an adult. If infancy was a harrowing time for "habit formation" (weaning, thumb-sucking, and toilet training now required precisely timed interventions), then so was adolescence, when a boy like Kenneth could develop an "unhealthy" interest in masturbation.[10] Steering her child away from these dangers was the modern mother's quasi-professional (unpaid) duty. It required vigilance, evaluation, and revision.[11]

It was easier for some mothers to meet the exacting standards of scientific motherhood than for others. Working-class caregivers like Nova McClure had less money than their well-off peers to spend on the tools of the new parenting wisdom: tonics, salves, vitamin-enriched cereals, childcare magazine subscriptions, and appointments with specialists. Time, too, was a scarce resource for women doing both in-home and out-of-home labor. Scientific motherhood demanded free time for reading, shopping, consulting, and diagnosing that amounted to a part-time second job.[12] Those who failed to provide the new bare minimum risked being judged a failure as both a woman and a mother—roles that remained as culturally inseparable in the 1910s as they had been in the mid-1800s.

Nova faced additional pressure as a new parent in the 1910s because she was a single mother. Though she claimed to have married "Mr. Carr," the man himself was nowhere to be seen, so she was single in appearance, practice, and income. De facto singlehood, for Nova, was a material as well as a social problem. It was also one that would have been less serious if Nova had raised Kenneth as a single mother in the 1850s, especially in a rural area. In that earlier decade, society sympathized, to a degree, with the plight of a woman caring for children without a man at home. If circumstances forced her to claim leadership of her household—a perversion of "natural" gender roles—neighbors were willing to overlook the impropriety when it benefitted children. By the 1910s, this benefit of the doubt had dried up.[13] As communities urbanized, a woman claiming authority over both her family and a business in a city context posed more of a competitive threat to men than her predecessors, who had limited themselves to farm management, food production, and household crafts. As the "normal" family form shrank from a multigenerational network to a nuclear unit headed by one man and one woman, single motherhood became all but equivalent to child neglect.[14] A woman parenting without a man alongside her had failed before she'd started.

The material side of Nova's challenge in mothering Kenneth was tied to her eligibility for government aid, but also to her gender. Pensions for struggling mothers were available as early as 1917, but they were hard to get unless you could prove you were married and your husband was present—something Nova could not do.[15] She therefore faced the prospect of supporting herself and a child on whatever income she could piece together from inconsistent jobs until Kenneth was old enough to work. Until that time, their household was limited to the income Nova could bring in. In Kansas between 1916 and 1924, the most common jobs for unskilled women workers like Nova were in laundries, shops, boardinghouses, and factories, with a rising number finding work as telephone operators.[16] When the US Bureau of Labor compiled statistics on women working in Kansas in 1921, it reported the median weekly earnings of those employed in "general mercantile" jobs at $11.95; in laundries at $10.50; in telephones at $10.80; and in "miscellaneous manufacturing" at $12.70.[17] Men, meanwhile, were making about 40 percent more than women in agricultural and manufacturing sectors across the United States.[18] The compiler of the 1921 report offered this grim assessment: "Annual earnings, weekly earnings, hourly earnings, all point to the same thing—the insufficient wage paid to the women in industry in Kansas."[19]

The realities of gender and labor in Kansas made the 1910s and 1920s a difficult time for a woman to afford single motherhood. Logistically, however, Nova was fortunate to adopt Kenneth when she did. The US government introduced restrictions in this period that complicated adoption, transforming what had been a relatively informal practice into a strictly regulated one. Before the 1910s, families could absorb abandoned children like Kenneth with relative ease. Legal adoption was prohibitively expensive and therefore rare, but also socially unnecessary; parents believed that cohabitation and care were enough to make adoptees their "real" children.[20] Then, in 1909, the White House Conference on the Care of Dependent Children called attention to the children without parents who were placed in institutions like orphanages and hospitals. In response, Congress created the United States Children's Bureau (USCB) in 1912 to regulate the removal of orphans and otherwise neglected or dependent children from their birth families. The Child Welfare League of America (CWLA) followed suit after its creation in 1921, pledging to standardize the placement of adoptees.[21] Some parents were now deemed unfit to adopt and prevented from doing so. By the 1920s, both the USCB and the CWLA promoted the idea that the best families for children were their "natural" ones, meaning their relatives by blood.[22] If the "natural" family failed, social workers tried to find the next-best thing: a "normal" family, defined increasingly in the 1920s as two married, middle-class, heterosexual, and gender-normative parents.

Since Nova Carr did not align with these expectations, she might have struggled to convince a social worker to let her adopt Kenneth legally after the 1920s. So her timing was lucky; by bringing a child into her home in 1913, she sidestepped the bureaucratic struggle that she would have faced in the decades that followed. I've found no surviving records that document a formal transfer of guardianship to Nova from Kenneth's birth parents. Instead, they simply lived together for the next fourteen years, and Nova introduced him to the people they met as her son.[23]

~

By 1915 Nova and Kenneth had moved to Parsons, Kansas, a city in northern Labette County. It was a homecoming of sorts for Nova, who had been out of the state since 1890. Belmont's last base in Kansas before moving to Missouri in 1890 had been Independence, less than thirty miles away from Parsons, and he'd sold washing machines in Oswego, the county seat. Nova found rooms for herself and Kenneth in a boardinghouse at 2221 Main Street in Parsons and, to pay for them, a job as a masseuse.[24]

When Kenneth moved with Nova to Parsons, he was the same age (thirteen) that Addie Walker had been when she'd worked in the cotton mill in Massachusetts. He was the same age, too, that Addie had been when Columbus Orcutt had embraced her as a surrogate father. Was Nova moved to offer the same kindness to Kenneth that Orcutt had shown to Addie? She did, even as a single parent, engineer for him the kind of middle-class young adulthood that Addie had never enjoyed. Where Addie had been a black sheep in West Warren, Kenneth emerged as an upright young citizen of his community. By 1915, Nova had signed him up for the Sunday school class at the local Presbyterian church, which hosted wholesome social events like Halloween parties for children.[25] She sent him to McKinley School, where he became a member of the Garden Club in 1917 and applied himself with such dedication that the *Parsons Daily Sun* singled him out for praise:

> Kenneth McClure who lives at 2221 Main and attends the McKinley school has done garden work that may help the Third ward folks to arouse interest. Kenneth, who is not yet 14 years old, handled about 3 acres on the south side of Main Street last year. The part that he put into corn was a loss because of the drouth. However after the corn crop failed he put in some turnips and on the other part of the plot he had carrots, parsnips and other vegetables. Besides what has been sold he still has on hand about 40 bushels of turnips and parsnips.[26]

Since it was the spring of 1917, and the United States was rushing to ship food overseas to the Allied nations fighting Germany, Kenneth's efforts gave off a patriotic glow.[27] The boy wasn't just a vegetable-growing dynamo; he was an emerging model citizen. If neighbors had judged him for being a newcomer to town with unknown birth parents, his exemplary work ethic suggested that they had nothing to fear from his difference.

As Kenneth grew up, Nova succeeded in steering him away from the bad reputation that she'd found so hard to shake in Massachusetts. Teenage Addie Walker had "run wild"; Kenneth did the opposite. By the summer of 1917 he had joined a Junior Boy Scout troop; attended its first picnic; and performed in a drill-work exhibition at church.[28] He was liked by his peers as well as adults. When the sixty-one members of the Parsons Pig Club (a 4-H–style organization for local teenagers) met in July 1918, they elected Kenneth their vice president.[29] Local newspapers, meanwhile, printed his name in their descriptions of community get-togethers, letting it be known that Kenneth McClure was the sort of boy who attended Valentine's Day–themed church parties and appeared in a Thanksgiving pageant called "American[s] in

Pilgrim Days."[30] He honed a talent for singing, scoring a bass solo in the church's 1921 Christmas oratorio *The Nativity*, composed by H. J. Stewart.[31] A year later he was chosen to perform a vocal solo during a local live radio broadcast—a huge event for Parsons residents in the early days of the technology.[32]

While Kenneth was thriving in Parsons in the years around 1920, his mother was leaving behind a fainter imprint. City directories published after 1916, when Nova was identified as a masseuse, do not list a profession. A source from 1927 refers to her involvement in women's organizations at her church.[33] If she made time for leisure activities (especially after 1918, when Kenneth started working), Parsons offered an array of state-of-the-art options attractive even to someone with Belmont's high standards. Since 1909, Parsons citizens had used for their public library a monumental Beaux Arts structure in Carthage stone paid for by Andrew Carnegie.[34] In 1915 a public baths complex—grandly called a natatorium—opened at the intersection of Fifteenth Street and Felix Avenue. Owner E. E. Dudley promised that "the pool will be brilliantly lighted at night by electricity and will leave nothing undone for the comfort of our bathers."[35] After a renovation in 1921, the Orpheum Theatre at 118–122 South 18th Street seated up to twelve hundred people and cooled them with electric fans while they enjoyed the latest musical comedies.[36] But the Orpheum faced stiff competition from the biggest innovation of all, open around the block at 1819–1821 East Main Street as of 1919: moving pictures.[37] If Nova and Kenneth got bored on a Saturday night, they could walk a few blocks east from their house at 2221 Main Street and lose themselves in the latest Charlie Chaplin farce or Dorothy Gish melodrama.

Parsons had a big enough population—16,828 people by 1923—to sustain demand for these businesses during the window of prosperity before the Great Depression.[38] The town owed that prosperity to its status as the headquarters of the Missouri–Kansas–Texas Railroad (known as the MKT, or Katy), which employed five hundred people in 1920 and two thousand in 1922.[39] The Katy complex took up the rough equivalent of twenty blocks northeast of the center of town, from Crawford Avenue in the south to Maple Avenue in the north.[40] Roundhouses, turntables, foundries, machine shops, coal tipples, sawdust houses, and locomotive repair pits, all of them laid out within a spider's web of overlapping tracks, staked out an industrial core at the city's center.[41] The Parsons depot served multiple rail lines, including the St. Louis–San Francisco Railway, and brought newcomers to town from as far away as the California coast.[42] Between 1915, when the Katy emerged from a financial crisis, and 1923, when it reorganized to compensate for overexpansion,[43] the company's success made Parsons a well-connected, forward-looking city unique in Labette County.

The Katy's gravitational pull at the center of Parsons life drew in Nova and Kenneth around the turn of the decade, when Kenneth went to work for the railroad as a foreman.[44] He was seventeen. Although it was not his first job (the 1918 Parsons directory had noted he was employed as a driver),[45] it was more demanding, as well as more adult: as a foreman he was responsible for the training and coordination of his own crew of machinists. The fact that he was chosen to lead other workers at such a young age suggests that he showed promise even as a new hire. By 1922, his daily routine involved waking up at 2221 Main, taking a short (less than five-minute) walk into the middle of town, and continuing north along the train tracks before ambling into the MKT shops to report for work.[46]

Early in the summer of 1922, Nova's future in Parsons seemed secure. Her son had a steady income, with the prospect of promotion within the MKT and receiving a legacy on his twenty-fourth birthday.[47] But forces were in motion that threatened the safety of her family. In yet another season of her life, Nova was about to fight for self-preservation against the currents of historical change.[48]

~

The American organized labor movement had struggled to hold on to its Progressive-era gains in the years after World War I. In spite of postwar inflation, trade unions demanded higher wages from employers in a series of national strikes. The labor-suspicious climate of the first Red Scare, meanwhile, eroded support for union activities increasingly seen as radical, unpatriotic, and even un-American.[49] A record number of strikes in 1919, coinciding with anarchist bombings in June of that year, further piqued public appetite for a "return to normal," expressed in the election of pro-business candidate Warren G. Harding as president in 1920. US Supreme Court rulings during the subsequent Harding administration (*Duplex Printing Press Co. v. Deering* and *Truax v. Corrigan,* both 1921) further diminished the power of labor. National corporations, sensing a turning of the tide, committed to an anti-labor crackdown that reached deep into the railroad industry, and through it, into Kansas.[50]

Railroad companies relied on more than 400,000 shopmen nationwide to build and maintain their trains by the early 1920s.[51] By 1921, more than 9,000 of them were at work in Kansas, in shops like the Katy's Parsons headquarters.[52] They watched with alarm as their collective power shrank throughout the year, undone by layoffs, outside contracting, and the management-friendly decisions of the Railroad Labor Board (RLB).[53] Then there were the wage cuts, which on June 1 amounted to a 12.5 percent loss for workers.[54] The closed-shop system itself was under threat. Mediation by the National Civic Federation failed to resolve conflicts between workers and management in December, and the RLB announced another wage cut planned for the summer of 1922. In response, railroad unions across the country prepared to use the most powerful tool at their disposal: a nationwide walkout. On July 1, nearly all 400,000 railroad shopmen (including 3,500 KATY employees) simultaneously left their jobs in the middle of work.[55] Kenneth McClure was one of them.[56] The Great Railroad Strike of 1922 had begun.

In Kansas, tensions escalated quickly. Governor Henry Allen called for the arrest of two union leaders, then ordered a newspaper editor in Emporia to take down the pro-union signs he'd hung in his office windows. When the editor refused, the Kansas Industrial Court issued an arrest warrant for him, too.[57] In Parsons, business owners sympathetic to the strikers refused to serve customers who'd crossed the picket line, leading the US Department of Justice to send in federal marshals for their protection. A local militia was organized for the same purpose after harassment continued.[58]

The tension boiled over into violence at 3:00 a.m. on September 8, when residents on the west side of Parsons were jolted awake by a series of explosions.[59] Two bombs had gone off in a residential area at 2600 and 2605 Morgan Avenue, half a mile from Nova and Kenneth's house. The explosives damaged the homes of two MK&T boiler washers who had continued working during the strike, though the families sleeping inside were spared from injury. The National Guard swept in and arrested four suspects. The mood of the neighborhood, and the town, turned from anxious to panicky as people wondered what would happen next.[60] The mayor agreed to withdraw local police to make way for partial martial law. Union leaders, doing damage control, denied involvement in the bombings and announced a resolution denouncing "this cowardly act as the most outrageous that was ever perpetrated on our community of liberty loving people."[61]

US Attorney General Harry M. Daugherty issued a broad injunction against union activity on September 1 that ended the strike in most US towns.[62] But in Parsons, MK&T workers continued their protest into October, and then into November. By this point, Kenneth McClure had gone for four months without a Katy paycheck. He was also losing time in finishing the professional training he needed to qualify for his legacy when he turned twenty-four. Nova pressed this point with her son and even asked M. C. Taylor, the chairman of Kenneth's craft union, to let him return to work.[63] Taylor didn't respond. One of Kenneth's friends in the union, meanwhile, warned him not to go back to the shops. Forced to choose between betraying his union and risking his family's security by continuing to strike, Kenneth had no good options. But Nova's will prevailed. He submitted a new application for employment to MK&T management, received a positive reply, and promised to go back to work on the morning of November 16.[64]

On the night of Thursday, November 15, Kenneth attended a dance sponsored by the MK&T shops union. It was an odd choice for someone about to cross that union's picket line—one that shows a resolve to remain friendly with striking coworkers. But when the sun rose on November 16, he hadn't come home.[65] It was out of character for him to stay out all night, especially when he had to report to the shops the next day. As the morning went on and there was still no sign of him at 2221 Main, at MK&T headquarters, or anywhere in Parsons, Nova started worrying. The week before, a coworker of Kenneth's who'd returned to work had been surrounded by a gang of men and beaten in an alley.[66] This may have been on her mind as she rushed to the US marshal's office to report that her son was missing.

When deputies investigated Kenneth's disappearance, the conflict between striking and returning workers was on their minds as well. They tracked down a witness named C. E. Ervin, the owner of a local electrical company, who reported that he'd seen Kenneth at 11:00 p.m. on the night of the dance. Then they found Parsons Station Master M. S. McElwee, who claimed to have seen Kenneth board a train for Oklahoma City in the company of two men in the early hours of Friday morning. He had "acted queer, as if he had been drugged."[67] The officers began to suspect, and Nova with them, that Kenneth had been smuggled out of town by strikers intent on punishing him for going back to work.[68]

Until this moment in the fall of 1922, Nova's name had never appeared in local newspapers. She'd succeeded in lying low, as might have been a relief for someone who'd endured the media hoopla around Addie Walker and the examinations forced on Leon Belmont. Now, with her son in danger and police struggling to locate him, Nova Carr spoke to the press—first, the *Parsons Daily Republican*:

> Kenneth McClure, nineteen years old foster son of Mrs. A. N. Carr, was still missing from Parsons last night and the United States marshal's office here was conducting a rigid search for him on the theory that he had been spirited away in violation of the federal injunction against interference with the operation of the railroads. . . . Mrs. Carr said the boy was of exemplary habits and she fears he was drugged or spirited out of town.[69]

Then the *Coffeyville Daily Journal* joined in:

> The strike situation at Parsons is tense, with the throwing of bricks at the homes of two men employed in the Katy shops. Kenneth McClure, a 19-year-old Katy striker at Parsons, has been missing since Wednesday night. His mother has been urging him to return to work and she fears that he has been drugged and sent out of town. He is believed to have been put on the southbound Katy train Wednesday night by two men,

with whom he was seen shortly before the arrival of the train.[70]

Even the *New York Tribune* picked up the story, with help from a Kansas correspondent:

> TOPEKA, Kan., Nov. 19—Striking shopmen in Parsons and Oskaloosa, Kan., who characterized the election of Jonathan B. Davis for Governor as a direct repeal of the Industrial Court law, apparently are staging guerilla warfare. Fresh outbreaks at these points caused the order lifting martial law to be canceled to-day. Houses of shopmen are targets for bricks and rocks. Kenneth McClure, of Parsons, who declared he was going to return to work November 16, has disappeared.[71]

As with Walker and Belmont, it's risky to rely on newspapers for the truth of Carr's emotional state during these uncertain days. Reporters called her worried, fearful, and even "frantic," but they may have leaned on the stock figure of the anxious mother for dramatic effect. What's clear is that on November 19, after Kenneth had been missing for four days, and with Governor Henry J. Allen citing her son's disappearance as a reason for the return of martial law, Nova was concerned enough to take action.[72] She decided to find Kenneth herself.

For a person trying to line up the facts of Kenneth's experience between November 16 and 20—who kidnapped him, if anyone; where he went; how he was treated—the path forward is blocked. Newspaper accounts contradict each other, and themselves. The *Parsons Daily Republican* reported in its November 17 article that McElwee had seen Kenneth get on a train to Oklahoma City, but it also repeated his coworkers' claim that he'd planned in advance, and by choice, to go to Kansas City.[73] The *Coffeyville Daily Journal* repeated the story that he'd headed south rather than east.[74] The *Parsons Daily Republican* implied on November 20 that Nova had gone looking for Kenneth in St. Louis before sharing indirect news from Kenneth himself that he'd been in Kansas City looking for jobs.[75]

Oklahoma City, St. Louis, and Kansas City were equally likely destinations for Kenneth, whether he was going freely or under duress. Each of them had an MK&T station directly down the line; a person drugged and put on a train in Parsons could find himself waking up and disembarking in any of them.[76] Each city was also a place where a shopman might look for a new MK&T job away from the conflict in Parsons. Nova, however, set out for St. Louis, more than three hundred miles away from home. The train ride out took more than five hours—a long time for a mother to contemplate the fate of her missing son. By the time she made her return trip to Parsons on the same day, she had less hope to ward off thoughts of the worst; she hadn't found Kenneth in St. Louis and was coming back to Kansas alone.

In Parsons, however, Nova found a joyful surprise: Kenneth had returned on his own. He was in bad shape, but alive, and his ordeal, whatever it had been, appeared to be over. Nova immediately returned with him to their apartment and cut off communication with the press, leaving the *Parsons Daily Sun* reporter to wrap up the story with almost no information:

> Kenneth McClure, the 19-year-old striking shopman who mysteriously disappeared last Wednesday night on the eve of his return to work at the shops, returned to his home Sunday as mysteriously. His foster mother, Mrs. A. N. Carr, also returned from St. Louis, where she had gone in her search for him. Efforts were made today to get an interview with Kenneth. Mrs. Carr, when asked over the telephone for information as to his return, refused to say anything further than that he had returned alive. A later call at the Carr home on West Main street was fruitless. Mrs. Carr was not at home and other parties in the house refused to ascertain whether or not Kenneth was in their apartment, saying that Mrs. Carr had left instructions that no one was to be taken to the rooms and that anyhow they would not mix up in the affair.[77]

For the *Parsons Daily Republican*, the message was the same. With Belmont-like resolve, Carr "refused to comment."[78] Whatever had happened to Kenneth, and wherever he'd gone, mother and son were not talking. Chief Deputy Zimmerman only confirmed Kenneth's return and that he was "in a bad physical condition," leaving reporters to speculate whether this meant injured or sick.[79] Deprived of new information, the story of the disappearance fizzled out. The public never learned precisely what had happened—only that Nova Carr was fiercely protective of her son.

~

By the end of 1922, the Great Railroad Strike was over in Parsons. Shopmen went back to work, found jobs outside the MK&T, or left the trade. In spite of his experience in November, Kenneth chose to go back to his original job.[80] He and Nova also chose to stay in the house they'd lived in for nearly a decade. They appear on the Kansas state census of 1925 living as two of the lodgers of Ida Peters at 2221 Main Street; Nova's listed birthplace is Massachusetts and Kenneth's is Wisconsin. Nova has no profession, but Kenneth is a "machinist apprentice" for the MK&T railway.[81]

Kenneth also returned to his community. Even after the violence of the strike, Parsons remained his home. He rededicated himself to his talent for singing, performing solos with the choir at a church on Central Avenue.[82] He appeared with a quartet of singers during an Easter pageant at the Presbyterian church—the same one whose Sunday school he had attended a decade earlier.[83] At a YMCA "musical meeting" he sang solos in four songs: "Mate O' Mine," "A Sleep in the Deep," "Bells of the Sea," and "Smilin' Through." The *Parsons Daily Sun* singled him out in a notice on the performance as "Kenneth McClure, who works in the shops and who is a well known bass."[84]

His social life remained as wholesome as ever. As part of a committee, "Mr. Kenneth McClure" organized an outdoor church picnic held on August 20, 1925.[85] Having participated in Boy Scouts as a teenager, as an adult he dedicated himself to bringing in the next generation, becoming an assistant scout master of Parsons's Troop 2 by 1926.[86] He led a camping trip in December of the same year—indoors, but still no easy task in the middle of a Kansas winter.[87] Nova, meanwhile, slipped back into the anonymity she had enjoyed before Kenneth's disappearance. The town's newspapers were as silent about her as they were quick to mention her son. She attended church, and there is evidence that she participated in local women's organizations, probably as a volunteer.[88]

In this final chapter of her life, Nova's experience with gender was less obvious than it had been for Addie Walker and Leon Belmont. But it was no less impactful. Nova Carr was now an elder as well as a mother, and this was a social role that had changed dramatically since Walker's youth in the 1870s. In the early Gilded Age, American society had venerated old women (those in the white, middle-class, and "respectable" category) as the pillars of the Cult of Domesticity. Social segregation by sex had made them the undisputed authorities of gender to their younger peers, teachers of the right way to be "feminine." By the 1920s, however, segregation by sex had ceded to a new kind of social sorting: segregation by age. Young women increasingly spent their leisure time not among female relatives of multiple generations but with each other, and with young men. A distinct youth culture thrived that prioritized dating, working, and attending parties without elders. In the new gender regime, women like Nova Carr lost the prestige they had once enjoyed as the reward of their maturity. Maturity itself paled in comparison to what was new, young, and exciting—particularly the phenomenon of the flapper.[89] Femininity, meanwhile, became more contingent on youth. Hollywood movies and *Photoplay* magazine announced that to be feminine was to look young, energetic, and up-to-date.[90] Popular writers stereotyped old women as backward-looking and stodgy; some compared them unfavorably with their more energetic descendants.[91] While many critics attacked the new generation as much as the old, they consistently relegated women to one of two seemingly unbridgeable islands, pitting them against each other and emphasizing their difference.

These social changes added a layer of otherness to old women's experience of gender in the 1920s. They shaped, too, Carr's relationship to gender in her old age—but with a likely twist. In 1922, a former neighbor in Springfield had remembered Carr (then McClure) in the 1900s as "a masculine course looking woman."[92] If Carr continued to express this masculinity as she aged, she stood in opposition to normative gender before age emerged as a factor. And even if her gender presentation became more feminine over the years, Carr was still a single parent living with her adopted son in a boardinghouse. As the married-in-name-only and female head of her chosen family, she represented an alternative to the nuclear standard determined by blood lineage. In a quieter way than Walker and Belmont, Carr was continuing to challenge gender conventions in her old age.

~

On January 1, 1927, Nova Carr was seventy-four years and six months old. Although the average life expectancy for a person born in the United States in 1926 was fifty-nine—an increase of ten years over the rate for people born in 1900[93]—Carr was stuck with the health prospects of someone born in 1853. She had lived a taxing life, especially in her first three decades. As that first day of the new year began, she had spent twenty-five years as Nova Carr (1902–1927) after about twenty-four as Leon Belmont (1878–1902) and twenty-five as Addie Walker (1853–1878). Now, after these three phases, her time was coming to an end. There is no record of her health in those final days, of whether she was active or injured or ill, if she was hospitalized, or if Kenneth cared for her. But on Sunday, January 23, 1927, at about 4:00 p.m., Nova Carr died, as did the memories of Leon Belmont and Addie Walker she carried with her.[94] A notice appeared in the *Parsons Daily Sun* the following day.

> **OBITUARY: MRS. A. NORA CARR**
>
> Mrs. A. Nova Carr who for several years past had made her home with Mrs. Ida Peters, 2221 Main, died Sunday evening at about 4 o'clock. Mrs. Carr came to Parsons about 15 years ago from Missouri. She is survived by one adopted son, Kenneth McClue, of this city. Mrs. Carr was born in Boston, in 1860. She was a member of the Christian church and as long as she was able to do so she was a consistent worker in the women's organizations. Funeral services will be Tuesday afternoon at 2:30 from the Kersey Jones funeral home conducted by Rev. Bert E. Stover and burial in Oakwood cemetery.[95]

The unmarked burial place (indicated by a rock to the left of the flowers) of Nova McClure Carr in Oakwood Cemetery, Parsons, Kansas. Photograph by Lizzie Ehrenhalt, October 4, 2023.

Even at the moment of Carr's death, a newspaper got the details wrong. Here, however, the errors were honest mistakes rather than sensation-building fantasies. Her first name was misspelled in the headline. Kenneth's last name was misspelled. She was born in West Warren, not Boston, in 1853, not 1860. The outlines, at least, matched the overall shape of her life, and Belmont's, and Walker's. For her to have a personal obituary at all shows her importance to the survivor (whoever it may have been) who wrote and submitted a few sentences to the *Parsons Daily Sun*.

Oakwood Cemetery, a burial ground for Parsons residents since 1872, was already running out of space in 1927, so Nova Carr was buried near the property's southern perimeter, in a section called the Coffey addition.[96] It was a site used for burials of poor people, people without family members, and unknowns.[97] The spot itself has no marker, suggesting that whatever money was scrounged together for the burial was not enough to cover a gravestone.[98] Carr's final resting place is therefore a flat piece of unremarkable land—unshaded but within view of deep woods—set back from the tombs, pillars, and memorials dedicated to Parsons's prominent citizens.

After a lifetime of striving, hustling, and moving, Leon Belmont was still. The change could not have been starker. Movement had been the uniting theme of Belmont's life: movement through space, gender, class, vocation, and identity. The urge to move had been the driving force behind his migration across the United States, but also the source of Addie Walker's resolve to undo the limitations of her birth, and of Nova Carr's drive to become a mother in her late middle age. Observers had sometimes played up this instinct to move as unusual—particularly during the Belmont sensation, when newspaper reporters marveled at the distance between where he'd started and where he'd finished. But crossing that distance, putting as much space as possible between one's birth circumstances and one's fate as an adult, was the defining accomplishment of Belmont's generation. It was the era of the self-made man, who conquered business and politics through guile rather than inheritance. But it was also the age of the gender migrant, who claimed manhood for himself even though he, too, hadn't been born with it. Men had "made" themselves in the United States before Belmont's lifetime, and people had always migrated from one gender to another. But their pace accelerated and their visibility soared in the second half of the nineteenth century. Newfangled financial chiseling enriched them; railroads brought them to faraway markets and social settings; wire news services and sensational journalism spread their myths. Settler colonialism, meanwhile, both assured white migrants that they were entitled to make their fortunes in the "undeveloped" West and drove the land-cession treaties that permitted their occupation of Native territory.

Individualism, bank fraud, railways, mass communication, Native land theft: these are the real sensations of Belmont's lifetime. Gender migrants who reinvented themselves in the Gilded Age relied on them as supports. So did Addie Walker. Without them, she wouldn't have translated fraud into independence. Ernest Ellwood wouldn't have made it to Chicago. Nova Carr wouldn't have ended up in Parsons. And Leon Belmont wouldn't have bought a ranch in Kansas (Wahzhazhe land), traveled to Dakota Territory (Lakota land), become a celebrity in Minneapolis (Dakota land), and met his boyfriend, girlfriends, and wife. These events were products of Gilded Age history rather than deviations from it.

I've tried to show in *Romantic Sensation* that Leon Belmont was not the outlier the media made him out to be. Each of his seemingly unusual traits, it turns out, has a precedent, and often a contemporary echo. People migrated from one gender to another in the 1800s. Their expressions of masculinity and femininity challenged the norm and changed as they aged. They submitted, under duress, to exams at the hands of doctors because of their gender variance. Some also moved across the country, claimed to have famous relatives, made shady business deals, and exploited trusting people in their lives. Gender-normative people did all of these things, too. The newspapers that printed the Belmont legend in 1880 ignored the evidence that normalized him, preferring to imagine him as a phenomenon that had never existed before, and would never emerge again.

It had, and it did. Trans, queer, and intersex people living in the twenty-first century are Belmont's descendants. When we trans gender, choose same-sex partners, build chosen families, and contend with doctors, reporters, and police, we continue the story that began, for Belmont, next to a river in Massachusetts, and ended in an unmarked Kansas grave. It's a story that shows the inseparable origins of trans, queer, and intersex identities in an age often assumed to leave no space for life outside the norm. Belmont opened up pockets of that space when he embraced the curious, restless, and even gender-questioning era in which he lived. He lived his queer lives not in spite of the course of American history, but because of it.

Postscript
Unanswered Questions

Why did Addie Walker become Leon Belmont? Why did Leon Belmont become Nova McClure?

As I explain in this book's introduction, Belmont did not leave behind evidence of his motivations or feelings about himself, except to say, "I couldn't wear women's clothing, and I couldn't go naked."[1] As a result, I've tried to do a minimum of speculating about why Addie Walker transitioned. This approach avoids the trap of assuming that a person's decision to trans gender demands an explanation, while deciding to stay aligned with a gender assigned at birth does not (see the introduction).

Belmont's transition to living as Nova McClure, on the other hand, offers an example of a gender migrant moving back into a normative identity, and I briefly examine the historical context that might have inspired that choice. For details, see chapter 8.

Where did Kenneth McClure come from?

My only sources on Kenneth's arrival in Kansas are from depositions to an examiner from the US Bureau of Pensions conducted in Springfield, Missouri, in 1922. When the examiner interviewed Melvina Belmont, she said that Kenneth was "a little boy that was abandoned on the train."[2] Melvina's neighbor Jennie M. Gehrett told the same examiner that Kenneth "was a child that was found on a train abandoned and first taken by a Mrs. Blood and Miss McClure got the child from Blood."[3] Since Kenneth was born in Wisconsin (see "What Happened to Kenneth McClure?" below), it's possible that he boarded a train in that state, whether alone or with a guardian, rode south as far as Kansas, and was discovered in Parsons.

What was Nova Carr's relationship to Ida Peters?

Carr's obituary in the *Parsons Daily Sun* begins with the detail that she "for several years past made her home with Mrs. Ida Peters, 2221 Main."[4] The phrase makes it easy to imagine an intimacy between them; you can't "make a home" with someone unless you commit yourself to them, whether in friendship or romance. But as satisfying as it would be to discover that Carr found a partner in the last decades of her life, I've found no evidence of a relationship between Carr and Peters more personal than that of a renter and her landlady. Peters rented out rooms in her house at 2221 Main to as many as seven people at a time, as is shown on censuses taken in 1910, 1920, and 1925. The 1920 census lists Peters at 2221 and Carr and Kenneth McClure at 2221½, which suggests that, at least in that year, they lived in separate apartments.

Like Carr, Peters (Adeliza B. Roberts West Peters) was born in the early 1850s.[5] She was married twice, first to William West Sr. in Missouri in 1868 and then to Oliver E. Peters in Kansas in 1901.[6] She remained a widow after Peters's death in 1901 and worked as the superintendent of the Parsons Home and Hospital for Old Ladies in the 1910s.[7]

Was Kenneth McClure kidnapped during the Great Railroad Strike of 1922?

Because Kenneth and Nova refused to talk to reporters after his return to Parsons, the cause of Kenneth's disappearance and possible abduction from town in November was never publicly resolved. The known facts are these. Kenneth went missing on November 16, the night before he was scheduled to return to work at the Katy shops, and just after he had attended a dance for workers sponsored by the union.[8] Two days into his disappearance, rocks and a brick were thrown into the homes of two Katy employees who had crossed the picket line (police never identified the people responsible).[9] Two months earlier, bombs had exploded in the homes of two other Parsons workers who had crossed the picket line.[10] Once Kenneth was back in Parsons on November 20, Nova confirmed only that he was "alive"; the police chief described him as being in "bad physical condition."[11] This points to a violent confrontation, if not to kidnapping.

How did Nova Carr die? Why didn't you find Carr's death certificate?

Death certificates are treasure troves of vital statistics that reach into multiple domains of a person's life. American death certificates from 1927, the year in which Nova Carr died, listed a person's assigned sex, occupation, birthplace, and parents' names as well as the cause, location, and date of death. Carr's death certificate would therefore explain not only how she died but also how she represented herself in her final years. If Kenneth McClure was the source of the information reported to Carr's doctor, the certificate would reveal how much he knew about his mother's origins, or at least what she told him to report. Did McClure know the names of Carr's real birth parents, or did Nova take to her grave the information that she'd been born Addie Walker? Did she die of illness? Injury? Something else?

I regret that I wasn't able to answer these questions. The Office of Vital Statistics of the state of Kansas provides access to pre-1940 death certificates only to people who are related to the deceased by blood, at the level of cousin and closer. Since I am not a blood relative of Nova Carr, I relied on the information in her obituary, which does not include a cause of death.

What happened to Kenneth McClure after Nova Carr died?

At some point in the three years between Carr's death and 1930, Kenneth McClure left Kansas and made a new home for himself in Michigan. Since he'd been born in Wisconsin,[12] it was a kind of return to his Upper Midwest origins. By 1930 he was working as a "toolmaker" in an automobile shop in Flint—a profession that he stuck with for the rest of his life.[13] It turned out to be a smart career move, since it allowed Kenneth to transfer the skills he'd learned in railroad maintenance (a declining industry) to car manufacturing (a growing one, especially in Flint).

In 1936 Carr married a stenographer named Berneatha Baker in Flint, and the marriage license the couple filled out provides his age (thirty-three) and the names of his parents, given as Kenneth and Nova McClure.[14] The 1940 US Census recorded Kenneth and Berneatha living in Flint, where Kenneth was still working as a toolmaker in a car factory.[15] Their lives were disrupted two years later, in 1942, when the draft called Kenneth to service in World War II. His draft card shows that at that time, he was working for the Chevrolet Motor Company.[16] After the early 1940s, when his timeline crossed the border of living memory, I stopped searching out of respect for his family. I did find his name in the US Death Index for the state of Michigan covering the year 1984.[17]

Acknowledgments

I owe special thanks to two people who were researching Belmont/Walker for years before I came along: BJ Alderman and Thomas G. Perkins. Although he didn't know it at the time, Thomas was piecing together Addie Walker's history in Massachusetts at the same time BJ was hundreds of miles away in Kansas, uncovering the story of Leon Belmont's affair with her great-great-grandfather, James W. Weakley. Bringing together their work to tell a unified story has been one of the joys of this project. It's only because of their hours of archival digging in the early 2000s that I was able to get a head start.

Sylvia Buck's book on Walker's birthplace (*Warren: A Town in the Making, 1741–1991*) connected me with photographs, background, and the historical context of central Massachusetts in the mid-1800s. BJ's papers (the Barbara J. Alderman collection) at Pittsburg State University provided the raw materials for her four published articles on Belmont. I'm grateful to both Sylvia and BJ for the resources they shared with me, for their kindness, and especially for the conversations we carried on via email. At the end of a notes document from the early 2000s that Sylvia shared with me in 2023, she had written, "What happened to Addie? Where did she go?" I hope this book answers those questions.

Historians are nothing without librarians and archivists, but also without indexers, microfilm techs, curators, digitizers, interns, and volunteers. Workers in all of these areas helped me, sometimes invisibly, during the writing process, and I appreciate their labor. On the Massachusetts side of my research, I'm grateful to Melissa Murphy (reference librarian, Baker Library and Special Collections, Harvard Business School); John Devine (reference librarian, Boston Public

Library); Susanna Sigler, Rakashi Chand, and Emily Peterman (Massachusetts Historical Society); Naomi Allen (librarian, Massachusetts State Library); Sara DeCaro (Curator of Special Collections and University Archivist, Pittsburg State University); Cliff McCarthy and Zoe Cheek (archivist and MassMutual special projects archivist, respectively, at the Wood Museum of Springfield History); Jennifer Pino (Judicial Archivist, Massachusetts Supreme Judicial Court); and the rest of the staff of the Massachusetts Supreme Judicial Court Records Center.

At the Minnesota Historical Society, library manager Jenny McElroy inspired me to attempt a biography of Leon Belmont through her project on Lord Gordon Gordon, another elusive figure of 1870s America. Laura Weber, the former editor of *Minnesota History* magazine, encouraged me by publishing an early version of my Belmont research in 2021. MNHS reference technicians Ashley Sierra and Rose Winter enabled me to get the best possible surviving image of Belmont from a digital scan of a newspaper on microfilm. Ulysses Swanson fact-checked the manuscript with characteristic skill, finesse, and attention to detail.

In Kansas, I was helped by Shanda Lofgren (Deputy City Clerk, City of Parsons); Susan Boss (librarian, Parsons Public Library); and multiple staff of the Kansas State Historical Society and Kansas State Archives: Lauren Gray (head of reference); Lisa Keys and Amber Draper (reference assistants); and Michael Church (librarian). I received remote assistance from reference services volunteer Christine S. Windheuser and client services archivist Kay Peterson at the National Museum of American History's Archives Center. Many of these workers have moved on to new positions since I interacted with them.

I'm grateful to the Mastodon group @histodons@a.gup.pe for collective help deciphering the 1869 Warren Cotton Mills payroll register, with particular thanks to Karl Ewalds, Michael Meckler, Chris Bond, and Richard Van Noorden. Elizabeth Foxwell of the same group provided me with the original place of publication of Virginia Woolf's essay "Lives of the Obscure," and John Awbrey responded to one of my queries by connecting morbus coxalgia with rickets and Tiny Tim.

Matt Cornett, the sexton of Oakwood Cemetery in Parsons, guided me to the place where Nova Carr is buried. He didn't bat an eye when I texted him from the public library to say that the reason we hadn't been finding Carr in the cemetery's burial register was that she'd been listed as "Karr," and that was I driving back to the cemetery (surprise!) to keep snooping around. More than once, Matt dropped what he was doing in his office to help me and, in the end, to confirm that a patch of unmarked grass was Carr's burial spot. I'm grateful for this help, for his interest in my project, and for his dedication to maintaining the cemetery.

Most of all, I thank my parents, Suzanne and Alan; my sibling, Jey; my sister-in-law, Kate; and my spouse, Perry. To Perry, I owe this mission statement: "Well, everybody knows Belmont was a romantic sensation. What this book *presupposes* is . . . maybe he wasn't?"

Notes

Author's Preface on Pronouns

1. Ann Heilmann, *Neo-/Victorian Biographilia and James Miranda Barry: A Study in Transgender and Transgenre* (Palgrave Macmillan, 2018), 63.
2. Jen Manion, *Female Husbands: A Trans History* (Cambridge University Press, 2020), 14.
3. Cameron Awkward-Rich, "She of the Pants and No Voice: Jack Bee Garland's Disability Drag," *Transgender Studies Quarterly* 7, no. 1 (2020): 20–36. Compare with Lou Sullivan's *From Female to Male: The Life of Jack Bee Garland* (Alyson Books, 1990), which uses he/him pronouns for the same person.
4. Clare Sears, *Arresting Dress: Cross-Dressing, Law, and Fascination in Nineteenth-Century San Francisco* (Duke University Press, 2014), 20–21.
5. Rebecca L. Davis, *Fierce Desires: A New History of Sex and Sexuality in America* (W. W. Norton, 2024), xx.
6. Emily Skidmore, *True Sex: The Lives of Trans Men at the Turn of the Twentieth Century* (New York University Press, 2017), 10.

Introduction

1. For an explanation of why I use he/him pronouns for Belmont and she/her pronouns for Walker and Carr, see this book's preface.
2. Other newspapers, including the *Boston Globe* ("He or She?," December 5, 1880, 10), followed the *Tribune*'s lead in linking Belmont's name with the word "sensation." The *Minneapolis Evening Journal* doubled down with the headline "THE LAST SENSATION: Another Exciting Incident in the Man–Woman Sensation" (November 2, 1880, 4).
3. Birth record of Addie Liona Walker, register of births in Warren, Massachusetts, 120, https://www.ancestry.com.
4. Sarah Scovill Whittelsey and Arthur Twining Hadley, "Massachusetts Labor Legislation, An Historical and Critical Study," *Annals of the American Academy of Political and Social Science* 17, suppl. 15 (January 1901): 9–34.

5. This reputation was not entirely deserved. See Robert R. Dykstra, "Quantifying the Wild West: The Problematic Statistics of Frontier Violence," *Western Historical Quarterly* 40, no. 3 (Autumn 2009): 331–47.
6. See especially Peter Boag, *Re-Dressing America's Frontier Past* (University of California Press, 2011). For a case study of a single Western city, see Clare Sears, *Arresting Dress: Cross-Dressing, Law, and Fascination in Nineteenth-Century San Francisco* (Duke University Press, 2015).
7. B. J. Alderman, "Leon the Mysterious Lady," *Wild West,* December 2018, 20–21.
8. The reluctance to use contemporary identity categories to label historical figures dates to the rise (in the 1970s) of social constructionism—the idea that sexual orientation is a historically contingent, late-1800s invention that did not exist in all eras. Influential contributors to the constructionist turn include Michel Foucault (*The History of Sexuality,* vol. 1, *An Introduction* [Random House, 1990]); Jeffrey Weeks (*Coming Out: Homosexual Politics in Britain from the Nineteenth Century to the Present* [Quartet Books, 1977]); David M. Halperin (*One Hundred Years of Homosexuality* [Routledge, 1990]); John D'Emilio ("Capitalism and Gay Identity," in *Making Trouble: Essays on Gay History, Politics, and the University* [Routledge, 1992]); and Jonathan Ned Katz (*The Invention of Homosexuality* [University of Chicago Press, 1995]).
9. For an analysis of the emergence of bisexuality as a category of sexual orientation, see especially "Science and the Invention of (Bi)Sexuality," chapter 2 in Steven Angelides's *A History of Bisexuality* (University of Chicago Press, 2001), 23–48.
10. In Foucault's formulation, the homosexual was not yet "a species." *History of Sexuality,* vol. 1, *An Introduction,* 43.
11. On the sexological and diagnostic origins of the term "transsexual," see Susan Stryker, *Transgender History: The Roots of Today's Revolution* (Seal Press, 2017), 51–57; Joanne Meyerowitz, *How Sex Changed: A History of Transsexuality in the United States* (Harvard University Press, 2002), 4–7; Barry Reay, *Trans America: A Counter-History* (Polity Press, 2020), 18–55; and Alison Oram, "Cross-Dressing and Transgender," in *The Modern History of Sexuality* (Palgrave, 2006), 269–80. On the politics of the move from "transsexual" to "transgender," see Stryker, 151–52; Reay, 181–86; and Oram, 257.
12. "A Warren Girl on Her Travels," *Palmer (MA) Journal,* January 18, 1873, 2.
13. "On Her Travels," *Chicago Tribune,* January 11, 1873, 5; and "'Simonds and Son,'" *Chicago Daily Tribune,* January 19, 1873, 4.
14. Jesse Bayker, "Before Transsexuality: Transgender Lives and Practices in Nineteenth-Century America" (PhD diss., Rutgers University, May 2019), 25.

15. "'Simonds and Son,'" 4.
16. Bayker, "Before Transsexuality," 25.
17. "Belmont: Who and What Is She?—a Mystery That Is Still Unsolved," *Minneapolis Tribune,* November 13, 1880, 7.
18. Belmont's experience during the Minneapolis sensation recalls a figure at the center of intersex history: Herculine Barbin (1838–1868), the French memoirist interrogated by Catholic clergy, doctors, and judges because of her atypical genitalia and secondary sex characteristics. Whereas Barbin's examinations led to the legal reassignment of her sex as male (and her suicide at the age of thirty), Belmont's trials produced no such consensus, and Belmont was able to continue living in his gender identity. Barbin's case drew attention after the 1980 republication of her journals by Michel Foucault, who infamously resigned the child Barbin to the "happy limbo of a non-identity" (*Herculine Barbin* [Vintage Books, 2010], xiii). For rejoinders to Foucault's reading of Barbin, see Judith Butler, *Gender Trouble* (Routledge, 1991), 31–32, 119–35; Morgan Holmes, *Intersex: A Perilous Difference* (Susquehanna University Press, 2008), 82–87; Geertje Mak, *Doubting Sex* (Manchester University Press, 2012), 66–89; and Hil Malatino, *Queer Embodiment: Monstrosity, Medical Violence, and Intersex Experience* (University of Nebraska Press, 2019), 39–66.
19. "A Lakeside Romance," *Minneapolis Evening Journal,* November 11, 1880, 4.
20. "He took a strong liking to the youthful and stylish, soprano-voiced 'Mr. Belmont.' Mr. Belmont reciprocated the regard. Like liked like. . . . He suggested that they should go down to the pebbly margin, disrobe themselves, and plunge into the rippling, crystal tide of coolness and refreshment. He desired his nobby friend to join him in a bath beneath the elm-trees' wavering shade down where the water-lilies blow." "A Lakeside Romance," 4. "Too awfully awful" recalls the phrase "quite too utterly utter," associated with Wilde and aestheticism. See the song sheet cover of that name (S.34–1993), ca. 1881, at the Victoria and Albert Museum, https://collections.vam.ac.uk/item/O81539.
21. Eve K. Sedgwick, *Tendencies* (Duke University Press, 1993), 8.
22. Sedgwick, *Tendencies,* 8. Picking up Sedgwick's language in their lecture/manifesto "Thinking the Transience of the Living/Promising a Queer Philosophy," Esther Hutfless and Elisabeth Schäfer reiterated in 2015 that queer subjects "do not signify monolithically"; they "suspend traditional representations without founding them new." Belmont appears to thrive on this kind of suspension at the heart of queerness, leaving himself "open, fluid, and dynamic" and preserving the ambiguity from which he "derive[s] his force." Unpublished lecture, University of Vienna Symposium, "Body Discourses/Body Politics and Agency," https://www.academia.edu/10600314.

23. David Halperin, *Saint Foucault: Toward a Gay Hagiography* (Oxford University Press, 1995), 62.
24. bell hooks, "Are You Still a Slave?," Eugene Lang College roundtable, YouTube, May 7, 2014, https://www.youtube.com/watch?v=rJk0hNROvzs.
25. Susan Stryker, Paisley Currah, and Lisa Jean Moore, "Introduction: Trans-, Trans, or Transgender?" *Women's Studies Quarterly* 36, no. 3/4 (Fall/Winter 2008): 13.
26. Sears, *Arresting Dress,* 8–9.
27. Hongwei Bao, *Queer China: Lesbian and Gay Literature and Visual Culture Under Postsocialism* (Routledge, 2020), 153.
28. Rachel Hope Cleves, "Six Ways of Looking at a Trans Man? The Life of Frank Shimer," *Journal of the History of Sexuality* 27, no. 1 (January 2018): 34.
29. Scott Larson, "Laid Open: Examining Genders in Early America," in *Trans Historical: Gender Plurality Before the Modern,* ed. Greta LaFleur, Masha Raskolnikov, and Anna Kłosowska (Cornell University Press, 2021), 357.
30. Jesse Bayker, "Some Very Queer Couples: Gender Migrants and Intimacy in Nineteenth-Century America," *Gender & History* 33, no. 2 (July 2021): 121n12; and Jen Manion, *Female Husbands: A Trans History* (Cambridge University Press, 2020), 11.
31. Manion, *Female Husbands,* 11.
32. Kadji Amin, *Disturbing Attachments: Genet, Modern Pederasty, and Queer History* (Duke University Press, 2017), 2.
33. Amin, *Disturbing Attachments,* 4.
34. Amin, 4. On the toll of these expectations on scholars searching for "ideal" objects of trans scholarship, as well as on objectified trans people themselves, see especially Jules Gill-Peterson, "Feeling Like a Bad Trans Object," *Post 45,* December 19, 2019, https://post45.org/2019/12/feeling-like-a-bad-trans-object. For related issues in feminist research, see Jessica Enoch and Elizabeth Ellis Miller, "Historiographic Disappointment: Archival Listening and the Recovering of Politically Complex Figures," in *Ethics and Representation in Feminist Rhetorical Inquiry,* ed. Amy E. Dayton and Jennie L. Vaughn (University of Pittsburgh Press, 2021), 70–88.
35. Power relations, as mapped by Foucault, guided articulations of queer subjectivity in the 1990s. Carolyn Dinshaw, for example, stated that "queerness articulates not a determinate thing but a relation to existent structures of power" ("Chaucer's Queer Touches/A Queer Touches Chaucer," *Exemplaria* 7, no. 1 [March 1995]: 77). In general, what is queer occupies a position of relative disempowerment. Belmont's exploitation of positions of power (particularly the racial power activated by his whiteness) complicates any reading of him as "ideally" or "entirely" queer. Summarizing Foucault as well as Judith Butler, Jack Halberstam likewise states that queer resistance in this framework "must produce creative new forms

of being by assuming and empowering a *marginal positionality*" ("Telling Tales: Brandon Teena, Billy Tipton, and Transgender Biography," *Auto/Biography Studies* 15, no. 1 [2000]: 66; italics added). Belmont slid between marginal and marginalizing positions throughout his life; he sometimes defrauded others in order to move into a position of power.

36. Rani-Henrik Andersson and David C. Posthumus, *Lakȟóta: An Indigenous History* (University of Oklahoma Press, 2022).
37. On Belmont's purchase of the ranch, see [Untitled], *Arkansas City Traveler,* March 8, 1882, 3. On the Drum Creek Treaty, see Louis F. Burns, *A History of the Osage People* (University of Alabama Press, 2004), 300–13.
38. Devon A. Mihesuah, "Diabetes in Indian Territory: Revisiting Kelly M. West's Theory of 1940," *American Indian Culture and Research Journal* 40, no. 4 (2016): 3–4.
39. Measuring Worth, https://www.measuringworth.com/dollarvaluetoday/?amount=0&from=1876.
40. "A Clever Piece of Systematic Swindling—A West Warren Scandal," *Boston Globe,* March 11, 1876, 7.
41. "The Last of the Strange Addie Stanley Case," *Springfield (MA) Republican,* December 12, 1876, 6.
42. Belmont composed a history for himself that sampled the greatest hits of Gilded Age melodrama: an "illegitimate" birth in the antebellum South; education among the English aristocracy; a secret millionaire father; a formerly enslaved nurse; a childhood deformity cured by visiting German baths; travels in Italy; and a family inheritance. For details, see chapter 3.
43. Belmont requested, and received, reimbursement. See "Council Proceedings," *Winfield Courier,* February 22, 1883, 3, and [Untitled], *Winfield Courier,* April 5, 1883, 2.
44. [Untitled], *Galena Times,* June 14, 1895, 3.
45. "Belmont's Rival," *St. Paul Globe,* November 13, 1880, 3.
46. "Pre-1950 Gender Variance History in Minnesota" (spreadsheet), collection of the author.
47. Two of the scholars named above discuss gender variance well before Belmont's lifetime. In *Female Husbands,* Jen Manion starts a discussion in 1740; Elizabeth Reis begins *Bodies in Doubt: An American History of Intersex* (Johns Hopkins University Press, 2009), with a case from 1637 (3).
48. Reis, *Bodies in Doubt,* 63–65.
49. Quoted in Reis, *Bodies in Doubt,* 67.
50. Reis, 72–73.
51. Boag, *Re-Dressing America's Frontier Past,* 1–2.
52. On Charley Pankhurst, see Boag, 46, 52–53, and 117–18; on Tom Johnson, see 37; on Milton Matson, see 48–49; on Joe Monahan, see 95–104; on Jack Hall and Dick Wells, see 125–26; and on bandits, see 118–23.

53. Sears, *Arresting Dress,* 3. Sears is careful to problematize the term "cross-dressing": "It erroneously assumes that the type of clothing that 'belongs' to each sex is easily agreed upon" and that "people can also be easily and consensually classified as 'belonging' to one of two discrete, opposite sexes" (21).
54. Emily Skidmore quotes Harry Gorman's response to a question from a reporter: "Did we have an organization? No, hardly an organization, but we run across each other once in a while[,] and over our beer and cigars in saloons[,] we have had many a good hearty laughs [*sic*] at the expense of the men." *True Sex,* 1–2.
55. Skidmore, *True Sex,* 2.
56. Like Belmont, Dubois moved west from his hometown in the 1870s, legally married a woman, and insisted under interrogation that his clothes were natural to him. Manion discusses him at length in *Female Husbands,* a book that (as its title suggests) uses the identity conveyed by marriage as an organizing theme.
57. Bayker, "Before Transsexuality," 12 and ii.
58. Bayker, "Before Transsexuality," 6 and 8.
59. For profiles of gender migrants living outside of the United States during the Gilded Age/Belle Époque, see Rachel Mesch's *Before Trans: Three Gender Stories from Nineteenth-Century France* (Stanford University Press, 2020).
60. Civil War veteran Albert Cashier maintained his post-transition identity for much longer than Belmont (fifty-three years), but he never transitioned a second time. Larson, "Laid Open," 360–61.
61. Special examinations of John Williams and Jennie M. Gehrett, April 19, 1922, US Bureau of Pensions, US Civil War Widows' Pensions, 1869–1910, pension file of Allen E. Barry (WC38058), 106 and 108–9, https://www.fold3.com.
62. Jules Gill-Peterson (@gp_jls) on Twitter, January 25, 2022. Finn Enke echoes this point in an overview of approaches to trans history, insisting that "the purview of queer history has always been animated by transness, or embodiment that begs more attention to the human creation of significant gender articulations, taxonomies, vocabularies and instabilities." "Transgender History (and Otherwise Approaches to Queer Embodiment)," chapter 17 in *The Routledge History of Queer America,* ed. Don Romesburg (Routledge, 2018), 225. Kit Heyam attends to the same intersections in "'A Feminine Soul Confined by a Masculine Body': The Entangled History of Gay and Trans Experience," chapter 4 of *Before We Were Trans: A New History of Gender* (Seal Press, 2022), 112–36. On the intersections of trans and intersex history, see "'I Am Both Man and Woman': Defiant Bodies in Early America and Beyond" (chapter 5 of *Before We Were Trans,* 137–66).

63. Hil Malatino, *Queer Embodiment: Monstrosity, Medical Violence, and Intersex Experience* (University of Nebraska Press, 2019), 6.
64. Active in San Francisco from the 1970s until his death from an AIDS-related illness in 1991, Lou Sullivan was one of the first activists to advocate on behalf of queer trans men, separating their sexual orientations from their gender identities. See Susan Stryker, "Portrait of a Transfag Drag Hag as a Young Man: The Activist Career of Louis G. Sullivan," in *Reclaiming Gender: Transsexual Grammars at the Fin de Siècle* (Bloomsbury Academic, 2016), 62–82. On Sullivan's identification with Garland, see *We Both Laughed in Pleasure: The Selected Diaries of Lou Sullivan, 1961–1991* (Nightboat Books, 2019).
65. Cameron Awkward-Rich, "She of the Pants and No Voice: The Life of Jack Bee Garland," *Transgender Studies Quarterly* 7, no. 1 (February 2020): 174.
66. Betty T. Bennett, *Maria Diana Dods: A Gentleman and a Scholar* (William Morrow, 1991), book jacket and 260.
67. Bennett, *Maria Diana Dods,* 95, 207, and 267. Geraldine Friedman's reading, following Bennett's, adds queer theoretical insights but dismisses the possibility that Lyndsay/Douglas identified as a man. See Friedman, "Pseudonymity, Passing, and Queer Biography: The Case of Mary Diana Dods," *Romanticism on the Net* 23 (August 2001), https://www.erudit.org/en/journals/ron/2001-n23-ron435/005985ar.
68. Men assigned a male sex at birth did not have a monopoly on "real" manhood in the nineteenth century. Geertje Mak has demonstrated that Western Europeans living before/outside sexology in the 1800s derived the reality of sex from a combination of personal representation, physical appearance, and social role. In other words, if someone said he was a man, looked like a man, and acted in a role seen as a man's (uncle, laborer, doctor, etc.), then in the eyes of his community, he was as real a man as anyone. See Mak, *Doubting Sex,* 2.
69. Ann Heilmann, *Neo-/Victorian Biographilia and James Miranda Barry: A Study in Transgender and Transgenre* (Palgrave Macmillan, 2018), 62.
70. Heilmann, 67, referring to Michael du Preez and Jeremy Dronfield, *Dr. James Barry: A Woman Ahead of Her Time* (Oneworld, 2016).
71. The rationalizing impulse ignores nonmaterial motives for gender migration. In *Inventing Loreta Velasquez: Confederate Soldier Impersonator, Media Celebrity, and Con Artist* (Southern Illinois University Press, 2016), William C. Davis attributes his subject's decision to trans gender to a desire for notoriety, money, adventure, and mobility (14). There's no doubt that Velázquez lied to get rich and famous; Davis untangles multiple deceptions, and Velázquez's own memoir describes "masculine aspirations" in the service of "dreams of glory" (*The Woman in Battle* [Dustin, Gilman, 1876], 42). But the same section shows Velázquez as a child "haunted with

the idea of being a man" and secretly dressing in a male cousin's clothes (*Woman in Battle,* 42). There is room among Velázquez's overlapping motives for affinity-based ones; insisting on a "practical" explanation crowds them out.

72. Halberstam, "Telling Tales," 68. The same essay was published in *Passing: Identity and Interpretation in Sexuality, Race, and Religion,* ed. Maria C. Sanchez and Linda Schlossberg (New York University Press, 2001), 13–37.
73. Halberstam, "Telling Tales," 68.
74. Halberstam, 68.
75. Larson, "Laid Open," 351.
76. Not making sense is a signature of being human, and Belmont's right. I'm influenced by Ilya Maude's argument that "to write about transness, we do not need to disambiguate the true gender identities of historical figures from their social and material circumstances. . . . When we do not demand a consistent and isolate gender identity of historical and literary figures, we free them, and ourselves, to read transly." See Ilya Maude, "'Selective Historians': The Construction of Cisness in Byzantine and Byzantinist Texts," *Gender & History* 36, no. 1 (March 2024): 37, https://onlinelibrary.wiley.com/toc/14680424/2024/36/1.
77. I claim Belmont as an ancestor not in the cishet sense but in the queer one, which values chosen family over genetics, and affinity over bloodline. Shared lived experience is the binder of LGBTQIA+ kinship and, for that reason, of our ancestry, too. Nevertheless, the work of claiming historical figures as ancestors remains fraught. Three especially sensitive discussions of its challenges and rewards are Kai Pyle's "Naming and Claiming: Recovering Ojibwe and Plains Cree Two-Spirit Language" (*Transgender Studies Quarterly* 5, no. 4 [2018]: 574–88); Morgan Thomas's *Guernica* essay "A Snapshot Diagnosis" (September 13, 2022, https://www.guernicamag.com/a-snapshot-diagnosis); and Hil Malatino's "Something Other Than Trancestors: History Lessons," in *Trans Care* (University of Minnesota Press, 2020), 47–59.
78. At the same time, I question the assumed need to establish motive, as if transing gender were a crime. Historians do not search for explanations for people's decisions to live in accord with their sex assignments at birth; they accept such choices as unconscious and unremarkable. Gender migrants like Belmont deserve the same treatment. In Finn Enke's words, "Historians are compelled to prove trans-ness, never to prove or define non-transness, which seems to go without saying until we historicize this, too" ("Transgender History," 232).
79. Well-documented F to M examples include Joseph Israel Lobdell (1829–1912), George Green (1833–1902), Frank Gray (ca. 1835–?), Eugene de Forest (1849–?), Joe Monahan (1850–?), Frank Dubois (active 1880s), William C.

Howard (1860s–1902), Jack Bee Garland (1869–1936), Nikolai De Raylan (1874–1907), and Ralph Kerwineo (1876–1932). This list excludes the many Americans who transed gender (F to M) for fewer than about five years at a time—especially those who enlisted as soldiers during the Civil War.

80. See Catherine J. Lavender, "Notes on the Cult of Domesticity and True Womanhood," prepared for Students in HST 386: Women in the City, Department of History, College of Staten Island/CUNY (1998), http://www.ghhsapush.com/uploads/8/0/6/2/80629020/cult_of_domesticity.pdf.
81. Reis, *Bodies in Doubt,* 23–54, and Mak, *Doubting Sex,* 17.
82. See Carroll Smith-Rosenberg, "The New Woman as Androgyne: Social Disorder and Gender Crisis, 1870–1936," in *Disorderly Conduct: Visions of Gender in Victorian America* (Oxford University Press, 1986), 245–96, as well as John D'Emilio and Estelle B. Freedman, *Intimate Matters: A History of Sexuality in America* (University of Chicago Press, 2012), 171–222.
83. Bayker, *"Before Transsexuality,"* 194–95.
84. Reis, *Bodies in Doubt,* 90–98.
85. Reay, *Trans America,* 31–38.
86. Virginia Woolf, "Lives of the Obscure," *The Dial* 78, no. 5 (May 25, 1925): 382.

1. The Child, 1853–1867

1. Cheryll Toney Holley, "A Brief Look at Nipmuc History," in *Dawnland Voices: An Anthology of Indigenous Writing from New England* (University of Nebraska Press, 2014), 404.
2. On the results of the conflict, see Lisa Brooks, *Our Beloved Kin: A New History of King Philip's War* (Yale University Press, 2018).
3. Nipmuc scholar D. Rae Gould has argued that settler-colonist exaggerations of the retreat of Nipmuc people after King Phillip's war created a "myth of Nipmuc erasure" that persists in present-day Massachusetts. See Gould's "The Cisco Homestead and Hassanamisco Reservation: Past, Present, and Future of the Nipmuc Nation," in *Historical Archaeology and Indigenous Collaboration: Discovering Histories That Have Futures* (University Press of Florida, 2020), 157.
4. Gould, "The Cisco Homestead and Hassanamisco Reservation," 149–56.
5. Massachusetts Historical Commission, *Reconnaissance Survey Town Report: Warren* (Massachusetts Historical Commission, 1984), 7. On the development of Western/Warren between 1731 and 1852, see Olney Irman Darling, *History of Warren, Massachusetts* (T. Morey, 1874), 5–11.
6. Massachusetts Heritage Landscape Inventory Program, *Warren Reconnaissance Report* (Spring 2008), 3. On the relationship between Warren's topography and waterways and the development of local industry, see Jeff Robbins, "A History of Local Capitalism in Warren and West Brookfield,

Massachusetts, 1870–1900" (MA thesis, Worcester State University, 2015), 2–3.

7. Massachusetts Historical Commission, *Reconnaissance Survey Town Report: Warren,* 4.
8. For a summary of the industrial and demographic evolution of Massachusetts between 1800 and 1860, see Michael B. Katz, *The Irony of Early School Reform: Educational Innovation in Mid-Nineteenth-Century Massachusetts* (Beacon Press, 1968), 5–11.
9. At least one of the children in the family had a father other than Albert Walker. The marriage and death records of Harriet A. Walker Smith (1840–1922) list her father as Tyler Walker. Since Tyler Walker's and Albert Walker's fathers had the same name (Gideon), it's likely that the two men were brothers. Harriet A. Walker was therefore Addie Walker's half sister.
10. 1840 US census (Worcester County, MA), https://www.ancestry.com. On Warren/Worcester County as a center of shoe and boot manufacturing, see Robbins, "History of Local Capitalism," 5–7, and Sylvia G. Buck, *Warren: A Town in the Making* (Roberts & Sons, 1994), 39.
11. 1850 US census (Worcester County, MA), and Warren register of births, 1853, both https://www.ancestry.com.
12. For the details of the two doctors' medical examinations of Belmont, see chapter 4.
13. Elizabeth Reis weaves several of these developments into the narrative of *Bodies in Doubt: An American History of Intersex* (Johns Hopkins University Press, 2021). On psychology, see Reis, 115–26; on bioethics, see 153–69; on surgery, see 71–72 and 86–88; and on patient-centered care, see 152, 160–62, and 178–79.
14. Reis, *Bodies in Doubt,* 1–22.
15. Reis, 23–54.
16. This happened in Salisbury, Connecticut, in 1843, when Levi Suydam attempted to vote in a local election. A doctor examined him and pronounced him a man, then looked a second time after Suydam's sister reported that he menstruated. Reis, 34–35.
17. Writing on Western Europe, Geertje Mak elaborates on this trend as "a strategy of non-intervention." "In many cases of hermaphroditism until around the 1860s and 1870s," she writes, "the initial response was not to disclose the sexual body to a physician in order to have it examined objectively. . . . In cases of doubtful sex, secrecy and non-intervention were to a certain extent preferred to disclosure to a physician." See *Doubting Sex: Inscriptions, Bodies, and Selves in Nineteenth-Century Hermaphrodite Case Histories* (Manchester University Press, 2012), 17 and 22.
18. Mak, *Doubting Sex,* 39.

19. Mak gives the example of a French father in the 1840s who asked for a doctor's help in determining his baby's sex, and then paid him for his silence. He also ensured a midwife's secrecy. Mak, 24.
20. Mak, 23.
21. On sex as inscription, see Mak, 43. On the overlapping concept of sex as a social construction, see especially the introduction of Judith Butler's *Bodies That Matter: On the Discursive Limits of "Sex"* (Routledge, 2011) and Anne Fausto-Sterling, *Sexing the Body: Gender Politics and the Constructions of Sexuality* (Basic Books, 2020).
22. Mak, *Doubting Sex,* 43.
23. Albert Walker in the US federal census of 1850, the Massachusetts state census of 1855, and the US federal census of 1860, all Worcester County.
24. Two hundred dollars was a decent amount of money in 1860—but less decent when you had eight children to support, as Albert Walker did in that year. By 1868, he had twelve children.
25. Massachusetts Registers of Deaths, 1856, Warren, MA, 215, https://www.ancestry.com.
26. Massachusetts Registers of Deaths, 1855 and 1856, Warren, MA, 215 and 164, respectively, https://www.ancestry.com.
27. Marriage certificate application of Albert Walker and Caroline I. Howard (Warren, MA, December 1, 1856), 22, https://www.ancestry.com.
28. Almus Bliss in the Massachusetts state census of 1865 (Worcester County), https://www.ancestry.com.
29. "'The What Is It,'" *Minneapolis Tribune,* February 21, 1881, 2. Similar details appear in "The Story of a Bad Girl: The Brilliant 'Confidence' Career of Addie Walker of West Warren," *Springfield Republican,* March 10, 1876, 10.
30. "Warren," *Palmer Journal,* December 29, 1877, 2.
31. "Warren," 2. The Walker family's poverty is also mentioned in "A Warren Girl on Her Travels" (*Palmer Journal,* January 18, 1873, 2); and "Arrest of a Suspicious Character" (*Hampshire Gazette,* March 14, 1876, 2).
32. Table 9 in *Report of the Bureau of Statistics of Labor Embracing the Account of Its Operations and Inquiries from August 2, 1869, to March 1, 1870, Inclusive* (Wright & Potter, 1870), 410.
33. Albert Walker's horse sales are recorded in Records of the Town of Warren, 1863–1873, 88, 102, 104, 111, 139, and 142, https://archive.org/details/recordsoftownofw1863warr.
34. "Another Scene in the Addie Walker Romance.—She Is Put Under Heavy Bonds for Appearance at the Superior Court," *Palmer Journal,* March 18, 1876, 6.
35. Patricia J. Cummings, "Worcester County Soldiers in the Civil War," *Historical Journal of Massachusetts* 20, no. 1 (Winter 1992): 32, https://www

.westfield.ma.edu/historical-journal/wp-content/uploads/2018/06/Cummings-combined.pdf.

36. Darling, *History of Warren, Massachusetts,* 19–20.
37. Massachusetts Heritage Landscape Inventory Program, "Warren Reconnaissance Report," 5.
38. *Abstract of the Census of the Commonwealth of Massachusetts* (William White, 1857), 213–15.
39. "Map of Warren" (E. M. Woodford, 1855), in Buck, *Warren,* 85.
40. To gauge the growth of West Warren and the Warren mills between 1855 and 1870, I compared the 1855 Woodford map with "Warren, Warren Town, Warren West, Brookfield West, West Brookfield," an 1870 map in *Atlas of Worcester County, Massachusetts, 1870* (F. W. Beers, 1870), https://www.historicmapworks.com/Map/US/6938.
41. "'The What Is It,'" 2.
42. Anne Bugbee, "Recollections of a Mill Worker," *Walloomsack Review* 12 (Autumn 2013): 31, https://benningtonmuseum.org/library/walloomsack/volume-12/mill-worker-recollections-of-a-mill-worker.pdf.
43. On the view from Marks Mountain, see *Warren Reconnaissance Report,* 3.
44. Barbara Welter, "Coming of Age in America: The American Girl in the Nineteenth Century," chapter 1 in *Dimity Convictions: The American Woman in the Nineteenth Century* (Ohio University Press, 1976), 3–20.
45. For Barbara Welter's original formulation, see "The Cult of True Womanhood: 1820–1860," *American Quarterly* 18, no. 2 (Summer 1966): 151–74. For her subsequent book chapter, see "The Cult of True Womanhood," 21–41. For an extended criticism of the Cult of True Womanhood, see Frances B. Cogan's *All-American Girl: The Ideal of Real Womanhood in Nineteenth-Century America* (University of Georgia Press, 1989). See also Mary Louise Roberts's "True Womanhood Revisited"; Nancy A. Hewitt's "Taking the True Woman Hostage"; Tracy Fessenden's "Gendering Religion"; and Donna J. Guy's "True Womanhood in Latin America," all part of a Welter retrospective in *Journal of Women's History* 14, no. 1 (Spring 2002).
46. Kunigunde Duncan, ed., *Blue Star: The Story of Corabelle Fellows* (Minnesota Historical Society Press, 1990), 22.
47. Duncan, *Blue Star,* 27–28.
48. Sarah Gooll Putnam Diaries, 1860–1912, vol. 1, Massachusetts Historical Society, images 11 and 13, https://www.masshist.org/collection-guides/digitized/fa0176/vol1#11 and https://www.masshist.org/collection-guides/digitized/fa0176/vol1#13.
49. Sarah Gooll Putnam Diaries, images 47 and 48, https://www.masshist.org/collection-guides/digitized/fa0176/vol1#47 and https://www.masshist.org/collection-guides/digitized/fa0176/vol1#48.

50. Sarah Gooll Putnam Diaries, image 82, https://www.masshist.org/collection-guides/digitized/fa0176/vol1#82.
51. Sarah Gooll Putnam Diaries, image 35, https://www.masshist.org/collection-guides/digitized/fa0176/vol1#35.
52. Sarah Gooll Putnam Diaries, image 35.
53. Marjorie Housepian Dobkin, ed., *The Making of a Feminist: Early Journals and Letters of M. Carey Thomas* (Kent State University Press, 1979), 39.
54. Dobkin, *The Making of a Feminist,* 49.
55. Dobkin, 39.
56. On the clothing of working-class New England children in the early 1860s, see Bugbee, "Recollections of a Mill Worker," 31–32.
57. Howard Chudacoff, *Children at Play: An American History* (New York University Press, 2008), 99.
58. Rebecca Yamin, "Working-Class Childhood in Nineteenth-Century New York City," in *The Oxford Handbook of the Archaeology of Childhood* (online ed.), ed. Sally Crawford, Dawn M. Hadley, and Gillian Shepherd (Oxford University Press, 2018), 198 and throughout, https://academic.oup.com/edited-volume/28280. On the material culture of childhood play in Addie Walker's era, see also "The Stuff of Childhood, 1850–1900," in Chudacoff, *Children at Play,* 67–97.
59. Katz, *Irony of Early School Reform,* 34.
60. "An Act Concerning the Attendance of Children at School" (chap. 240), in *Acts and Resolves Passed by the General Court of Massachusetts, in the Year 1852* (White & Potter, 1852), 170, https://www.google.com/books/edition/Acts_and_Resolves_Passed_by_the_General/Sf-SABzHajMC.
61. Buck, *Warren,* 114. For photographs of Warren's public schools before 1900, see the same, 114–19. For a survey of education in Warren between 1795 and 1874, see Darling, *A Brief History of Warren,* 12–13.
62. Buck, *Warren,* 117; Darling, *A Brief History of Warren,* 12–13; and *Reconnaissance Survey Town Report: Warren,* 8.
63. Amy Susan Green, "Savage Childhood: The Scientific Construction of Girlhood and Boyhood in the Progressive Era" (PhD diss., Yale University, 1995), 24. Green draws from Katz, *Irony of Early School Reform,* 11–14.
64. Green, "Savage Childhood," 24.
65. "Who Is She?" *Minneapolis Tribune,* November 1, 1880.
66. *Report of the Special Commissioner of the Revenue for the Year 1868,* 40th Congress, 3rd Session, ex. doc no. 16 (Government Printing Office, 1868), 16 and 122.
67. I based this rounded weekly estimate on the average daily wage of $2.69 (without board) made by a Massachusetts shoemaker in 1870, according to US Bureau of Statistics Chief Edward D. Young's *Special Report on*

Immigration; Accompanying Information for Immigrants (Government Printing Office, 1871), 213. It assumes a Monday through Saturday work schedule.

68. On the ubiquity of working children in all corners of American life in the 1800s, see Michael Schuman, "History of Child Labor in the United States—Part 1: Little Children Working," *Monthly Labor Review*, US Bureau of Labor Statistics, January 2017, https://www.bls.gov/opub/mlr/2017/article/history-of-child-labor-in-the-united-states-part-1.htm.
69. Robbins, in "History of Local Capitalism" (4), calls the Warren Cotton Mills "the backbone of economic prosperity" in mid-1800s Warren.
70. Darling (*A Brief History of Warren*, 23) lists Warren's 1865, 1870, and 1874 populations as 2,180; 2,623; and 3,100, respectively. In *Warren* (90), Buck mentions that the West Warren Mills employed 900 people at its peak, but does not specify a year.
71. Inset image of West Warren in *Atlas of Worcester County, Massachusetts, 1870* (F. W. Beers, 1870), https://www.historicmapworks.com/Map/US/6938.
72. Compare with Massachusetts Heritage Landscape Inventory Program, *Warren Reconnaissance Report*, which states that "by 1864 the Warren Cotton Mills owned more than thirty-four tenement homes in West Warren" (4).
73. *Warren Reconnaissance Report*, 14, and *Fifth Annual Report of the [Massachusetts] Bureau of Statistics of Labor* (Wright & Potter, February 1874), 152.
74. Susan to Mary, April 1844, *Lowell Offering*, series 2, vol. 4 (June 1844): 170.
75. Jamie H. Eves, "The Din of Machines: The Technology of Textile Production," Windham Textile and History Museum, undated but ca. 2010s, https://millmuseum.org/din-of-machines.
76. A worker in a mill dressing room told the Massachusetts Bureau of Statistics of Labor in 1869, "The heat of the room in which I work ranges, usually from a 100 to 110 degrees, and frequently goes above that if ever below that, the work will be but imperfectly dried." *First Annual Report of the [Massachusetts] Bureau of Statistics of Labor* (Wright & Potter, March 1870), 294, https://archives.lib.state.ma.us/handle/2452/757004.
77. Vera Shlakman, *Economic History of a Factory Town: A Study of Chicopee, Massachusetts* (Smith College, 1915), 184–185. On the 1874 law, see also Sarah Scoville Whittelsey, "Massachusetts Labor Legislation, An Historical and Critical Study," *Annals of the American Academy of Political and Social Science* 17, suppl. 15 (January 1901): 12–13.
78. For a demonstration of the industrial carding process from a worker's perspective, see "Lancashire Cotton Mill Tour" (YouTube video), Arnold's Attic, https://www.youtube.com/watch?v=kmJm63xxlm0&t=870s. The video cap-

tures a tour of the spinning and carding room in the Helmshore Cotton and Wool Mill (Helmshore, UK), which retains the technology Addie would have used.

79. James D. Schmidt, "'Restless Movements Characteristic of Childhood': The Legal Construction of Child Labor in Nineteenth-Century Massachusetts," *Law and History Review* 23, no. 2 (August 18, 2010): 339.
80. The mill owner maintained that the workers injured themselves "through their own carelessness." *First Annual Report of the [Massachusetts] Bureau of Statistics of Labor,* 85.
81. *First Annual Report of the [Massachusetts] Bureau of Statistics of Labor,* 215.
82. *First Annual Report of the [Massachusetts] Bureau of Statistics of Labor,* 270.
83. *Sixth Annual Report of the [Massachusetts] Bureau of Statistics of Labor* (Wright & Potter, March 1875), 85. Massachusetts mills had been using cotton-carding strippers since 1852. See Thomas R. Navin Jr., "The Wellman-Woodman Patent Controversy in the Cotton Textile Machinery Industry," *Bulletin of the Business Historical Society* 21, no. 5 (November 1, 1947): 146.
84. Letter from Susan to Mary, June 1844, *Lowell Offering,* series 2, vol. 4 (Greenwood Reprint, 1970), 169.
85. "Lancashire Cotton Mill Tour," 16:09.
86. Lucy Larcom, "Among Lowell Mill-Girls: A Reminiscence," *Atlantic,* November 1881, 595 and 602, https://cdn.theatlantic.com/media/archives/1881/11/48-289/131951852.pdf. Larcom's nostalgic recollection leaves out the Lowell strikes of 1834 and 1836, in which 1,500 women and children participated, as well as the push for a ten-hour workday by the members of the Lowell Female Labor Reform Association in 1845. On both, see Timothy R. Lane, "Industrial Independence: Working Class Women's Creation of the Public, Political Female in Antebellum America" (PhD diss., Northeastern Illinois University), 2019.
87. On the contradictory conclusions of historians looking at working conditions in cotton mills—were they good, horrible, or merely subpar?—see Ray Ginger, "Labor in a Massachusetts Cotton Mill, 1853–1860," *Business History Review* 28, no. 1 (March 1954): 67–91.
88. Letter from Susan to Mary, 170–71.
89. Juliana, "Written for the 'Improvement Circle,'" *Voice of Industry,* June 12, 1846, 2, https://www.industrialrevolution.org/original-issues/1846/1846-06-12.pdf.
90. "Factory Life—Romance and Reality," *Voice of Industry,* December 3, 1847, 2.

91. Mary Palmer, a mill worker and contemporary of Addie Walker, dated the change to the beginning of the Civil War, when companies demanded more work for less pay. Bugbee, "Recollections of a Mill Worker," 33.
92. "The [cotton] mills do nothing in supplying any kind of intellectual or physical recreation; there are no libraries, no reading rooms, no lectures, nor excursions." *First Annual Report of the [Massachusetts] Bureau of Statistics of Labor,* 116.
93. A worker in the Chicopee Manufacturing Company's carding room told the Massachusetts Bureau of Statistics of Labor that in 1869, "I was injured by cutting my arm in July; was laid up about two weeks; I received nothing; never knew of any one's pay going on. My work is all over the room in different positions." *First Annual Report of the [Massachusetts] Bureau of Statistics of Labor,* 215.
94. "Regulations to be Observed by Persons Employed in the Boott Cotton Mills" [broadside], L. B. H. Penhallow, [1866], Massachusetts Historical Society, https://www.masshist.org/database/2289.
95. Volume 100 (Payrolls, 1865–1870), Thorndike Company records (MSS:442 1836–1918 T455), Baker Library, Harvard Business School.
96. *First Annual Report of the [Massachusetts] Bureau of Statistics of Labor,* 119.
97. *First Annual Report,* 119.
98. *First Annual Report,* 119.
99. *First Annual Report,* 116.
100. Volume 100 (Payrolls, 1865–1870), Thorndike Company records (MSS:442 1836–1918 T455), Baker Library, Harvard Business School.

2. The Youth, 1867–1873

1. Map of "Warren, Warren Town, Warren West, Brookfield West, West Brookfield," in *Atlas of Worcester County, Massachusetts, 1870* (F. W. Beers, 1870), 51–52. Leventhal Map & Education Center, State Library of Massachusetts,https://collections.leventhalmap.org/book_viewer/commonwealth:bz60gj62m#1/52.
2. Buck, *Warren: A Town in the Making,* 43 and 44.
3. Most of the 3,125 women working in mills in Essex County in 1865 lived in the cities of Boston and Lowell. Oliver Warner, dir., *Abstract of the Census of Massachusetts, with Remarks on the Same, and Supplementary Tables* (Wright and Potter, 1867), 166, https://babel.hathitrust.org/cgi/pt?id=uma.ark:/13960/t3qv3jr87&seq=5.
4. An 1868 timetable from a Lowell mill shows the unrelenting system of bells that structured each worker's day, from the first, at 4:30 a.m., to the last, at 6:30 p.m.—evidence that although the Lowell system's benefits had dried up by the 1860s, its punishing schedule persisted. "Time Table of the Lowell Mills," MIT Open Courseware, Massachusetts Institute of Technology,

https://ocw.mit.edu/ans7870/11/11.001j/f01/lectureimages/4/image24.html.

5. Edward Young (United States Treasury Department Bureau of Statistics), *Special Report on Immigration . . . in the Year 1869–1870* (Government Printing Office, 1871), 202 and 216, https://babel.hathitrust.org/cgi/pt?id=hvd.32044024335481&view=1up&seq=236.
6. Massachusetts Bureau of Statistics of Labor, *Report of the Bureau of Statistics of Labor, Embracing the Account of its Operations and Inquiries from August 2, 1869, to March 1, 1870, Inclusive, Being the First Seven Months Since Its Organization* (Wright & Potter, 1870), 362.
7. Map of "Warren, Warren Town, Warren West, Brookfield West, West Brookfield," 1870, https://collections.leventhalmap.org/search/commonwealth:2b88qf56v. The location of Orcutt's farm is confirmed by Henry F. Walling's 1857 map of Worcester County. For the acreage of Orcutt's farm, see the 1870 farm census of Massachusetts, US Selected Federal Census Non-Population Schedules, 1850–1880, 2–3, https://www.ancestry.com.
8. 1870 farm census of Warren, Worcester County, Massachusetts, and 1870 Massachusetts state census of Warren, Worcester County, Massachusetts, https://www.ancestry.com.
9. Massachusetts state census of 1870 (Worcester County), www.ancestry.com.
10. *Springfield Daily Republican,* May 27, 1876, 4.
11. "The Story of a Bad Girl," *St. Louis Globe Democrat,* March 13, 1876, 2.
12. "She lived with [Orcutt] a year, and since has 'worked out' in this city [Springfield]; been in the family of Dea[con] Graves at Athol, where it is said she went to school; and, according to her own telling, was at Chicago for a little." "Story of a Bad Girl."
13. "Story of a Bad Girl."
14. Lilley B. Caswell, *Athol, Massachusetts, Past and Present* (pub. by author, 1899), 136–38, https://archive.org/details/cu31924028819162/page/136/mode/2up; and School Street on "View of Athol, Massachusetts, 1878," Norman B. Leventhal Map Center, Boston Public Library, https://collections.leventhalmap.org/search/commonwealth:x633fd80q.
15. Teachers at Athol High School organized students by grades and offered formal courses of study beginning in 1873, so it's possible Walker was present during the transition. Caswell, *Athol, Massachusetts, Past and Present,* 137.
16. Walker's resolve to be seen as educated surfaced in an 1873 newspaper item: "She declined to give her name in a manner whose emphasis somewhat qualified her statement that she had been well educated—a statement, by the way, which appeared to be of great importance." "On Her Travels," *Chicago Daily Tribune,* January 11, 1873, 5.
17. [Untitled], *Springfield Republican,* March 13, 1876, 6. The 1870s rosters of the state normal school at Westfield do not mention Addie [L.] Walker. A

student named Ada Walker, of East Brookfield, is listed among the school's junior class in the summer term of 1873, but this refers to Ada V. Walker (1855–1933). See *Catalogue of the State Normal School at Westfield, Mass., 1873* (Clark & Story, 1873), 11, and Ada V. Walker in Oakham, Massachusetts (Worcester County), in the 1880 US federal census.

18. Daniel A. Cohen, ed., *The Female Marine and Related Works: Narratives of Cross-Dressing and Urban Vice in America's Early Republic* (University of Massachusetts Press, 1997), ix, https://archive.org/details/femalemarinerela00dani/page/n9.
19. Cohen, *The Female Marine and Related Works,* 71. On Shurtliff's life and its interpretation, see Greta LaFleur, Masha Raskolnikov, and Anna Kłosowska, "Introduction: The Benefits of Being Trans Historical," in *Trans Historical: Gender Plurality Before the Modern* (Cornell University Press, 2021), 1–3; and Manion, *Female Husbands: A Trans History*, 68–71 and 93–103.
20. Lieutenant Murray [Maturin Murray Ballou], *Fanny Campbell: The Real Female Pirate Captain* (E. D. Long, 1844), https://archive.org/details/fannycampbellfem00ball.
21. [Mary Simerton], *The Deserted Wife's Revenge, Or Life and Wonderful Adventures of Mary Simerton* (Elmer Barclay, 1852), https://www.digitaltransgenderarchive.net/files/70795785t.
22. Dion Haco, *Sue Munday: The Guerilla Spy* (T. R. Dawley, 1865), https://www.digitaltransgenderarchive.net/files/wm117p19f.
23. Burlesque programs often featured minstrel show divertissements, and burlesque and minstrelsy coevolved throughout the nineteenth century. On their overlap, see Robert C. Allen, *Horrible Prettiness: Burlesque and American Culture* (University of North Carolina Press, 1991), 163–78.
24. Advertisement, *Springfield Republican,* September 5, 1870, 1, and advertisement, *Boston Evening Transcript,* September 7, 1870, 3. See also Allen, *Horrible Prettiness,* 132–33.
25. Kurt Gänzl, *Lydia Thompson: Queen of Burlesque* (Routledge, 2002), 140–42.
26. Globe Theatre (Boston) playbill in Susan Ingalls Lewis and Morgan Gwenwald, "Year of the British Blondes," *New York Archives* 13, no. 2 (Fall 2013): 19.
27. *All the Daring of the Soldier: Women of the Civil War Armies* (W. W. Norton, 1999), 165, 310–11.
28. Some of the most famous cases of Civil War cross-dressing did not circulate until at least the mid-1870s. Loreta Janeta Velázquez, for example, did not publish her memoir, *The Woman in Battle,* until 1876; newspapers did not report on Albert Cashier's service until after his sex assignment at birth was known in the 1910s. Many such stories, however, appeared in

print before Belmont's first steps toward gender transition, in 1872. See [Untitled], *Burlington County News,* May 2, 1863, https://www.digitaltransgenderarchive.net/files/m613mx67m; "A Female Soldier," *Gallipolis Journal,* May 7, 1863, 2; "A Colored Fille du Regiment," *Cleveland Morning Leader,* September 11, 1863, 1; "A Female Soldier from Maine," *Portland Daily Press,* January 5, 1864, 4; "A Female Soldier," *Richmond Dispatch,* February 20, 1865, 4; and "Bridgeport Items," *Jackson County News,* June 16, 1865, https://www.digitaltransgenderarchive.net/files/fq977t99m.

29. "Lizzie Compton, a Soldier Girl," *Owensboro (KY) Monitor,* May 4, 1864, 1. Similar items on Compton appeared in newspapers in Kansas, Michigan, Pennsylvania, Iowa, Minnesota, and Louisiana. See [Untitled], *Leavenworth Times,* May 21, 1863, 2; [Untitled], *Lansing State Republican,* January 13, 1864, 1; "A Bold Soldier Girl," *Sunbury Gazette, and Northumberland County Republican,* June 13, 1863, 1; "News and Items," *North Iowa Times,* December 30, 1863, 2; "A Bold Soldier Girl in the Second Minnesota," *St. Paul Pioneer and Democrat,* May 22, 1863, 8; and "A Strange Story: Lizzie Compton, the Soldier Girl," *Daily True Delta,* March 9, 1864, 6.
30. Surveys of Civil War cross-dressing narratives include Elizabeth D. Leonard's *All the Daring of the Soldier: Women of the Civil War Armies* (W. W. Norton, 1999); DeAnne Blanton and Lauren M. Cook's *They Fought Like Demons: Women Soldiers in the American Civil War* (Louisiana State University Press, 2002); and Larry G. Eggleston's *Women in the Civil War: Extraordinary Stories of Soldiers, Spies, Nurses, Doctors, Crusaders, and Others* (McFarland, 2003).
31. Reports on Boulton and Park appeared in newspapers throughout Walker's part of the world, including the *Springfield Republican,* June 10, June 21, June 24, and August 11, 1870; the *Boston Evening Transcript,* June 23, 1870; and the *Fall River Evening News* (Bristol County, MA), May 16, 1870. See also *New York Herald,* May 23, June 22, and June 23, 1870; *New York Clipper,* June 4, 1870; and *New York Times,* May 16, 1871. For an evaluation of coverage in British papers, see Michelle Liu Carriger, "Performers in the Audience: The Boulton and Park Case of 1870–1871" (MA thesis, Pepperdine University, 2006). On Boulton and Park in general, see H. G. Cocks, *Nameless Offences: Homosexual Desire in the 19th Century* (Bloomsbury Academic, 2003), 105–14.
32. "Goddesses in Disguise; Or, Women in Masquerade," *The Days' Doings* (New York), November 15, 1870, https://www.digitaltransgenderarchive.net/files/ww72bb66k.
33. See, for example, "Women in Men's Clothes," *Public Ledger* (Memphis), June 28, 1866, https://www.digitaltransgenderarchive.net/files/x346d420r.
34. "Free-Love and Trousers," *World,* May 27, 1871, https://www.digitaltransgenderarchive.net/files/w0892b04g.

35. Walker not only addressed her women readers directly ("I place in your hands that power which shall emancipate you from the bondage of all that is oppressive"); she also insisted that in the future, all women would wear pants. *Hit: Essays on Women's Rights* (Humanity Books, 2003), 29 and 94.
36. Although newspapers of the early 1870s rarely interpreted cross-dressing as evidence of identity, one example survives from the *Massachusetts Weekly* (based in Addie Walker's own Worcester County). Reporting on Joseph Israel Lobdell, the paper noted that "[Lobdell] dresses in male attire, and is evidently laboring under the delusion that she is a man" ("Plymouth County," *Massachusetts Weekly,* October 31, 1873, https://www.digitaltransgenderarchive.net/files/z603qx51g). For discussion of the Lobdell case with attention to its place in queer and trans history, see Boag, *Re-Dressing America's Frontier Past,* 159–66; Skidmore, *True Sex,* 27–36; and Manion, *Female Husbands,* 198–230.
37. In addition to the newspaper articles cited above covering the period between 1865 and 1873, see also "A Female 'Husband' Robs His Wife and Decamp," [Publication unknown], April 22, 1865; "A Man-Woman," *Last Sensation,* January 25, 1868; "A Disguised Female Becomes Pugilistic in a New York Bar Room," [Publication unknown], December 4, 1869; "A Cleveland Girl in Male Attire," *Toledo Blade,* December 30, 1869; "The Female Husband and Male Wife," *New Republic,* March 21, 1868; and "About a Man-Woman," *Moore's Rural New-Yorker,* August 5, 1871, 83.
38. In *Gaylaw: Challenging the Apartheid of the Closet* (Cambridge, MA, 1999), 27, William N. Eskridge Jr. counted nineteen US cities with such ordinances before 1900 (27); Jesse Bayker expanded the tally to sixty-nine (https://map.transpast.org). Ulysses Swanson, meanwhile, documented more than 120 put in place between 1848 and 1899 (https://www.google.com/maps/d/u/0/viewer?mid=1p99OaGS_nnikYJCY3bKOItYGeJX3Q-s&ll).
39. As Elizabeth Reis has observed, "Urbanization and new interpersonal commercial networks . . . [created] opportunities to remake one's self and perhaps to deceive others." See Reis, *Bodies in Doubt,* 30. Referencing San Francisco, Clare Sears has similarly pointed out that "rapid population growth produced large-scale anonymity that robbed people of their ability to order public life through personal ties" (Sears, *Arresting Dress,* 67). The concurrent growth of American cities and confidence crime at midcentury intensified "concerns about the opacity of urban things," which were themselves "a product of both the most rapid period of urbanization in American history and the radical restructuring of the older socioeconomic orders that such urbanization provoked." James W. Cook, *The Arts of Deception: Playing with Fraud in the Age of Barnum* (Harvard University Press, 2001), 201.

40. This is a cissexist question. Historians do not agonize over why cis people of the past kept their gender presentations the same over time. Uncoupled from the assumption that transing gender is baffling and demands an explanation, the search for a "motive" loses its urgency.
41. By "practical fallacy" I mean the invalid reasoning that leads historians to discount identity-based motives for transing gender in favor of practical explanations (obtaining money, freedom, a job, etc.). Jack Halberstam calls this process rationalization. "Telling Tales," 68.
42. "In Disguise," *Minneapolis Tribune,* October 30, 1880, 6.
43. "Addie Walker—the Girl in Boy's Clothes," *Palmer Journal,* January 25, 1873, 2.
44. "Springfield," *Springfield Daily Republican,* May 27, 1876, 4.
45. "Addie Walker—the Girl in Boy's Clothes."
46. A twenty-three-year-old woman used a similar strategy to buy a man's suit in a Philadelphia department store in 1885, assuring the salesman she was buying it for her brother. See Jesse Bayker, "Before Transsexuality: Transgender Lives and Practices in Nineteenth-Century America" (PhD diss., Rutgers University, 2019), 171.
47. Bayker, "Before Transsexuality," 171. Bayker's analysis of Harry T. Buford/ Loreta Velázquez highlights the dimensions of nineteenth-century gender migration that went beyond clothing. In Buford's case, Bayker explains, a "masculine" gait, facial hair, a male mentor, and a professional haircut help him to pass as a man in homosocial settings like saloons. "Before Transsexuality," 144–45.
48. Ernest was a common name in 1876, but the choice hints at self-awareness and a sense of humor. Ellwood was in earnest, even if he had not always been Ernest. Oscar Wilde later crafted his play *The Importance of Being Earnest* (1895) to hinge on this pun. "Ernest," spelled without the "a," was also the first name of Ernest Boulton, whose 1870 arrest for cross-dressing in London was well publicized in the United States. On the writing and production of *The Importance of Being Earnest,* see Matthew Sturgis, *Oscar Wilde: A Life* (Alfred A. Knopf, 2021), 478–85. On Ernest Boulton, see Cocks, *Nameless Offences,* 105–14.
49. A newspaper report published eight years later mentioned that Ellwood spent his evenings walking around Warren in order to flirt with young women, evidently with no negative consequences. "'The What Is It,'" *Minneapolis Tribune,* February 21, 1881, 6.
50. "A Warren Girl on Her Travels," *Palmer Journal,* January 18, 1873, 2.
51. At some point in December or January, Ellwood visited Brattleboro, Vermont, where he stayed at the Revere House. See "Suspicious Individual," *Argus and Patriot,* January 23, 1873, 2.
52. [No title], *Palmer Journal,* January 4, 1873, 2.

53. "'The What Is It,'" 6.
54. According to the *Palmer Journal,* during his stay in town, Ellwood (called Addie Walker by the paper) paid "some eight or ten dollars for livery bills" ("A Warren Girl on Her Travels," 2). A Massachusetts farm laborer earned an average wage of six dollars a week, with board, by working sixty hours a week. *Annual Report of the Board of Statistics of Labor* (Wright & Potter, State Printers, 1874), 55 and 102.
55. The Boston & Albany Railway had been called the Massachusetts Western Railway from 1833 until 1867, at which point multiple mergers over multiple years led to its renaming. For the route's stops, see "Colton's Railroad Map of the US and Canada, 1873," Norman B. Leventhal Map Center Collection, Boston Public Library, https://collections.leventhalmap.org/search/commonwealth:cj82kp61c.
56. "'Simonds and Son,'" *Chicago Daily Tribune,* January 19, 1873, 4.
57. "'Simonds and Son.'"
58. "Donning Doublet and Hose; and Doing Other Foolish Things Which Lead to His-Her Arrest," *Chicago Evening Post,* January 10, 1873, 1.
59. On the conductor's surveillance and subsequent report to the police, see "Donning Doublet and Hose," 1. The Gault House is referred to as "second-rate" and "small" in "On Her Travels," 5. "On Her Travels" also offers details about Ellwood's arrival in Chicago.
60. On the scale and pace of rebuilding after the Great Fire of 1871, see *Chicago Illustrated's One Year From the Fire* (J. M. Wing, 1873); "New Chicago," chapter 14 of Carl Smith's *Chicago's Great Fire: The Destruction and Resurrection of an Iconic American City* (Atlantic Monthly Press, 2020); and Scott Berg's *The Burning of the World: The Great Chicago Fire and the Fight for a City's Soul* (Pantheon, 2023). On Chicago's population relative to the population of other American cities in 1870, see Campbell Gibson, *Population of the 100 Largest Cities and Other Urban Places in the United States: 1790 to 1990* (US Census Working Paper POP-WP027), June 1998, https://www.census.gov/library/working-papers/1998/demo/POP-twps0027.html.
61. "Donning Doublet and Hose," 1, does not specify that Ellwood and the train passenger from Rochester shared a room—only that they ate breakfast together.
62. The clothes Ernest wore on January 11 are described in "Donning Doublet and Hose," 1.
63. Eskridge, *Gaylaw,* 27.
64. "Donning Doublet and Hose," 1.
65. "Donning Doublet and Hose."
66. For a contemporary perspective of Washburn's sometimes controversial tenure as superintendent of the Chicago Police Department, see John J.

Flinn, *History of the Chicago Police: From Settlement to 1886* (Police Book Fund, 1887).

67. "On Her Travels," 5.
68. "On Her Travels."
69. "'Simonds and Son,'" *Chicago Daily Tribune,* January 19, 1873, 4.
70. "On Her Travels."
71. "On Her Travels."
72. Although this plot point applies to five of Shakespeare's characters (Portia in *The Merchant of Venice*; Rosalind in *As You Like It*; Viola in *Twelfth Night*; Julia in The *Two Gentlemen of Verona*; and Imogen in *Cymbeline*), the phrase "doublet and hose" in the context of cross-dressing appears only in *As You Like It,* II.4.6.
73. "Donning Doublet and Hose," 1. For "Fair Ines," see Thomas Hood, *The Plea of the Summer Fairies, Hero and Leander, Lycus the Centaur, and Other Poems* (Longman, Rees, Orme, Brown, and Green, 1827), 158.
74. "On Her Travels," 5.
75. "'Simonds and Son.'"
76. "The Police Board," *Chicago Inter-Ocean,* March 11, 1873, 2.
77. "Addie Walker—the Girl in Boy's Clothes." See also "A Warren Girl on Her Travels."
78. "'Simonds and Son.'"
79. US federal census, 1870 (Hampden County, MA), https://www.ancestry.com. Dexter Smith was a son of Horace Smith, the Smith half of the Smith & Wesson gun-manufacturing company, based in Springfield. He married Harriet (Hattie) Walker in 1860 (marriage registry, Springfield, Massachusetts, 1860, https://www.ancestry.com). The 1870 US census listed his personal estate at $20,000.00.
80. "'Simonds and Son.'"
81. "Determined to Go West," *Chicago Daily Tribune,* January 26, 1873. The article states that Walker wrote from "South Brookfield," which did not exist in 1873 (or ever). It's likely that Walker wrote instead from Brookfield or West Brookfield, which is about five miles from her hometown of West Warren.

3. The Con Artist, 1873–1878

1. *The Greatest Burglary on Record: Robbery of the Northampton National Bank* (Steam Press of Gazette Printing, 1876), 10–21, https://www.google.com/books/edition/The_Greatest_Burglary_on_Record/B6M7AAAAYAAJ. See also "The Northampton Bank Robbery," J. North Conway's discussion of the 1876 heist as a precursor to the 1878 one (accomplished by the same gang) that eclipsed it, in *King of Heists: The Sensational Bank Robbery of 1878 That Shocked America* (Lyons Press, 2010), 137–52.

2. "Springfield," *Springfield Republican,* March 9, 1876, 6.
3. "'The What Is It.'"
4. "Arrest of a Suspicious Character," *Hampshire Gazette,* March 14, 1876, 2.
5. On Hiram Day, see Charles Forbes Warner, *Representative Families of Northampton,* vol. 1 (Northampton Picturesque Publishing, 1917), 236–40. On the election of Day as Northampton city treasurer, see "Hampshire County Items," *Greenfield Gazette and Courier,* April 5, 1875, 3. For Day's change in address circa 1874, see the *Northampton, Holyoke & Chicopee Directory and Historical Register,* 1873–1874, 38, and the *Northampton Directory and Historical Register,* 1875, 131, https://www.ancestry.com.
6. Scott Reynolds Nelson, "The Real Great Depression," *Chronicle of Higher Education* 55, no. 8 (October 17, 2008), B9–B10. For the economic details of the Panic of 1873, see Daniel Schulman's *The Money Kings: The Epic Story of the Jewish Immigrants Who Transformed Wall Street and Shaped Modern America* (Alfred A. Knopf, 2023).
7. Nineteenth-century children contracted hip disease through tuberculosis, sometimes with deadly results. See Peter G. Jones, "Dickens' Literary Children," *Australian Pediatric Journal* 8 (1972), 240; and "Morbus Coxalgia," M. Macfarlan, MD, "Surgical Clinic of Hahnemann College," in *American Journal of Homeopathica Materia Medica and Record of Medial Science* 1, no. 1 (1871), 151.
8. Brookfield, Massachusetts, death register, 1874, 314, https://www.ancestry.com.
9. Brookfield, Massachusetts, death register, 1874, 314.
10. Dexter Smith, Addie Walker's brother-in-law, invented and manufactured the shotgun named after him. His father (Horace Smith) had co-developed the Smith & Wesson revolver in 1857. William Richard Cutter, ed., *Geological and Personal Memoirs Relating to the Families of the State of Massachusetts,* vol. 2 (Lewis Historical Publishing, 1910), 982.
11. Household of Dexter Smith, US census of 1870 (Hampden County, MA), https://www.ancestry.com.
12. "The Bad Girl Again," *Springfield Republican,* March 17, 1876, 5.
13. *The Greatest Burglary on Record,* 22.
14. "'The What Is It.'"
15. The idea of Walker bringing a lawsuit was not far-fetched. She had threatened to sue Orcutt himself for defamation in 1873, after returning from Chicago as Ernest Ellwood (she settled and received $400). At about the same time, she had sued a railroad company after falling through a depot platform and suffering minor injuries. She asked for $600 and received $100. "A Clever Piece of Systematic Swindling—A West Warren Scandal," *Boston Globe,* March 11, 7, and "A Confidence Operation," *Fall River Daily Evening News,* March 11, 1876, 1.

16. "The Story of a Bad Girl," 6; "Addie Walker Again," *Palmer Journal,* March 11, 1876, 2; and "A Clever Piece of Systematic Swindling."
17. "The Story of a Bad Girl" and "A Clever Piece of Systematic Swindling."
18. I've found no evidence of a marriage between Addie Walker and a man named Stanley, or a man by any name, in any decade.
19. "The Story of a Bad Girl"; "Addie Walker Again"; "A Clever Piece of Systematic Swindling"; and "Arrest of a Suspicious Character."
20. "The Bad Girl Again."
21. Walker may have been simultaneously conning and blackmailing Orcutt, with the latter project aiding the former. An otherwise unrelated article in the *Palmer Journal* in 1877 referred to "Addie Walker of black-mail notoriety" without explanation ("County Politics," September 1, 1877, 2).
22. "A Female Fraud," *Fitchburg (MA) Sentinel,* March 9, 1876, 2; "The Story of a Bad Girl"; and "The Bad Girl Again."
23. "The Story of a Bad Girl."
24. Mark Wahlgren Summers is careful to point out that popular memory has inflated the corruption of 1865–1877 beyond its real scope (*Era of Good Stealings* [Oxford University Press, 1993], x). For Summers, it was the public discussion of fraud that created the era's corrupt reputation rather than an actual increase in crime.
25. Summers, *The Era of Good Stealings.*
26. Timothy Rives, "Grant, Babcock, and the Whiskey Ring," *Prologue* 32, no. 3 (Fall 2000): 144, https://babel.hathitrust.org/cgi/pt?id=uva.x006095816&seq=159.
27. Black Friday's broad effects included "a string of Wall Street bankruptcies, a decline in farm prices, and a bankers' riot on Broad Street (where the Gold Exchange was located)." Jeffrey D. Broxmeyer, "Bringing the 'Ring' Back In: The Politics of Booty Capitalism," *Journal of the Gilded Age and Progressive Era* 19, no. 2 (2020), 238. See also Kenneth Ackerman, *The Gold Ring: Jim Fisk, Jay Gould, and Black Friday, 1869* (Dodd, Meade, 1988).
28. Historians have complicated Tweed's image as a one-dimensional villain since the 1960s. See Seymour J. Mandelbaum, *Boss Tweed's New York* (Ivan R. Dee, 1990); Leo Hershkowitz, *Tweed's New York: Another Look* (Anchor Press, 1977); and Kenneth Ackerman, *Boss Tweed: The Rise and Fall of the Corrupt Pol Who Conceived the Soul of Modern New York* (Carroll and Graf, 2005).
29. On the joint contributions of *New York Times* reporting and Nast's cartoons to Tweed's downfall, see Fiona Deans Halloran, "Tweed," chapter 6 in *Thomas Nast: The Father of American Political Cartoons* (University of North Carolina Press, 2012), 119–44. The symbolic language of Nast's drawings, Halloran suggests, harnessed "the power of the visual" to inspire indignation against Tweed (133, 143).

30. Vernon L. Parrington, *The Beginnings of Critical Realism in America, 1860–1920,* vol. 2 of *Main Currents in American Thought* (Harcourt, Brace, 1927), 17.
31. The title of Mark Twain and Charles Dudley Warner's novel *The Gilded Age: A Tale of Today* (1873) introduced the phrase; critics seized on it in the 1920s and brought it into wide use. See Richard Schneirov, "Thoughts on Periodizing the Gilded Age: Capital Accumulation, Society, and Politics, 1873–1898," *Journal of the Gilded Age and Progressive Era* 5, no. 3 (July 2006): 194.
32. Balleisen, *Fraud: An American History from Barnum to Madoff* (Princeton University Press, 2017), 76 and 77.
33. Parrington, *Beginnings of Critical Realism,* 11.
34. On the culture and mechanics of corporate financial corruption in the Gilded Age, see George Robb, "Before Madoff and Ponzi: Nineteenth-Century Business Frauds," *Phi Kappa Phi Forum* (Spring 2012): 7–9, as well as Richard White, "Information, Markets, and Corruption: Transcontinental Railroads in the Gilded Age," *Journal of American History* 90, no. 1 (June 2003), 19–43, https://academic-oup-com.ezp3.lib.umn.edu/jah/article/90/1/19/741922.
35. Balleisen, *Fraud,* 75.
36. [James Houston], "Police Intelligence: Arrest of the Confidence Man," *New-York Herald,* July 8, 1849, 2. For a discussion of the *New-York Herald* article's role in the acceptance of the term "confidence man," as well as William Thompson's place in the history of the con, see Jean Braucher and Barak Orbach, "Scamming: The Misunderstood Confidence Man," *Yale Journal of Law & the Humanities* 27, no. 2 (Summer 2015), 249–90.
37. Karen Halttunen, *Confidence Men and Painted Women: A Study of Middle-Class Culture in America, 1830–1870* (Yale University Press, 1982), 198.
38. James W. Cook, *The Arts of Deception: Playing with Fraud in the Age of Barnum* (Harvard University Press, 2001), 202.
39. "The Confidence Woman," *Palmer Journal,* March 26, 1870, 1.
40. "The Confidence Woman."
41. "A Confidence Woman," *Palmer Journal,* December 21, 1867, 2. Depending on the length of their interaction, the incident may have been a case of pickpocketing rather than a con; either way, it illustrates the use of the term "confidence woman" in Massachusetts as early as 1867.
42. "A Female Swindler Abroad," *Springfield Republican,* July 24, 1867, 10.
43. "A Female Swindler Abroad."
44. "Local Affairs," *Springfield Republican,* July 27, 1867, 2; and "Arrest of a Confidence Woman," *Springfield Republican,* November 23, 1870, 8. Dutton received more attention in 1875 after pretending to be the wife of Civil War veteran Colonel Wesley Merritt during a visit to New York. See "The

Alleged Tug Boat Outrage in New York," *Portland Daily Press,* July 24, 1875, 2; "From New York," *Springfield Republican,* July 24, 1875, 5; and "Connecticut," *Springfield Republican,* July 26, 1875, 6.

45. Mitchell Zuckoff, *Ponzi's Scheme: The True Story of a Financial Legend* (Random House, 2006), and Tamar Frankel, *The Ponzi Scheme Puzzle: A History and Analysis of Con Artists and Victims* (Oxford University Press, 2012).
46. Herald Freiberger, "Diese Frau hat den Betrug per 'Schneeballsystem' groß gemacht," *Süddeutsche Zeitung,* November 11, 2017, https://www.sueddeutsche.de/muenchen/schneeballsystem-es-begann-in-der-au-1.3743735.
47. George Robb, "Depicting a Female Fraud: Sarah Howe and the Boston Women's Bank," *Nineteenth-Century Contexts* 34, no. 5 (December 2012): 445–59; and Henry A. Clapp, "Sympathetic Banking," *Atlantic,* July 1881, 121–36.
48. On the intersections of spiritualism and confidence crime, including the early careers of Chadwick and Diss Debar, see Kerry Segrave's *Women Swindlers in America, 1860–1920* (McFarland, 2007).
49. "Lola the Second: The Young King of Bavaria Captured by a Cincinnati Adventuress," *Springfield Republican* [from the *Cincinnati Times*], June 22, 1872, 7.
50. Segrave devotes two chapters of *Women Swindlers in America* to peers of Walker's "who passed bad paper, checks, and drafts. They swindled financial institutions, retailers, and individuals for amounts ranging from a few dollars to perhaps over $100,000" (3).
51. "Springfield and Vicinity," January 1, 1869, 4; "The Last Confidence Woman," January 8, 1869, 4; "Springfield and Vicinity," January 9, 1869, 8; "General News Items," January 4, 1871, 22; "General News Items," May 12, 1871, 5; "Political Notes," September 26, 1968, 5; "Connecticut," July 16, 1872, 2; "Connecticut," July 26, 1872, "A Confidence Woman Nabbed," January 24, 1871, 2; and "From New York," January 26, 1871, 3. Other women con artists appear in the same newspaper in "Gleanings and Gossip," March 22, 1873, 8; "A New York Confidence Woman," October 15, 1870, 8; "From New York," March 21, 1873, 5; "Gleanings and Gossip," December 31, 1872, 5; and "From Boston," January 8, 1873, 6.
52. Although I've argued that Walker's dealings with Orcutt fit within the context of the golden age of the con, I've stopped short of claiming that her swindles were cons in the strict sense of the word. A con transpires between two people with no existing relationship: the perpetrator and her target, or mark (Braucher and Orbach, "Scamming," 287). The perpetrator must be a stranger to the mark in order for his grant of "confidence" to bear weight. Walker and Orcutt were not strangers. In

their case, Walker drew on powers of persuasion strengthened by their closeness rather than the expectation of trust between presumed social equals.

53. Robb, "Depicting a Female Fraud," 448.
54. "Arrest of a Suspicious Character," *Hampshire Gazette,* March 14, 1876, 2.
55. "Hampshire County: Northampton," *Springfield Republican,* March 8, 1876, 6, and "The Bad Girl Again." On Judge Robinson, see *Pictorial Palmer Massachusetts: Descriptive and Illustrative* (Carpenter and Cady, 1896), 69–70, https://archive.org/details/pictorialpalmerma/page/68.
56. Josiah Howard Temple, *History of the Town of Palmer, Massachusetts* (Town of Palmer, 1889), 470, https://archive.org/details/historyoftownofp00temp/page/470/mode/2up.
57. "Addie Walker Again."
58. "The Bad Girl Again."
59. "Another Scene in the Addie Walker Romance," *Palmer Journal,* March 18, 1876, 6.
60. "Another Scene in the Addie Walker Romance."
61. "The Bad Girl Again." For summaries of both Orcutts' remarks, see also "Another Scene in the Addie Walker Romance."
62. "Stephen S. Taft Dead," *Boston Globe,* May 17, 1912, 12.
63. "Another Scene in the Addie Walker Romance" and "The Bad Girl Again."
64. "The Bad Girl Again."
65. "The Bad Girl Again."
66. "The Bad Girl Again" and [Untitled], *Boston Globe,* March 18, 1876, 7.
67. "The Grand Jury's Report," *Springfield Republican,* May 18, 1876, 6, and [Untitled], *Palmer Journal,* May 20, 1876, 9. The *Springfield Republican* later claimed she faked her illness. See "The Last of the Strange Addie Stanley Case," *Springfield Republican,* December 12, 1876, 6.
68. [Untitled], *Palmer Journal,* May 26, 2; and "Springfield," *Springfield Republican,* May 26, 1876, 6.
69. "Springfield."
70. "Springfield."
71. [Untitled], *Springfield Republican,* May 25, 1876, 6.
72. [Untitled], *Palmer Journal,* May 26, 1876, 2; and [Untitled], *Springfield Republican,* May 27, 1876, 6.
73. [Untitled], *Palmer Journal,* June 3, 1876, 2.
74. [Untitled], *Springfield Republican,* May 27, 1876, 6.
75. *First Annual Report of the Commissioners of Prisons, January, 1872* (Wright and Potter, 1872), 18, https://archives.lib.state.ma.us/entities/archivalmaterial/9a22e2a7-c824-48ba-8d3e-012ca17528c4.
76. See the folder "State Street Jail: Building Specs for Additional Accommodations," box 21 of Hampden County Courthouse Records: House of

Corrections Records, 1827–1881, Lyman and Merrie Wood Museum of Springfield History, Massachusetts.

77. State Street Jail House blueprint, undated, box 21 of Hampden County Courthouse Records: House of Corrections Records, 1827–1881, Lyman and Merrie Wood Museum of Springfield History.
78. *Fifth Annual Report of the Prison Commissioners, January 1, 1876* (Wright & Potter, 1876), 35; and *Sixth Annual Report of the Prison Commissioners, January 1, 1877* (Albert J. Wright, 1877), 35.
79. "Springfield: Certain Facts About the Jail," *Springfield Republican,* September 13, 1886, 5–6.
80. "Jail and House of Correction in Springfield, Mass.: Answers of Ralph Day, March 21, 1848," in *Twenty-Third Annual Report of the Board of Managers of the Prison Discipline Society* (T. R. Marvin, 1848), 225, https://babel.hathitrust.org/cgi/pt?id=mdp.39015039712800, and *Annual Report of the Prison Commissioners, January 1, 1875,* 9.
81. *Fifth Annual Report of the Prison Commissioners, January 1, 1876,* 11.
82. On the manufacture of slippers at Springfield Jail and Correctional Facility, see *First Annual Report of the Commissioners of Prisons, January, 1872,* 18, as well as *Springfield City Directory and Business Advertiser, 1875–6* (Clark W. Bryan, 1875), 60, https://archive.org/details/1875SpringfieldMADirectory/page/n45/mode/2up. For the location of the workshop, see State Street Jail House blueprint, Wood Museum of Springfield History.
83. *Sixth Annual Report of the Prison Commissioners, January 1, 1877,* 34.
84. *First Annual Report of the Commissioners of Prisons, January, 1872,* 18.
85. *Springfield City Directory and Business Advertiser, 1875–6,* 60. The routine seems to have changed little since 1848. See "Jail and House of Correction in Springfield, Mass.: Answers of Ralph Day, March 21, 1848," 225.
86. "Springfield: Certain Facts About the Jail." The State Street Jail House blueprint (Wood Museum of Springfield History) shows that the women's bathing room also contained only two tubs.
87. Nicole Hahn Rafter, "Gender, Prisons, and Prison History," *Social Science History* 9, no. 3 (Summer 1985): 237. See also Rafter's book *Partial Justice: Women, Prisons, and Social Control* (Routledge, 1990).
88. Rafter, "Gender, Prisons, and Prison History," 238.
89. *Fourth Annual Report of the Prison Commissioners, January 1, 1875,* 21; State Street Jail House blueprint, Wood Museum of Springfield History; and "Springfield: Certain Facts About the Jail," 6.
90. Nicole Hahn Rafter, "Prisons for Women, 1790–1980," *Crime and Justice* 5 (1983): 142. Here, again, I've applied Rafter's research on women in prison to women in jails, since the Hampton County Jail and House of Corrections housed women in the same block. See State Street Jail House blueprint, Wood Museum of Springfield History.

91. Henry G. Clark, report to the Massachusetts House of Representatives, in *Twenty-Third Annual Report of the Board of Managers of the Prison Discipline Society,* 19.
92. The state of Massachusetts did not build a new Hampden County Jail and House of Corrections until 1887. See *Out of the Darkness: History of Corrections Reform at the Hampden County, MA Sheriff's Department, 1661–2021* (Republican Inc., 2021), 19.
93. *First Annual Report of the Commissioners of Prisons, January, 1872,* 18.
94. *First Annual Report of the Commissioners of Prisons, January, 1872,* 5.
95. *Out of the Darkness,* 17–19.
96. *Sixth Annual Report of the Prison Commissioners, January 1, 1877,* 16.
97. "Springfield: Certain Facts About the Jail," 5–6. The *Republican* reporter did go on to note that in that year, "Thanks to the unusually tough constitutions of the prisoners, however, the percentage of the sick is small."
98. *Seventh Annual Report of the Commissioners of Prisons, January 1, 1878,* 48.
99. *Sixth Annual Report of the Prison Commissioners, January 1, 1877,* 35.
100. Although it's possible women prisoners had a separate workroom, the prison's floor plan does not indicate this. See State Street Jail House blueprint, Museum of Springfield History.
101. "Jail and House of Correction in Springfield, Mass.: Answers of Ralph Day, March 21, 1848," 228.
102. *Fourth Annual Report of the Prison Commissioners, January, 1875,* 19; and *Prison Commissioners' Report, January, 1877,* 35.
103. Charles H. Barrows, *The History of Springfield in Massachusetts, for the Young* (Connecticut Valley Historical Society, 1921), 182, https://archive.org/details/historyofspringf01barr/page/182/mode/2up; and *View of Springfield, Mass.: 1875* (O. H. Bailey, [1875]), Norman B. Leventhal Map Center Collection, Boston Public Library, https://collections.leventhalmap.org/search/commonwealth:x633fc72t.
104. *Map of the City of Springfield, Massachusetts, 1870,* https://collections.leventhalmap.org/search/commonwealth:9s161d22h, shows footprints for a "soap factory" and a second building owned by "R. M. C." An 1875 map of Springfield does not show the factory building. The Springfield city directory for that year, however, states that R. M. Cooley was operating as a soapmaker at the 1870 address: 259 State Street. *Springfield City Directory and Business Advertiser, 1875–6,* 60.
105. "Pioneer Life: Soap Making," YouTube video, Okefenokee Swamp Park, https://youtu.be/QdmyWZqEmJg?t=29.
106. *View of Springfield, Mass.: 1875* and *Map of the City of Springfield, Massachusetts, 1870* (Bees, Ellis, & Soule, 1870), Norman B. Leventhal Map Center Collection, Boston Public Library.

107. "Palmer and Vicinity," *Palmer Journal,* December 16, 1876, 2; "Springfield," *Boston Globe,* December 12, 1876, 2; and "The Last of the Strange Addie Stanley Case."
108. "The Last of the Strange Addie Stanley Case."
109. "Palmer and Vicinity."
110. "The Last of the Strange Addie Stanley Case."
111. "Springfield and Vicinity," *Palmer Journal,* May 5, 1877, 2.
112. "Addie Walker Discharged," *Hampshire Gazette,* November 17, 1877, 2.
113. *Argus and Patriot* (Montpelier, VT), November 21, 1877, 2; and "Addie Walker Discharged."
114. "Addie Walker Discharged."
115. "Addie Walker Once More: The Naughty Girl Turns Up Out West in Men's Clothes," *Springfield Republican,* December 4, 1880, 8.

4. The Rancher, 1878–1879

1. "Howland–Belmont: The Brilliant Society Wedding at Newport Yesterday," *New York Herald,* 7.
2. S. S. Howland (1849–1925), a son of Gardiner Greene Howland (1787–1851), was named for his uncle Samuel Shaw Howland (1790–1853), the shipping merchant and descendant of Mayflower Compact signer John Howland. On the Howland family, see Edward Pessen, *Riches, Class, and Power Before the Civil War* (D. C. Heath, 1973), 101.
3. "Howland–Belmont: The Brilliant Society Wedding at Newport Yesterday" as well as "New England News," *Boston Globe,* September 19, 1877, 2.
4. "Miss Belmont's Wedding: The Event of the Newport Season—$50,000 in Presents," *New York Times,* September 19, 1877, 1.
5. David Black, *The King of Fifth Avenue: The Fortunes of August Belmont* (Dial Press, 1981), 20–25, 33–34, 39, and 418–20.
6. Black, *The King of Fifth Avenue,* 434.
7. An 1882 print by the Buek & Linder Lithography Company included August Belmont among the "Kings of Wall Street," alongside Jay Gould and Cornelius Vanderbilt. Library of Congress Prints & Photographs Division, Washington, DC, https://loc.gov/pictures/resource/pga.02540.
8. On Belmont's mansion and highbrow tastes, see Stephen Birmingham, *Our Crowd: The Great Jewish Families of New York* (Harper & Row, 1967), 71–72 and 148.
9. John Collins, "Up-Town Sketches: August Belmont," *New York Sun,* November 19, 1877, 2, quoted in Black, *The King of Fifth Avenue,* facing page viii.
10. Black, *King of Fifth Avenue,* 6.
11. Black, 67 and 76.
12. Black, 410.

13. Norman Lebrecht, *Genius & Anxiety: How Jews Changed the World* (Scribner, 2019), 47–48.
14. "Lord Gordon Gordon: Particulars of His Death—Result of the Coroner's Inquest," *New York Times,* August 13, 1874, 8; and "'Lord' Gordon Gordon: The Career of a Pseudo-Nobleman," *New York Times,* August 5, 1874, 3.
15. Christopher A. Kent, "Victorian Self-Making, or Self-Unmaking? The Tichborne Claimant Revisited," *Victorian Review* 17, no. 1 (Summer 1991), 18–34.
16. "From New York," *Springfield Republican,* July 24, 1875, 5; and "Connecticut," *Springfield Republican,* July 26, 1875, 6. See also "The Alleged Tug Boat Outrage in New York," *Portland Daily Press,* July 24, 1875, 2.
17. "In Disguise," *Minneapolis Tribune,* October 30, 1880.
18. Black, *King of Fifth Avenue,* 11.
19. "The Belmont Sensation Out West," *Farmer and Mechanic,* November 18, 1880, 1.
20. My use of "myth" here is influenced by Richard Slotkin's discussion of the word in *The Fatal Environment: The Myth of the Frontier in the Age of Industrialization, 1800–1890* (University of Oklahoma Press, 1998), 19.
21. Although "Go West, young man!" is attributed to Greeley, its origins are unclear. See Thomas Fuller, "'Go West, Young Man!'—an Elusive Slogan," *Indiana Magazine of History* 100, no. 3 (September 2004): 231–42.
22. Horace Greeley, "Migration—Colonization—Homes," *Wood's Household Magazine,* May 1872, 209–11, quoted in Fuller, "'Go West, Young Man!,'" 238.
23. David M. Wrobel, *Global West, American Frontier: Travel, Empire and Exceptionalism from Manifest Destiny to the Great Depression* (University of New Mexico Press, 2013), 8. On Western travel writing by British authors, see also Monica Rico, *Nature's Noblemen: Transatlantic Masculinities and the Nineteenth-Century American West* (Yale University Press, 2013), 57.
24. "Western Outlaws: Train Robbers, Road Agents, and Cattle Thieves," *Illustrated Police News* (Boston) 23, no. 573 (October 20, 1877): 6.
25. Gary Scharnhorst with Jack Bales, *The Lost Life of Horatio Alger, Jr.* (Indiana University Press, 1985), 111.
26. Rico, *Nature's Noblemen,* 170–71.
27. On the homoerotic currents of the Western formula, see Geoffrey W. Bateman's "Horatio Alger's Queer Frontier," chapter 2 in *Queering the Countryside: New Frontiers in Rural Queer Studies,* ed. Mary L. Gray, Brian J. Gilley, and Colin R. Johnson (New York University Press, 2016), 49–68.
28. Scharnhorst, *The Lost Life of Horatio Alger, Jr.,* 111.
29. Sometimes the dime novel hero was a heroine who transed gender, as in Edward Wheeler's *Deadwood Dick on Deck, or, Calamity Jane, the Heroine of Whoop-up* (1878) and *Philip S. Warne's Hard Crowd: Or, Gentleman Sam's Sister* (1878). The former involved two cross-dressing characters, and the latter three. As Peter Boag has shown, however, the plots of these

novels contained gender transgressions by linking them to heterosexuality. See Boag, *Re-Dressing,* 107.

30. George A. Custer, *My Life on the Plains* (Applewood Books, 2009), facsimile edition of 1874 original, 11.
31. These eras overlapped with and informed one another. Jacksonian manliness, with its emphasis on physical strength, individualism, and aggression, prefigured the cowboy archetype that emerged in later decades. See David G. Pugh, *Sons of Liberty: The Masculine Mind in Nineteenth-Century America* (Praeger Press, 1983); and David Laverenz, *Manhood and the American Renaissance* (Cornell University Press, 1989). On the transition from the masculine ideal of the yeoman farmer (e.g., Thomas Jefferson) to the big-game hunter (e.g., Theodore Roosevelt), see Karen R. Jones, *Epiphany in the Wilderness: Hunting, Nature, and Performance in the Nineteenth-Century American West* (University Press of Colorado, 2015), 5.
32. Sarah Watts, *Rough Rider in the White House: Theodore Roosevelt and the Politics of Desire* (University of Chicago Press, 2003), 123–24. Christopher Herbert dates the origins of this reshaping of white American manliness to the Gold Rush era (1848–1871), when migrating miners negotiated between incentives to show restraint (restrained manhood) and to indulge in violence (martial manhood). *Gold Rush Manliness: Race and Gender on the Pacific Slope* (University of Washington Press, 2018), 20.
33. Rico, *Nature's Noblemen,* 11. Bateman has illustrated a similar zero-sum game of masculine questing in the novels of Horatio Alger, whose characters achieve manhood, in some cases, by feminizing Chinese immigrant men ("Horatio Alger's Queer Frontier," 60–66).
34. Watts, *Rough Rider in the White House,* 124.
35. Jones, *Epiphany in the Wilderness,* 20.
36. On Alger's Western novels as homoerotic and masculinist fantasy, see Bateman, "Alger's Queer Frontier." On Alger's trip to California and subsequent novels, see Scharnhorst, *The Lost Life of Horatio Alger, Jr.,* 111–16; and Edwin Palmer Hoyt, *Horatio's Boys: The Life and Works of Horatio Alger, Jr.* (Chilton Book Company, 1974), 186–200.
37. Bateman, "Horatio Alger's Queer Frontier," 57.
38. Bateman, 53.
39. Watts, *Rough Rider in the White House,* 126; and Edmund Morris, *The Rise of Theodore Roosevelt* (Coward, McCann & Geoghegan, 1979), 144.
40. Morris, *The Rise of Theodore Roosevelt,* 144.
41. Morris, 149.
42. Morris, 156.
43. Watts, *Rough Rider in the White House,* 127, and "Elkhorn Ranch, National Park Service," https://home.nps.gov/thro/learn/historyculture/elkhorn

-ranch.htm. These ranchland experiences formed the basis for the gender assumptions Roosevelt articulated in his book *The Wilderness Hunter* (1893), a "manifesto of manliness" (Jones, *Epiphany in the Wilderness,* 39).

44. Rico, *Nature's Noblemen,* 184. Christopher Knowlton covers the same period in Roosevelt's life in *Cattle Kingdom: The Hidden History of the Cowboy West* (Houghton Mifflin Harcourt, 2017), 87–96, https://archive.org/details/cattlekingdomhid0000know/page/56/mode/2up, as does Peter Boag, more briefly, in *Re-Dressing America's Frontier Past* (152–54).
45. Rico, *Nature's Noblemen,* 65.
46. Rico, 66–67.
47. Rico, 74–75. Knowlton discusses Frewen's intersecting personal and business lives in the late 1870s in *Cattle Kingdom,* 79–84 and 142–55.
48. Mayne Reid, *The Scalp-Hunters: A Thrilling Tale of Adventure and Romance in Northern Mexico* (1851; repr., M. A. Donohue, 1899), 21–22. Read from a contemporary perspective, the trope of the hero on the cusp of adulthood growing and strengthening into a man—transitioning—takes on a special resonance for trans masc people.
49. On the mythical West as a landscape of testosterone and restoration ("testoration"), see Jones, *Epiphany in the Wilderness,* 57.
50. Boag, *Re-Dressing America's Frontier Past,* 50. Writing from a trans-affirmative point of view, I propose that they *were* male, and *were* men. That they arrived at those identities by transitioning to them does not make them less real.
51. Boag, *Re-Dressing America's Frontier Past,* 116 and 124–25.
52. *Weekly Register-Call,* quoted in Boag, *Re-Dressing America's Frontier Past,* 32.
53. [No title], *Kinsley Graphic,* January 25, 1879.
54. Boag, *Re-Dressing America's Frontier Past,* 114, 117, 126–27.
55. Emily Skidmore, *True Sex,* 63–68; and Boag, *Re-Dressing America's Frontier Past,* 95–106.
56. Clare Sears, *Arresting Dress,* 35–36; and Boag, *Re-Dressing America's Frontier Past,* 52–53.
57. Historians have used trans-inflected language to describe the masculine quests of men we would today consider cisgender. Moreton Frewen aimed "to remake himself into a different, new man" (Rico, *Nature's Noblemen,* 65). Eastern gentlemen sought to "cross the divide into essential manhood" and "construct a new physical image" (Watts, *Rough Rider in the White House,* 126). Theodore Roosevelt "epitomized the evolutionary turn of the hunter hero" by "claiming an identity" amid "an expansive landscape of transformation" (Jones, *Epiphany in the Wilderness,* 56).
58. Michael Woods, *Bleeding Kansas: Slavery, Sectionalism, and Civil War on the Missouri-Kansas Border* (Routledge, 2016).

59. The Bleeding Kansas narrative's focus on violence among settler colonists obscures the violence they committed against Native people, as demonstrated by Jeffrey Ostler, *Surviving Genocide: Native Nations and the United States from the American Revolution to Bleeding Kansas* (Yale University Press, 2019), 355.
60. Dale E. Watts, "How Bloody Was Bleeding Kansas? Political Killings in Kansas Territory, 1854–1861," *Kansas History* 18, no. 2 (Summer 1995): 123.
61. On the Exodusters, see Robert G. Athearn, *In Search of Canaan: Black Migration to Kansas, 1879–80,* chapter 3 of Brent M. S. Campney's *This Is Not Dixie: Racist Violence in Kansas, 1861–1927* (University of Illinois Press, 2015); the essential *Exodusters: Black Migration to Kansas After Reconstruction,* by Nell Irvin Painter (W. W. Norton, 1992); and Robert G. Athearn's *In Search of Canaan: Black Migration to Kansas, 1879–80* (University Press of Kansas, 1978).
62. M. W. Reynolds of Parsons, Kansas, quoted in Charlotte Hinger's *Nicodemus: Post-Reconstruction Politics and Racial Justice in Western Kansas* (University of Oklahoma Press, 2016), 67. As noted by Hinger (217), Reynolds's words originally appeared in a newspaper editorial but were presented as evidence in the testimony of F. M. Stringfield before a US Senate Committee (the Voorhees Committee) in 1880.
63. Glen Schwendemann, "Wyandotte and the First 'Exodusters' of 1879," *Kansas Historical Quarterly* 26, no. 3 (Autumn 1960), https://www.kancoll.org/khq/1960/60_3_schwendemann.htm.
64. Hal D. Sears, *The Sex Radicals: Free Love in High Victorian America* (University Press of Kansas, 1977), 33. See also Andrea M. Weingartner, "Sex Radicals in America's Heartland: Redefining Gender and Sexuality, 1880–1910" (PhD diss., University of Missouri–Columbia, 2013), 30.
65. Moses Harman and Edward C. Walker, "Retrospect," *Lucifer, the Light-Bearer,* April 3, 1885, 2. Partially quoted in Weingartner, "Sex Radicals in America's Heartland," 30. Italics original.
66. On the first election of women as clerks in the Kansas House of Representatives, see *House Journal of the Legislative Assembly of the State of Kansas, Sixteenth Annual Session* (George W. Martin, 1876), 59–61, https://www.google.com/books/edition/_/LPlFAQAAMAAJ. On the first election of girls (ages ten through fifteen) as pages, see *House Journal,* 63–64.
67. The members and officers of the Kansas House of Representatives during the sixteenth annual session, beginning January 11, 1876, included Mrs. C. A. Anderson (enrolling clerk); Emma R. Bristol (engrossing clerk); Jessie True (page); Rose Blanton (page); Minnie A. Swafford (page); and Josie B. Anger (page). *House Journal,* 5.
68. "A New Kansas Question," *New York Times,* February 11, 1877, 6. For a counterargument to the idea of Western states as havens of professional

opportunity for women, with Colorado as an example, see Ashley Michelle Achée, "Criminal Womanhood: Colorado Women In-and-Out of Courts, 1873–1933" (PhD diss., University of California, Irvine, 2022), 42.

69. Other Kansas women challenged gender norms in public in the 1870s through militant temperance rhetoric. "Let every woman take off a head," one woman urged in a newspaper in 1874, "as Judith smote the head of Holofoornes." "About Women," *Leavenworth Daily Commercial,* March 6, 1874, quoted in Nancy G. Garner, "'A Prayerful Public Protest': The Significance of Gender in the Kansas Woman's Crusade of 1874," *Kansas History* 20, no. 4 (Winter 1997–1998): 215.
70. "Fertile Kansas: Valuable Points Regarding the Young State," *Boston Daily Globe,* July 31, 1877, 3.
71. "Homes in Kansas" (advertisement), *Palmer Journal,* September 22, 1877, 4.
72. "Where and How to Live," *Berkshire County Eagle,* November 29, 1877, 2.
73. Craig Miner and William E. Unrau, *The End of Indian Kansas: A Study of Cultural Revolution, 1854–1871* (University Press of Kansas, 1990), 125, https://archive.org/details/endofindiankansa0000hcra/page/138.
74. The Western (from an 1870s perspective) states admitted to the Union between 1858 and 1876 were Minnesota, Oregon, Kansas, Nevada, Nebraska, and Colorado. According to the US Census Bureau, these states have a combined total area of 559,607 square miles (State Area Measurements and Internal Point Coordinates, 2010, https://www.census.gov/geographies/reference-files/2010/geo/state-area.html). Indian Affairs Commissioner Francis A. Walker reflected the era's cresting tide of Manifest Destiny genocide when he wrote in 1872 that "if [Native people] stand up against the progress of civilization and industry, they must be relentlessly crushed." Quoted in Burns, *A History of the Osage People,* 275.
75. Tai S. Edwards, *Osage Women and Empire: Gender and Power* (University Press of Kansas, 2018), 110 and 124.
76. Burns, *A History of the Osage People,* 282.
77. Burns, 282–85.
78. Burns, 336.
79. Burns, 282 and 321.
80. David Parsons, "The Removal of the Osages from Kansas" (PhD diss., University of Oklahoma, 1940), 29–30.
81. Burns, *A History of the Osage People,* 283.
82. "The Osage Lands: Text of a Treaty with the Indians," *Kansas State Record,* September 17, 1870, 2. Quoted in Burns, 344.
83. Dennis McAuliffe, *Bloodland: A Family Story of Oil, Greed and Murder on the Osage Reservation* (Council Oak Books, 1999), 116. See also Miner and Unrau, *The End of Indian Kansas,* 139.

84. Some post-removal contact between Kansas settler colonists and Wahzhazheh people from across the border was peaceful—when it came in the context of entertainment for white people. Isais J. McCaffery, "Fear, Politics, Myth, and Memory: Governor Thomas A. Osborn and the Osage Border War of 1874–1875," *Kansas History* 42, no. 1 (Spring 2019), 8.
85. Burns, *A History of the Osage People,* 350–51; and McCaffery, "Fear, Politics, Myth, and Memory," 12–13.
86. Miner and Unrau, *The End of Indian Kansas,* 139.
87. Edwards, *Osage Women and Empire,* 122. See also the Osage population statistics in Ostler, *Surviving Genocide,* 400.
88. Anonymous laborer's diary, 1878 (MS-S840), Massachusetts Historical Society, [1].
89. Anonymous laborer's diary, [3].
90. Anonymous laborer's diary, [5].
91. G. F. Cram, *Railroad and Township Map of Kansas, 1877* (Missouri Publishing Company, 1878), David Rumsey Map Collection, https://www.davidrumsey.com/luna/servlet/s/o8g5qw.
92. Kansas Pacific Railway Company, *A Geographically Correct Map of Kansas & Colorado, Showing Principal Cities & Towns, 1878,* Denver Public Library, https://digital.denverlibrary.org/nodes/view/822280.
93. For the state's ecological regions, see Shannen S. Chapman et al., 2001, *Ecoregions of Nebraska and Kansas* (color poster with map, descriptive text, summary tables, and photographs) (US Geological Survey, 2001), https://store.usgs.gov/product/21635. For elevations, see *Digital Elevation Model Shaded Relief Map of Kansas,* State of Kansas GIS Data Access and Support Center, Kansas Geological Survey, https://www.kgs.ku.edu/General/demMap.html.
94. National Park Service, *Chisholm and Great Western National Historic Trail Feasibility Study / Environmental Assessment* (May 2019), 43, http://npshistory.com/publications/transportation/chisholm-great-western/fs-ea-2019.pdf. For a foundational text on the subject, see Robert Dykstra, *The Cattle Towns* (Bison Books, 1983). For a more recent source alert to the operation of cattle ranching within capitalism, see Knowlton, *Cattle Kingdom.*
95. Laurel Wilson, "American Cowboy Dress: Function to Fashion," *Dress: The Journal of the Costume Society of America* 28, no. 1 (2001): 40–43.
96. Sworn testimony of Henry Gregory to Russell County Justice of the Peace J. C. Burnett, January 16, 1879, B. J. Alderman papers, box 9, folder 173, Pittsburg State University. See also B. J. Alderman, "Where Is Leon Belmont?" *Chronicle of the Old West,* June 2005, 15.
97. State warrant issued by Justice of the Peace J. C. Burnett on January 16, 1879, B. J. Alderman papers, box 9, folder 173.

98. State warrant, B. J. Alderman papers.
99. B. J. Alderman, "Leon the Mysterious Lady," *Wild West,* December 2018, 20.
100. A Texas rancher named James Hickey sold a lot of 1,000 cattle in Dodge City for $17.00 a head in June 1879 (*Dodge City Times,* June 21, 1879, 8). If Belmont charged a similar price for 3,000 cattle in January of the same year, he stood to make $51,000.00.
101. [No title,] *Kinsley [KS] Graphic,* January 25, 1879.
102. Tom Clavin, *Dodge City: Wyatt Earp, Bat Masterson, and the Wickedest Town in the American West* (St. Martin's Press, 2017), 197–98, 200, and 203–4.
103. Dodge City ledger, 1878–1882, Dodge City Municipal Court, Ford County Historical Society, https://archive.org/details/dodge-city-ledger/page/n433/mode/2up.
104. "Iniquitous Dodge," *Hays City Sentinel,* September 14, 1877, 4.
105. Robert Dykstra has demonstrated the exaggeration of violent crime in 1870s/1880s Dodge City in multiple publications. See *The Cattle Towns*; "Overdosing on Dodge City," *Western Historical Quarterly* 27, no. 4 (Winter 1996): 505–14; and "Quantifying the Wild West: The Problematic Statistics of Frontier Violence," *Western Historical Quarterly* 40, no. 3 (Autumn 2009): 331–47. See also Dykstra's book with JoAnn Manfra, *Dodge City and the Birth of the Wild West* (University Press of Kansas, 2017). Christopher Knowlton echoes Dykstra's warning more generally in *Cattle Kingdom,* 56 and 59.
106. Dykstra and Manfra, *Dodge City and the Birth of the Wild West,* 5.
107. [No title], *Kinsley Graphic,* January 25, 1879.
108. *Russell Independent,* February 8, 1879, 3. Since the *Russell Independent* writer was following the information supplied by the warrant issued in Russell County, he referred to Belmont as "Dr. Stanley, the pretended woman physician" rather than as Belmont. Belmont's time in Dodge is also mentioned in Alderman, "Leon the Mysterious Lady," 20.
109. *Harper County Times,* February 6, 1879, 3. Alderman notes in "Leon the Mysterious Lady" (20) that since ulsters were unisex garments, the reference to Belmont's ulster underlines his androgyny.
110. Alderman, "Where Is Leon Belmont?," 15.
111. [No title], *Harper County Times,* February 20, 1879, 3, and letter in the B. J. Alderman papers (box 2, folder 48) dated March 15, 2004.
112. "Anthony News," *Harper County Times,* February 20, 1879, 2.
113. Alderman, "Where Is Leon Belmont?"
114. Alderman, "Leon the Mysterious Lady," 20.

5. The Outlaw, 1879–1880

1. B. J. Alderman, typescript of "Saga of Sheriff Weakley," B. J. Alderman papers, box 3, folder 71, Kansas Historical Society. The article was published in *Kansas Cowboy* in March 2003.
2. Alderman, "Weakley Family Black Sheep," 51, B. J. Alderman papers, box 3, folder 70.
3. B. J. Alderman papers, box 9, folder 173.
4. B. J. Alderman papers, box 9, folder 173.
5. Alderman, "Where Is Leon Belmont?" *Chronicle of the Old West,* June 2005, 20.
6. B. J. Alderman, *The Secret Life of the Lawman's Wife* (Praeger, 2007), 186.
7. *Russell Independent,* February 15, 1879. B. J. Alderman papers, folder 194, box 10.
8. "Odell," *Harper County Times,* February 27, 1879, 3. The notice got three things wrong: the spelling of Weakley's name; his origin (Russell County rather than Pawnee); and the spelling of Belmont's alias, Stanley.
9. "The Belmont Mystery," *Minneapolis Tribune,* November 12, 1880, 6.
10. B. J. Alderman, a great-great-granddaughter of James Weakley, describes Belmont's escape with the sheriff in multiple publications. For the most detailed narrative, see "Where Is Leon Belmont?" 16 and 20.
11. "A Fraud," *Cresset* (Medicine Lodge, KS), April 3, 1879, B. J. Alderman papers, box 10, folder 179.
12. "A Fraud." See also "Town and County News," *Cresset,* February 6, 1880, B. J. Alderman papers, box 10, folder 179.
13. "A Fraud" and "Belmont's Blue Blood: The Female Man Arraigned for Appearing in Male Attire," a *St. Paul Pioneer Press* article printed in the *Russell Record,* October 31, 1880, 6.
14. "A Fraud."
15. "Anthony News," *Harper County Times,* 3.
16. "The Governor and His Staff," *Dodge City Globe,* June 3, 1879, 3.
17. At the time of the murders, the seven men were returning with 353 other Ôhmésêhese (Northern Cheyenne) from their reservation in Indian Territory to their homeland in the northern plains as part of the Northern Cheyenne Exodus (1878–1879). For an Ôhmésêhese perspective on the exodus, as well as the leadership of Vóóhéhéve (Morning Star), see Leo Killsback, "Morning Star Rises: Peace, Power, and Righteousness in the Face of Colonization," *Wíčazo Ša Review* 33, no. 1 (Spring 2018): 5–37. On the planned trial of the seven (later six) Ôhmésêhese men, which was dismissed before it began, see Denise Low and Ramon Powers, *Northern Cheyenne Ledger Art by Fort Robinson Breakout Survivors* (University of Nebraska Press, 2020), 17–19.

18. See the *Russell Independent* items (published on April 19, April 26, May 3, May 17, and May 24, 1879) in the B. J. Alderman papers, folder 194, box 10.
19. *Russell Independent,* May 17, 1879, B. J. Alderman papers, folder 194, box 10.
20. *Russell Independent,* May 24, 1879, B. J. Alderman papers, folder 194, box 10.
21. John St. John to Henry Senft, June 25, 1879, Governor's Office letter press books, Gov. John P. St. John papers, box 5, No. 17, June 25–August 5, 1879, Kansas Historical Society. I've relied on the transcription in Alderman, "Weakley Family Black Sheep," 51–52.
22. "Belmont's Blue Blood," *Russell Record,* October 31, 1880, 6.
23. Undated *Anthony Republican* article in B. J. Alderman papers, box 10, folder 179. See also Alderman, "Leon the Mysterious Lady," 21.
24. "Belmont's Blue Blood," *Russell Record,* November 11, 1880, 6. Belmont's first-person narrative in "The What Is It" (*Minneapolis Tribune,* October 31, 1880, 2) suggests that Morris Clifford had a brother who accompanied the group to Dakota Territory.
25. Casey Tefertiller, *Wyatt Earp: The Life Behind the Legend* (John Wiley & Sons, 1999), 17.
26. Jan Cerney and Roberta Sago, *Black Hills Gold Rush Towns* (Arcadia Publishing, 2010), 7–8.
27. "Pictures of Life in the Black Hills," *Cheyenne Daily Sun,* May 11, 1878. Quoted in Karen R. Jones, *Calamity: The Many Lives of Calamity Jane* (Yale University Press, 2020), 68.
28. *Great Western Railway of Canada and Its Connecting Lines* (Rand McNally, 1881), David Rumsey Map Collection, https://www.davidrumsey.com/luna/servlet/s/j2i913.
29. "The Black Hills a Hard Road to Travel," *Hampshire Gazette,* March 7, 1876, 2.
30. "'The What Is It,'" *Minneapolis Tribune,* February 21, 1881, 6. Another article in the *Minneapolis Tribune* states that "Taylor had come to the Hills in the evident capacity of a companion of Belmont. They associated and lived together under the same canvas." "Who Is She?" November 1, 1880, 5.
31. On the Homestake Mine as the biggest and deepest gold mine in North America, see Andrew L. Yarrow, "Beneath South Dakota's Black Hills," *New York Times,* August 9, 1987, 21. On the mine's profits between 1878 and 1880, see Table 7.2, "Operating Costs for the Homestake Mine (May 1, 1878, through August 31, 1880)," in Steven T. Mitchell, *Nuggets to Neutrinos: The Homestake Story* (Xlibris ebook, 2009), pages unnumbered.
32. "Belmont in the Hills: How the Precious Fraud Duped Ladies in Lead City," *Minneapolis Evening Journal,* November 10, 1880, 4.
33. "Belmont in the Hills."

34. Boag, *Re-Dressing America's Frontier Past,* 1. Examples throughout Boag's book bear out this claim.
35. In *Re-Dressing America's Frontier Past,* Boag uses the term "progress narrative" to name a common excuse for gender migration used by female-assigned people in the American West: they did it because dressing as men brought them personal progress, freedom, and money (9). This excuse aligned with a narrative of *national* progress in whose service the state enlisted citizens to enrich, expand, and "settle" the United States.
36. In addition to the definitions of settler colonialism used in Patrick Wolfe's *Traces of History: Elementary Structures of Race* (Verso, 2016) and Lorenzo Veracini's *Settler Colonialism: A Theoretical Overview* (Palgrave Macmillan, 2010), I appreciate the definition of the term offered by Levi Gahman in "White Settler-Colonialist Society as Monster: Rural Southeast Kansas, Ancestral Osage (Wah-Zha-Zi) Territories, and the Violence of Forgetting," *Antipode* 48, no. 2 (2016): 319.
37. Darrell Ehrlick, "The Remarkable Life, Death and Tombstone of Manhattan's Sammy Williams," *Daily Montanan,* April 30, 2023. See also Boag, *Re-Dressing America's Frontier Past,* 31–32.
38. "Disguised Her Sex," *St. Paul Daily Globe,* January 28, 1888, 10.
39. Jones, *Calamity,* 60–61.
40. James D. McLaird, *Calamity Jane: The Woman and the Legend* (University of Oklahoma Press, 2005).
41. Canary's relationship to gender variance differed from Belmont's. While Belmont persistently identified himself as a man between 1879 and 1902, Canary did not. James D. McLaird, one of Canary's biographers, argues that dime novels presented her dressed as a man in order to burnish her transgressive appeal (*Calamity Jane,* 4–5). On newspaper coverage of Canary's Black Hills years, see Jones, *Calamity,* 65–71. On Canary's decision to wear a man's cavalry uniform in the 1870s, see pages 29–55 of the same volume.
42. "Pictures of Life in the Black Hills," 68.
43. In making this claim I'm in debt to Jamey Jesperson's concept of settler *trans*nationalism, which she defines as the route by which "trans bodies 'pass' into the US body politic, not just through gender, but through investment in, and allegiance to, the nation." "Settler *Trans*Nationalism: The Colonial Politics of White Trans Passing on Stolen Land," *Spectator* 42, no. 1 (Spring 2022), 33.
44. The example of one of Belmont's Black Hills contemporaries suggests that in some circumstances, settler colonist affinity trumped race as well as gender. Sarah Campbell, an African American woman born in Kentucky, participated in Custer's 1874 gold expedition as a cook and laundress, filed claims to prospect for gold and silver, and bought into the Custer Park

Mining Company. With these settler credentials, she claimed the title of the first white woman to enter the Black Hills (with "white" used a cipher for "non-Native"). Journalist William Curtis wrote approvingly of Campbell as an "old frontiersman"—a sign of acceptance that "alluded to the flexible boundaries of gender normativity for those seen as part of the 'rough and ready' pioneer vanguard" (Jones, *Calamity,* 36).

45. Killsback, "Morning Star Rises," 22.
46. The Ȟe Sápa are also sacred to Northern Cheyenne, Dakȟóta, and Nakȟóta people. With their Lakȟóta relatives, the Dakȟóta and Nakȟóta make up a single nation: the Očhéthi Šakówiŋ (Seven Council Fires). For contemporary reflections on the Ȟe Sápa from writers across the Očhéthi Šakówiŋ, see Craig Howe, Lydia Whirlwind Soldier, and Lanniko L. Lee, eds., *He Sapa Woihanble: Black Hills Dream* (Living Justice Press, 2011). See also Dakota Wind Goodhouse's "Makȟóčhe Wašté: The Beautiful Country" (MA thesis, North Dakota State University of Agriculture and Applied Science, October 2019).
47. Treaty of Fort Laramie, Article II, National Archives, https://www.archives.gov/milestone-documents/fort-laramie-treaty.
48. The "sale" of the Ȟe Sápa was illegal as well as coerced by threats of starvation, as pointed out by Rani-Henrik Andersson and David C. Posthumus. See *Lakȟóta: An Indigenous History* (University of Oklahoma Press, 2022), 170.
49. Office of Sen. Daniel Inouye, "1986 Black Hills Hearing on S. 1453: Introduction," *Wíčazo Ša Review* 4, no. 1 (1988): 11.
50. Mitchell, *Nuggets to Neutrinos,* unnumbered pages.
51. Gahman, "White Settler-Colonialist Society as Monster," 322.
52. Clare Sears, *True Sex: The Lives of Trans Men at the Turn of the Twentieth Century* (New York University Press, 2017), 178; and Boag, *Re-Dressing America's Frontier Past,* 157.
53. Charles (Chas.) L. Watts in the 1870 US census (Shasta County, CA), https://www.ancestry.com.
54. "'The What Is It.'"
55. "'The What Is It.'"
56. "Who Is She?"
57. "'The What Is It.'"
58. "A Double Character," *St. Paul Globe,* October 31, 1880, 5.
59. "A Double Character."
60. "'The What Is It.'"
61. "'The What Is It.'"
62. "Mary Belmont," *Minneapolis Evening Journal,* October 31, 1880, 4; and "In Disguise," *Minneapolis Tribune,* October 30, 1880, 6.
63. "'The What Is It.'"

64. "A Female Man at Large," *St. Paul Pioneer Press*, October 30, 1880, 6; and "In Disguise," *Minneapolis Tribune*, October 30, 1880, 6.

6. The Celebrity, 1880–1881

1. "The Belmont Mystery," *Minneapolis Tribune*, November 12, 1880, 6.
2. "In Disguise: The Curious and Romantic Sensation That Was Developed in the City Yesterday Afternoon," *Minneapolis Tribune*, October 30, 1880, 6.
3. Springfield, Massachusetts, population history, 1840–2025, https://www.biggestuscities.com/city/springfield-massachusetts.
4. The population of St. Anthony in 1870 was 5,073. See US census, 1870, Population, 178, 180; and manuscript census schedules, Minneapolis, 1857, cited in Lucile M. Kane, "Governing a Frontier City: Old St. Anthony, 1855–1872," *Minnesota History* 35, no. 3 (September 1956): 119.
5. "That Female Man," *Illustrated Police News*, November 13, 1880, 11.
6. On Belmont's arrival in Minneapolis, see "That Female Man." For the address and inhabitants of the Watts family's Fifth Avenue house, see the 1880 US census (Hennepin County), https://www.ancestry.com.
7. Sources disagree on Belmont's role in Dr. Goodrich's office, with some calling him a medical student and others suggesting he was an employee. See "That Female Man."
8. "That Female Man."
9. "In Disguise."
10. "The Last Sensation," *Minneapolis Evening Journal*, November 2, 1880, 4; and "Mary Belmont," *Minneapolis Evening Journal*, October 31, 1880, 4.
11. "'The What Is It,'" *Minneapolis Tribune*, February 21, 1881, 6.
12. "That Female Man," *Illustrated Police News*, November 11, 1880, 2.
13. The date of 1867 contradicts William N. Eskridge, *Gaylaw: Challenging the Apartheid of the Closet* (Harvard University Press, 1999), 339, but is shown in "An Ordinance Relative to Misdemeanors, Breaches of Peace and Disorderly Conduct," *Minneapolis Tribune*, June 5, 1867, 4 (I'm grateful to Ulysses Swanson for the citation). Municipal court clerk L. A. Dunn received a written and sworn complaint from Brackett on October 30 that was eventually published in the *Minneapolis Tribune* ("The Belmont," November 10, 1880, 6).
14. "In Disguise," and "A Female Man at Large," *St. Paul Pioneer Press*, October 30, 1880, 6. The *Pioneer Press* reported Belmont's address as "Fourth avenue south, between Sixth and Seventh streets," whereas the *Tribune* referred to him as living "on Second avenue south and Sixth street."
15. "Mary Belmont," *Minneapolis Evening Journal*, October 31, 1880, 4.
16. "A Double Character," *St. Paul Daily Globe*, October 31, 1880, 5.
17. "The Limboed Belmont." *Minneapolis Tribune*, November 2, 1880, 6. See also "The Last Sensation"; "Minneapolis Globelets," *St. Paul Daily Globe*,

November 1, 1880, 2; and "Who Is She?" *Minneapolis Tribune,* November 1, 1880, 5. For information about Beal's gallery, see Peter E. Palmquist and Thomas R. Kailbourn, *Pioneer Photographers from the Mississippi to the Continental Divide: A Biographical Dictionary, 1839–1865* (Stanford University Press, 2005), 97–99. For the role of photography in the development of American celebrity culture, see Leo Braudy, *The Frenzy of Renown: Fame and Its History* (Vintage Books, 1997), 491–94. For the effect of modern newspaper journalism on the same, see Braudy, *The Frenzy of Renown,* 508–10.

18. "'The What Is It,'" *Minneapolis Tribune,* October 31, 1880, 2. The phrase "the what is it," used in multiple Belmont headlines and articles, picks up on the language of Victorian freak shows. P. T. Barnum toured the United States in the 1870s with an African American man (William Henry Johnson) billed as "Zip, the What Is It?" See Lindsey B. Churchill, "What Is It? Difference, Darwin, and the Victorian Freak Show," in *Darwin in Atlantic Cultures: Evolutionary Visions of Race, Gender, and Sexuality* (Routledge, 2010), 128–42. On spectacles of gender transgression in Victorian freak shows, see Claire Sears, *Arresting Dress,* 101–11. On William Henry Johnson, see Cook, *The Arts of Deception,* 126–38 and 256.
19. "Who Is She?"
20. "The Limboed Belmont" and "Gossip About Town," *Minneapolis Tribune,* November 3, 1880, 6. The phrase "in durance vile" (in prison) turns up in, for example, Roberts Burns's "Epistle from Esopus to Maria" (1794): "In durance vile here must I wake and weep, / And all my frowzy Couch in sorrow steep."
21. "Mary Belmont," *St. Paul Daily Globe,* November 4, 1880, 3.
22. "The Farce Ending," *St. Paul Daily Globe,* November 5, 1880, 5.
23. The association of the word "abomination" with homosexuality is due in part to English translations of Leviticus 18:22. See Elizabeth Reis, "Impossible Hermaphrodites: Intersex in America, 1620–1960," *Journal of American History* 92, no. 2 (September 2005): 427n38.
24. For examples of this logic at work in later periods, see Toby Beauchamp, *Going Stealth: Transgender Politics and U.S. Surveillance Practices* (Duke University Press, 2019), 9; and David K. Johnson, *The Lavender Scare: The Cold War Persecution of Gays and Lesbians in the Federal Government* (University of Chicago Press, 2004).
25. "The Belmont," *Minneapolis Tribune,* November 10, 1880, 6; and "The Courts," *Minneapolis Tribune,* November 12, 1880, 7.
26. "Gossip About Town," *Minneapolis Tribune,* November 12, 1880, 6; "Belmont at Liberty," *St. Paul Daily Globe,* November 12, 1880, 2.
27. "The Belmont Mystery."

28. By sex and gender variance I mean a mutually inclusive range of nonconforming desires, bodies, and practices encompassing what we would today call intersex conditions, trans identities, drag or cross-dressing contexts, and non-straight sexual orientations.
29. Skidmore, *True Sex,* 15–16. See also Lisa Duggan, "Doctors of Desire," in *Sapphic Slashers: Sex, Violence, and American Modernity* (Duke University Press, 2000), 156–79; Chris Waters, "Sexology," in *Palgrave Advances in the Modern History of Sexuality,* ed. M. Houlbrook and H. Cocks (Palgrave Macmillan, 2006), 41–63; and Alison Oram, "Cross-Dressing and Transgender," also in *Palgrave Advances,* 256–85.
30. "Belmont: Who and What Is She?—a Mystery That Is Still Unsolved," *Minneapolis Tribune,* November 13, 1880, 7.
31. InterACT, "Intersex Variations Glossary," https://interactadvocates.org/wp-content/uploads/2022/10/Intersex-Variations-Glossary.pdf.
32. The vast majority of doctors diagnosed patients with "pseudohermaphroditism" rather than so-called true hermaphroditism. Sexologists spent much of the late nineteenth century in pursuit of what they called the "true" or "perfect" hermaphrodite: a person with "complete" male and female genitalia. See Reis, *Bodies in Doubt,* 50–52 and 57–59.
33. For a historical survey of gender variance in Indigenous cultures, see Gregory D. Smithers, *Reclaiming Two Spirits: Sexuality, Spiritual Renewal & Sovereignty in Native America* (Beacon Press, 2020). For additional perspectives, see Mark Rifkin's *When Did Indians Become Straight? Kinship, the History of Sexuality, and Native Sovereignty* (Oxford University Press, 2011), as well as Kai Pyle's "Naming and Claiming: Recovering Ojibwe and Plains Cree Two-Spirit Language," in *TSQ: Transgender Studies Quarterly* 5, no. 4 (November 2018): 574–88.
34. On the change from monsters to impostors, see Reis, *Bodies in Doubt,* 23–54.
35. Minnesota cases include "Belmont's Rival" (*St. Paul Daily Globe,* November 13, 1880, 3); "A Mixed Gender" (*St. Paul Daily Globe,* December 13, 1883, 6); a hotel waiter (*St. Paul Daily Globe,* July 27, 1886, 3); and Cecelia Regina Gonzaga (*Minneapolis Star Tribune,* August 21, 1885, 3; *St. Paul Daily Globe,* August 21, 1885, 2; and *St. Paul Globe,* August 22, 1885, 2). The first two were white, and the second two were African American. On race in narratives of sex and gender variance, see C. Riley Snorton, *Black on Both Sides: A Racial History of Trans Identity* (University of Minnesota Press, 2017); Duggan, *Sapphic Slashers,* 9–21; Skidmore, *True Sex,* 68–100; Boag, *Re-Dressing America's Frontier Past,* 130–58; and Sears, *Arresting Dress,* 121–38.
36. National media sensations comparable to Belmont's flared up around Joseph Israel Lobdell in the 1870s (see Jen Manion, *Female Husbands: A Trans History,* Cambridge University Press, 2020, 219–25), Frank DuBois in the 1880s (Skidmore, *True Sex,* 15–27), Milton Matson in the 1890s

(Sears, *Arresting Dress,* 103–5), and Joe Monahan in the 1900s (Boag, *Re-Dressing America's Frontier Past,* 95–104). All were white. This homogeny bears up Skidmore's claim that "whiteness (in terms of racial identity and American nationality) was a vital component to the popular stories of trans men in the first decades of the twentieth century" (*True Sex,* 70).

37. On the infrastructure of modern celebrity, including railways, the penny press, the telegraph, and paper manufacturing, see Sharon Marcus, *The Drama of Celebrity* (Princeton University Press, 2019), 10–12. On the development of daily and mass-circulation newspaper networks, see Fred Inglis, *A Short History of Celebrity* (Princeton University Press, 2010), 118–23; and Duggan, *Sapphic Slashers,* 32–36. On the international reach of fame in the mid-to-late nineteenth century, during which the celebrity became "an aspirational figure for the marginalized," see Páraic Finnerty and Rod Rosenquist, "Transatlantic Celebrity: European Fame in Nineteenth-Century America," *Comparative American Studies* 14, no. 1 (2016): 1–6.
38. Inglis, *A Short History of Celebrity,* 4.
39. On fame in the Romantic era, see Inglis, *A Short History of Celebrity,* 25–27 and 58–73; as well as Braudy, *The Frenzy of Renown,* 422–45.
40. Marcus, *The Drama of Celebrity,* 26–27.
41. Inglis, *A Short History of Celebrity,* 120.
42. Devon Cox, *The Street of Wonderful Possibilities: Whistler, Wilde, and Sargent in Tite Street* (Frances Lincoln, 2015).
43. Minnesota Governor R. W. Johnson had heralded Van Cleve as one of "the three oldest settlers in the state" ten years earlier, in a speech to the Old Settlers Association published in the *Minneapolis Tribune* ("R. W. Johnson's Address Before the Old Settlers' Association," February 24, 1870, 3). For an autobiographical overview of Van Cleve, see Bobbie Scott, "Charlotte Ouisconsin Clark Van Cleve: Mother, Patriot, Reformer," *Hennepin History* 72, no. 1 (Winter 2013): 14–34.
44. "Belmont at Liberty"; "Municipal," *Minneapolis Tribune,* November 12, 1880, 7; and "Belmont: Who and What Is She?"
45. "The Limboed Belmont." For the interview with Ames, see "The Belmont Located," *St. Paul Pioneer Press,* November 14, 1880, 6.
46. See "The Belmont: The Mystery Thickens—He, She or It Declared to Be a Man," *Minneapolis Tribune,* November 14, 1880, 1.
47. "The Belmont Mystery" and "The Belmont: The Mystery Thickens."
48. "The Great Unknown," November 16, 1880, 3.
49. "The Great Unknown," November 16, 1880, 3.
50. "A Mystery Cleared Up," *Minneapolis Tribune,* November 18, 1880, 6.
51. "Immediately after the release of Belmont from the county jail, it found a boarding place in a boarding-house in the lower part of town" ("'The What Is It'"). "The Belmont is about to commence the study of medicine

in Dr. Ames's office" ("Gossip About Town," *Minneapolis Tribune,* November 17, 1880, 6).

52. "Adieu," *Minneapolis Tribune,* November 17, 1880, 8.
53. "A Mystery Cleared Up." The *Tribune*'s offer to accept Belmont's gender variance on the condition of his "good" behavior mirrors what Emily Skidmore has identified as a more typically rural tolerance of gender variance. See Skidmore, *True Sex,* 44.
54. On the symptoms and incidence of CAH, see Hedi Claahsen-van der Grinten et al., "Congenital Adrenal Hyperplasia—Current Insights in Pathophysiology, Diagnostics, and Management," *Endocrine Reviews* 43, no. 9 (2022): 91–99 and especially 94–95. On Belmont's lack of a beard, see "That Female Man," *Illustrated Police News,* November 20, 1880, 2; "In Disguise," *Minneapolis Tribune,* October 30, 1880; and Melvina's 1922 deposition testimony (deposition of Melvina A. Barry, February 13, 1922, US Bureau of Prisons, pension file of Allen E. Barry, 114, https://www.fold3.com).
55. On the case of patient A. B. (Lawrence Register Payne), see Reis, *Bodies in Doubt,* 72–75, and Bayker, "Before Transsexuality," 196.
56. The panel of experts convened to testify in the Jumas case included the forensic scientist Auguste Ambroise Tardieu, whose work influenced the development of sexology in the 1880s and 1890s. Geertje Mak, *Doubting Sex: Inscriptions, Bodies, and Selves in Nineteenth-Century Hermaphrodite Case Histories* (Manchester University Press, 2012), 120.
57. Reis, *Bodies in Doubt,* 29.
58. Mak, *Doubting Sex,* 131 and 135.
59. Mak, 92.
60. Mak, 114.
61. Mak, 100, 136–37, 141–43, and 144.
62. Mak, 144.
63. *Illustrated Police News,* November 13, 1880, 11.
64. "The Belmont Located."
65. Another possibility remains: that Belmont bribed Ames to lie and proclaim him a man. Ames was Dirty "Doc" Ames, the infamously corrupt four-time mayor who earned the nickname "the Shame of Minneapolis." A court found him guilty of accepting a bribe from a sex worker in 1903, but his sentence was overturned. On Ames in general, see Erik Rivenes, *Dirty Doc Ames and the Scandal That Shook Minneapolis* (Minnesota Historical Society Press, 2018).
66. Hil Malatino has pointed to the examination table as a site of "radical disempowerment in the face of medical objectification" of intersex people. *Queer Embodiment: Monstrosity, Medical Violence, and Intersex Experience* (University of Nebraska Press, 2019), 126. See also Katrina Karkazis,

Fixing Sex: Intersex, Medical Authority, and Intersex Experience (Duke University Press, 2008).

67. Mak dates this shift toward "routines (or role-playing) necessary for the temporary dislodgement of a person from the body" to the 1870s and 1880s. See *Doubting Sex,* 143.
68. Mak, *Doubting Sex,* 119, 122, and 123.
69. "A Feminine Don Juan in Masculine Attire," *Boston Globe,* October 31, 1880, 1; "Sensation in Minneapolis: A Girl in Boy's Clothes," *Washington Evening Star,* November 1, 1880, 1; "Girl in Boy's Clothes Courts Another Girl," *Democrat and Chronicle* (Rochester, NY), 3; "Notes and Excerpts," *Oakland (CA) Tribune,* November 11, 1880, 2; *Swanton (VT) Courier,* 3; "Belmont's Blue Blood: The Female Man Arraigned for Appearing in Male Attire," *Russell (KS) Record,* 1; "A Girl in Boy's Clothes," *Opelika (AL) Times,* November 12, 1880, 1; [Untitled], *Louisville (KY) Courier-Journal,* November 3, 1880, 3. See also "Is It a Key?" *Minneapolis Tribune,* November 15, 1880, 6; "A Female Swindler," *Daily Milwaukee News,* December 10, 1880, 1; "A Girl in Men's Clothes," *Burlington (VT) Weekly Free Press* (via the *Springfield [MA] Republican*), December 24, 1880, 1.
70. "Is It a Key?," 6. See also Addie Liona Walker's birth record in the birth registry of Warren, Massachusetts, June 1, 1853, https://www.ancestry.com; "He or She?" *Boston Globe,* December 5, 1880, 10; "'The What Is It?'"; and records of the Albert Walker family in the 1860 US census (Worcester County, MA), https://www.ancestry.com.
71. "'The What Is It'" and the 1881 Minneapolis city directory, https://www.ancestry.com.
72. George Campbell and family in the 1880 US census (Hennepin County, MN), https://www.ancestry.com.
73. Barbara Mayes Boustead, Martha D. Shulski, and Steven D. Hilberg, "The Long Winter of 1880/81," *Bulletin of the American Meteorological Society* 101, no. 6 (June 2020): 797–813, https://journals.ametsoc.org/view/journals/bams/101/6/bamsD190014.xml.
74. "The Campbells Are Parted," *St. Paul Globe,* March 25, 1881, 2.
75. "The Campbells Are Parted."
76. The *Tribune* portrayed Belmont's relationship with Melvina as a May–December romance ("'The What Is It'"). Their age difference was, in fact, ten years. See the age of Melvina Lowell in the 1850 census of Whitneyville, Maine (Washington County), and the birth record of Addie Liona Walker in Warren, Massachusetts (Worcester County), 1853, https://www.ancestry.com.
77. "'The What Is It.'"
78. "The Campbells Are Parted."
79. For the details of Melvina's life before Belmont, see chapter 8.
80. "Gossip About Town," *Minneapolis Tribune,* April 15, 1881, 6.

81. "Society: Leon A. Belmont," *Minneapolis Tribune,* February 27, 1881, 7.
82. Legal marriages between people assigned a female sex at birth were not unheard of in the late nineteenth century, though they were not identified as such at the time. For a survey of examples, see Manion's *Female Husbands* as well as Rachel Hope Cleves's "'What, Another Female Husband?': The Prehistory of Same-Sex Marriage in America," *Journal of American History* 101, no. 4 (March 2015): 1055–81. For the details of Belmont's marriage to Melvina, see [No title], *Northern Pacific Farmer,* March 3, 1881, 3; "The Campbells Are Parted," *St. Paul Globe,* March 25, 1881, 2; marriage certificate, State of Minnesota, County of Isanti, issued on April 6, 1881, to Leon A. Belmont and Melvina A. Barry, personal collection of the author; and "Wedded: A Report That Leon A. Belmont's Latest Escapade Is Marriage," *Minneapolis Tribune,* April 8, 1881, 5.
83. "Minneapolis News: City Council," *St. Paul Globe,* April 13, 1881, 3.
84. "Gossip About Town," *Minneapolis Tribune,* April 15, 1881, 6.
85. Melvina's daughter with George Campbell appears on the 1880 US census (Hennepin County) as Josie M[aude] Campbell. On the 1885 state census of Kansas (Cherokee County), a child of the same age and sex appears as Maude Belmont, the daughter of Leon and Melvina Belmont. Both from https://www.ancestry.com.
86. "A Strange Affair," *St. Paul Globe,* August 11, 1881, 2.
87. Affidavit signed by Melvina Barry, September 28, 1921, pension file of Allen E. Barry.

7. The Hustler, 1881–1902

1. John P. Edwards, *Historical Atlas of Cowley County, Kansas* (John P. Edwards, 1883), 9, https://www.kansasmemory.org/item/223990/page/7.
2. Josie M. Campbell's age on the 1880 US census (Hennepin County, MN) is listed as five. The middle initial "M" may have stood for Maud, in which case her middle name served as her first name once she was in Kansas. Later records, however, including her marriage license and death certificate (both issued in Jasper County, Missouri), list her name as "Maud C. Belmont." All from https://www.ancestry.com.
3. Cowley County's total population in 1881 was 19,167; Winfield's in 1880 was 2,844. Edwards, *Historical Atlas of Cowley County,* 9 and 10.
4. Edwards, *Historical Atlas of Cowley County,* 10.
5. On Belmont's purchase of Cochran's ranch, see *Winfield Courier,* January 12, 1882, 3. For the mention of Belmont in the atlas, see Edwards, *Historical Atlas of Cowley County,* 11.
6. James D. Cochran (Cowley County, KS), Osage Trust Lands certificate no. 1278 (KS3580__.274), General Land Office Records, https://glorecords.blm.gov/details/patent/default.aspx?accession=KS3580__.274.

7. See "The Osage Removal," chapter 16 in Louis F. Burns, *A History of the Osage People,* 314–34.
8. "The Osage Lands: Text of a Treaty with the Indians," *Kansas State Record,* September 17, 1870, 2, quoted in Burns, *A History of the Osage People,* 344. See also Derby Historical Society and Museum, "Osage Trust Land," Travel Through Time blog, November 4, 2022, https://derbykshistorymuseum.org/blog/f/osage-trust-land.
9. Burns, *History of the Osage People,* 345.
10. "Treaty with the Great and Little Osage," Tribal Treaties Database, Oklahoma State University, https://treaties.okstate.edu/treaties/treaty-with-the-great-and-little-osage-1868-22827; and Burns, *History of the Osage People,* 300–113.
11. "The Courant," *Winfield Daily Courant,* January 26, 1882, 4; and "The Courant," *Cowley County Current,* January 26, 1882, 3.
12. "The Traveler," *Arkansas City Weekly Traveler,* March 8, 1882, 3.
13. "The Times," *Sedan (KS) Times,* July 27, 1882, 5.
14. Edwards, *Historical Atlas of Cowley County,* 9.
15. "The Courier," *Winfield Courier,* January 12, 1882, 3.
16. For the register of the Commercial Hotel, see "Personals," *Douglass Index,* March 16, 1883, 5.
17. "Town and Country," *Douglass Index,* March 30, 1883, 5; and "Town and Country," *Douglass Index,* April 13, 1883, 5.
18. "Town and Country," *Douglass Index,* April 6, 1883, 5.
19. "Town and Country," *Douglass Index,* June 8, 1883, 5; and "Town and Country," *Douglass Index,* October 26, 1883, 5.
20. Belmont, Melvina, and Maud appear on the 1885 Kansas state census of Cherokee Township in Montgomery County (https://www.ancestry.com). Belmont's profession is given as "doctor."
21. Advertisement for L. A. Belmont, *Burden Saturday Journal,* February 14, 1884, 3, and deposition of Melvina A. Barry, February 13, 1922, US Bureau of Pensions, pension file of Allen E. Barry, 9, https://fold3.com.
22. Deposition of Melvina A. Barry, February 13, 1922, 9. On the history of Cherokee Freedmen in this period, see Fay A. Yarbrough, *Race and the Cherokee Nation: Sovereignty in the Nineteenth Century* (University of Pennsylvania Press, 2008).
23. James N. Leiker and Ramon Powers, *The Northern Cheyenne Exodus in History and Memory* (University of Oklahoma Press, 2011), 44–45.
24. Devon A. Mihesuah, "Diabetes in Indian Territory: Revisiting Kelly M. West's Theory of 1940," *American Indian Culture and Research Journal* 40, no. 4 (2016): 3. See also Dianna Everett, "Medical Education," *Encyclopedia of Oklahoma History and Culture,* https://www.okhistory.org/publications/enc/entry.php?entry=ME004, which confirms that "like other

locations in the late nineteenth century, Oklahoma and Indian territories desperately needed qualified doctors and dentists, and a small number of them did come here."

25. Mihesuah, "Diabetes in Indian Territory." See also Everett, "Medical Education."
26. Mihesuah, "Diabetes in Indian Territory." Compare with the Guthrie Chamber of Commerce, which states that in August 1889 the city's directory listed thirty-nine doctors and nineteen pharmacists ("History of Guthrie," https://guthriechamber.com/history-of-guthrie).
27. Mihesuah, "Diabetes in Indian Territory."
28. Report of Indian Agent John Q. Tufts to the Commissioner of Indian Affairs, *Annual Report of the Commissioner of Indian Affairs to the Secretary of the Interior for the Year 1884* (Government Printing Office, 1884), 99, https://search.library.wisc.edu/digital/AZMFYFNKNNMHHT8J/pages/AG4DWR4AYAIJO287.
29. Deposition of Melvina A. Barry, April 19, 1922, 8.
30. Deposition of Melvina A. Barry, February 13, 1922, 9.
31. Deposition of Melvina A. Barry, February 13, 1922, 9.
32. Report of Indian Agent Robert L. Owen to the Commissioner of Indian Affairs, *Annual Report of the Commissioner of Indian Affairs to the Secretary of the Interior for the Year 1886* (Government Printing Office, 1886), 147.
33. Report of Indian Agent Robert L. Owen to the Commissioner of Indian Affairs, *Annual Report . . . for the Year 1886,* 157.
34. "Oswego Republican," *Oswego Courant,* March 13, 1886, 2.
35. Deposition of Melvina A. Barry, February 13, 1922, 8.
36. Deposition of Melvina A. Barry, February 13, 1922, 8.
37. Deposition of Melvina A. Barry, February 13, 1922, 9.
38. On *Orin Smith v. L. A. Belmont,* see *Coffeyville Weekly Journal,* December 4, 1886, 2. Belmont's attorneys are mentioned in "March Term of the District Court," *Coffeyville Weekly Journal,* March 3, 1887, 3.
39. "City Tidings," *Independence Daily Reporter,* June 10, 1887, 4.
40. "District Court Proceedings," *South Kansas Tribune,* August 10, 2.
41. Kellee Blake, "'First in the Path of the Firemen': The Fate of the 1890 Population Census," *Genealogy Notes* 28, no. 1 (Spring 1996): 64–81.
42. References to New Women first appear in British publications earlier (1870s) than in American ones (1880s). See Patricia Marks, *Bicycles, Bangs, and Bloomers: The New Woman in the Popular Press* (University Press of Kentucky, 1990), 10–23. For a foundational analysis, see Carroll Smith-Rosenberg's "The New Woman as Androgyne: Social Disorder and Gender Crisis, 1870–1936," in *Disorderly Conduct: Visions of Gender in Victorian America* (Oxford University Press, 1985), 245–96.

43. Martha H. Patterson, *Beyond the Gibson Girl: Reimagining the American New Woman, 1895–1915* (University of Illinois Press, 2005).
44. I have in mind Kate Chopin, Winnifred Harper Cowley, and Sarah Orne Jewett in the United States, as well as, in Britain, Sarah Grand and Ménie Muriel Dowie. On Grand and Dowie, see Heilmann, *Neo-/Victorian Biographilia and James Miranda Barry,* 84–85.
45. For example, Elizabeth Nourse, Ellen Day Hale, Alice Austen, Frances Benjamin Johnston, Cecelia Beaux, and Elizabeth Coffin.
46. On the athletic dimension of New Womanhood, see Brigid M. Boyle, "Athleticism and the New Woman: Lawn Tennis at the Staten Island Ladies' Club," *Winterthur Portfolio* 53, no. 3 (2019): 248–51.
47. For example, Jane Addams, Mary Rozet Smith, Lillian Wald, and Vida Scudder. See also Smith-Rosenberg's list of New Women in *Disorderly Conduct,* 177.
48. Marks, *Bicycles, Bangs, and Bloomers,* 2. See also 206: "For the average reader, then, women were no longer fixed in a definable locus but were as liable to be out on the playing field or in the office as they were in the home."
49. See Andrea Weingartner, "Sex Radicals in America's Heartland: Redefining Gender and Sexuality, 1880–1910" (PhD diss., University of Missouri–Columbia, July 2013). For a broader discussion, see Hal D. Sears, *The Sex Radicals: Free Love in High Victorian America* (University Press of Kansas, 1977).
50. *Lucifer* moved from Valley Falls to Topeka in the fall of 1890, and from there to Chicago in 1896. On *Patrick Henry*'s endorsement, see "On with the Fight," *Lucifer,* May 7, 1890, 2.
51. "List of Our Authorized Agents," *Lucifer,* September 17, 1886, 2.
52. Edwin Cox Walker, "The New Woman: What Is She?—What Will She Be?" *Lucifer,* August 23, August 30, and September 6, 1895, 1.
53. For examples of Springfield residents interacting with *Lucifer,* see "Our Press Fund," August 21, 1885, 2; "Our Press Fund," February 5, 1886, 2; "Various Voices," November 26, 1898, 6; "Various Voices," June 30, 1900, 6; and A. H. Tucker, "Infidel Women—My Opinion," *Lucifer,* April 6, 1901, 3. For the personal ad, see page 10 of the January 21, 1899 issue.
54. [Untitled], *Independence Daily Reporter,* May 18, 1899, 2; and "Dr. Hall's Lecture," *Independence Daily Reporter,* May 24, 1899, 2.
55. "The New Woman Defined," *Cherokee County Republican* (Baxter Springs, KS), January 8, 1897, 7. The item reported on a "competition for the best definition of the 'new woman' in an English newspaper."
56. Carry Nation biographer Fran Grace suggests that New Womanhood found a stronger foothold in states like Kansas than in the Northeast. See *Carry A. Nation: Retelling the Life* (Indiana University Press, 2001), 9.

57. Grace, *Carry A. Nation,* 144. Nation's use of hatchetation as a direct-action protest strategy was not original. According to Grace, squads of temperance activists had infiltrated Kansas saloons carrying hatchets as early as the 1850s (145).
58. Grace notices a divergence between Eastern and Western responses to Nation (*Carry A. Nation,* 223). For further discussion of Nation's gender trouble, see 161 and 223–25.
59. Grace, 6.
60. Grace, 25.
61. Brooke Speer Orr, *The "People's Joan of Arc": Mary Elizabeth Lease, Gendered Politics and Populist Party Politics in Gilded-Age America* (Peter Lang, 2014), 3.
62. Orr, *The People's Joan of Arc,* 1 and 56–89.
63. Orr, 3–4.
64. Orr, 143–44.
65. Brooke Speer Orr, "Mary Elizabeth Lease: Nineteenth-Century Populist and Twentieth-Century Progressive" (PhD thesis, George Washington University, 2002), 169.
66. Emily Toth, *Kate Chopin: A Life of the Author of "The Awakening"* (Morrow, 1990), 334, https://archive.org/details/katechopin00toth/page/334/mode/2up.
67. Toth sums up *The Awakening*'s reception by saying the book was "welcomed by most women, but despised by most men"; *Unveiling Kate Chopin* (University Press of Mississippi, 1999), xix and 226. On the depth of Chopin's critique of True Womanhood, see also Nancy A. Walker's *Kate Chopin: A Literary Life* (New York: Palgrave, 2001), in which she observes that "in the person of Edna Pontellier, the *Awakening* questions both the fulfillment of marriage and the universality of women's maternal instinct" (22).
68. Toth, *Unveiling Kate Chopin,* 222–23.
69. "Books of the Week," *Providence Sunday Journal,* June 4, 1899, 15; and "Review of The Awakening," *New Orleans Times-Democrat,* June 18, 1899, 14–15, both quoted in Sarah M. Corse and Saundra Davis Westervelt, "Gender and Literary Valorization: *The Awakening* of a Canonical Novel," *Sociological Perspectives* 45, no. 2 (2002): 144.
70. "Books and Authors," *Boston Beacon,* June 24, 1899, 4, quoted in Toth, *Kate Chopin,* 348.
71. "News and Gossip About Forthcoming Books," *St. Louis Republic,* March 25, 1899, quoted in Toth, *Kate Chopin,* 329. (Toth doesn't cite a page number.)
72. "100 Books for Summer Reading," *New York Times Saturday Review,* 1899, 408, quoted in Toth, *Kate Chopin,* 349.

73. Richard A. Kaye, "Sexual Identity at the Fin de Siècle," in *The Cambridge Companion to the Fin de Siècle,* ed. Gail Marshall (Cambridge University Press, 2007), 62. See Andreas De Block and Pieter R. Adriaens, "Pathologizing Sexual Deviance: A History," *Journal of Sex Research* 50, no. 3–4 (April 2013): 280.
74. Kaye, "Sexual Identity at the Fin de Siècle," 64.
75. Scholarship on the emergence of this stereotype owes a debt to Esther Newton, whose "The Mythic Mannish Lesbian: Radclyffe Hall and the New Woman" was published in 1984. More recently, Lisa Duggan concluded that "a genealogy of the 'lesbian' as she appears clearly on the cultural and social landscape by the 1930s leads back to the mannish 'invert,' the masculine woman of the late nineteenth century." Duggan, *Sapphic Slashers: Sex, Violence, and American Modernity* (Duke University Press, 2000), 28.
76. The phrase "lesbian love murder" comes from Duggan (*Sapphic Slashers,* 2). For Duggan, narratives of lesbian murder as well as lynching from this period coincide with "the birth of American modernity in the 1890s" (30).
77. Duggan, *Sapphic Slashers,* 46.
78. Duggan, 100, 113, and 164.
79. Duggan, 154.
80. This shift in the late Victorian period from an ideology of sexual acts (behavior) to one of sexual orientation (identity) is a focus of Michel Foucault's *History of Sexuality,* vol. 1, *An Introduction.*
81. *Galena Times,* June 14, 1895, 3.
82. "Warren–Belmont: A Union Between Joplin and Webb City Young People," *Joplin Herald,* November 12, 1895.
83. Lawrence O. Christensen and Gary R. Kremer, *A History of Missouri: 1875–1919* (University of Missouri Press, 1997), 93 and 149, https://archive.org/details/historyofmissour0004unse. See also Brandon Dupont, "Panic in the Plains: Agricultural Markets and the Panic of 1893," *Cliometrica* 3 (2009): 27–54.
84. "In Circuit Court," *Joplin Globe,* June 24, 1898, 2; and "Circuit Court," *Joplin Herald,* June 24, 1898, 4.
85. The 1900 US census schedule of Jasper County, Missouri (https://www.ancestry.com), lists Belmont's age as thirty-seven and Melvina's as thirty-nine. This is incorrect; they were born in 1853 and 1842, respectively. See the birth record of Addie Liona Walker (https://www.ancestry.com) and the letter from Melvina Barry Campbell Belmont to the US Commissioner of Pensions, September 20, 1916, US Bureau of Pensions, pension file of Allen E. Berry, https://www.fold3.com.
86. 1900 US census schedule, Jasper County, Missouri, https://www.ancestry.com.

87. Bayker, "Before Transsexuality," 165. I've also relied on details in "Fifteen Years in Man's Attire: The Protracted Masquerade of a Kansas City Woman," *Herald and Tribune* (Jonesborough, TN), November 19, 1885, https://www.digitaltransgenderarchive.net/files/p2676v599.
88. "Romance of a Poor Young Woman," *Bottineau (ND) Pioneer,* September 19, 1889, https://www.digitaltransgenderarchive.net/files/3j3332260.
89. Boag, *Re-Dressing America's Frontier Past,* 119–20. See also "Tom King," *Sierra County Advocate,* September 17, 1894, https://www.digitaltransgenderarchive.net/files/6969z078d.
90. The dedication to hustling shared by Belmont, Gray, Cox, and King may have less to do with their experiences as gender migrants than it does with their locations and the competitive capitalist era in which they lived. See Thomas J. Jablonsky, "The Middle West and Far West During the Gilded Age and Progressive Era," in *A Companion to the Gilded Age and Progressive Era,* ed. Christopher McKnight Nichols and Nancy C. Unger (John Wiley & Sons, 2017), 63.
91. "Forty-three Women Who Have Posed as Men," *St. Louis Republic,* April 27, 1902, https://www.digitaltransgenderarchive.net/files/gq67jr480. For a similar survey from the previous year, see "Females Posed as Men," *St. Paul Daily Globe,* February 3, 1901, https://www.digitaltransgenderarchive.net/files/73666477c.
92. Jen Manion's *Female Husbands* supports this claim, as does Emily Skidmore's *True Sex.*

8. The New Woman, 1902–1913

1. Manion, *Female Husbands,* 3.
2. See Jack Halberstam on the wives of Billy Tipton in "Telling Tales," 71.
3. Declaration for Remarried Widow's Pension, May 21, 1921, US Bureau of Pensions, pension file of Allen E. Barry, 37, https://www.fold3.com. See also Frank A. Beard and Robert L. Bradley, "Whitneyville Congregational Church," National Register of Historic Places nomination form, October 1978, https://npgallery.nps.gov/GetAsset/19276462-fae5–4217-b3f6–5bc8b04a7662.
4. Beard and Bradley, "Whitneyville Congregational Church."
5. Household of Simeon Lowell, US census of 1850 (Washington County, MA), https://www.ancestry.com.
6. Miranda Lowell married Irving Wardwell on May 9, 1858; Melvina Lowell married Allen E. Barry on October 19, 1858. Widow's declaration for Army Pension, October 8, 1863, US Bureau of Pensions, US Civil War Widows' Pensions, 1860–1910, pension file of Irving A. Wardwell (WC30975), 3, https://www.fold3.com; and marriage certification, August 16, 1864, pension file of Allen E. Barry, 7.

7. Increase of widow's pension, January 7, 1871, pension file of Allen E. Barry, 211.
8. Sworn statement of notary public L. M. Stewart, October 11, 1873, pension file of Allen E. Barry, 199–200.
9. Sworn statement of notary public L. M. Stewart, October 11, 1873, 199.
10. Households of Irving A. Wardwell (Hancock County, ME) and Simeon B. Lowell (Washington County, ME) in the US census of 1860, https://www.ancestry.com.
11. Donald W. Beattie, Rodney M. Cole, and Charles G. Waugh, eds., *A Distant War Comes Home: Maine in the Civil War Era* (Down East Books, 1996), 2.
12. Proof of soldier's service, pension file of Irving A. Wardwell, 7, and brief in the case of Mrs. Melvina A. Barry, December 31, 1864, pension file of Allen E. Barry, 2.
13. Proof of soldier's service, pension file of Irving A. Wardwell, 7.
14. Certification of death, pension file of Allen E. Barry, 16.
15. Agnes M. Larson, *History of the White Pine Industry in Minnesota* (University of Minnesota Press, 1949), 37.
16. Delmar R. Lowell, *The Historic Genealogy of the Lowells of America, from 1639 to 1899* (Tuttle, 1899), 413.
17. I've derived the population of Whitneyville, Maine, in 1865 by comparing the 1860 and 1870 US censuses, https://www.ancestry.com. For the populations of Minneapolis and St. Anthony, see Lucille Kane, "Governing a Frontier City: Old St. Anthony, 1855–1872," *Minnesota History* 35, no. 3 (September 1865): 117.
18. Household of Simeon Lowell, US census (Hennepin County, MN), 1870, https://www.ancestry.com.
19. Mrs. M. T. Wardwell in the Minneapolis city directory, 1867 (139), and Mrs. M. F. [*sic*] Wardwell in the Minneapolis city directory, 1872 (121), https://www.ancestry.com. See also Carole Zellie, *Minneapolis Public Schools Historic Context Study,* prepared for the Minneapolis Heritage Preservation Commission, April 2005, 10.
20. Mrs. M. T. Wardwell in the Minneapolis city directory, 1873 (416), https://www.ancestry.com.
21. Proof of marriage of George C. Campbell and Mrs. Melvina A. Barry, pension file of Allen E. Barry, 9. See also deposition of Melvina Barry, February 13, 1922, pension file of Allen E. Barry, 112.
22. Increase of widow's pension, January 7, 1871, pension file of Allen E. Barry, 211. See also the sworn statement of John Lowell and Simeon Lowell, October 20, 1870, 92.
23. Pension file of Allen E. Barry, 199–200.

24. Household of George A. Campbell, Minnesota state census, 1875 (Hennepin County), https://www.ancestry.com.
25. Households of George A. Campbell and Miranda Wardwell, Minnesota state census (Hennepin County), 1880.
26. "In Disguise," *Minneapolis Tribune,* October 30, 1880, 6.
27. I'm thinking here of Eve K. Sedgwick's effort to pluralize sexual ignorance(s), presented in "Privilege of Unknowing: Diderot's *The Nun,*" in *Tendencies* (Duke University Press, 1993), 25. For a broader philosophical discussion of the will to ignorance, see Mark Lilla, *Ignorance and Bliss: On Wanting Not to Know* (Farrar, Straus and Giroux, 2024).
28. Deposition of Melvina A. Barry, February 13, 1922, pension file of Allen E. Barry, 114.
29. Act of September 8, 1916, 39 Stat. 844, Chap. 470, sect. 1, 844–45, and *Increase of Civil War Pensions,* 1st Session, 69th Congress, House of Representatives, report no. 818, April 9, 1926, 3.
30. Mrs. Allen E. Barry to US Commissioner of Pensions, September 20, 1916, pension file of Allen E. Barry, 171–73.
31. G. M. Saltzgaber to Mrs. Allen E. Barry, September 22, 1916, pension file of Allen E. Barry, 131.
32. Melvina A. Barry to the Commissioner of Pensions, October 11, 1916, pension file of Allen E. Barry, 71.
33. Marriage certificate of Leon A. Belmont and Melvina Barry, Isanti County, Minnesota, personal collection of the author. See also the pension file of Allen E. Barry, 11–12.
34. Deposition of Melvina A. Barry, February 13, 1922, pension file of Allen E. Barry, 115–16.
35. Affidavit of Melvina A. Barry, September 28, 1920, pension file of Allen E. Barry, 78.
36. Melvina A. Barry to the Commissioner of Pensions, December 15, 1920, pension file of Allen E. Barry, 179.
37. G. M. Saltzgaber to Melvina A. Barry, January 27, 1917, pension file of Allen E. Barry, 133.
38. G. M. Saltzgaber to Melvina A. Barry, February 27, 1917, pension file of Allen E. Barry, 132.
39. G. M. Saltzgaber to Melvina A. Barry, May 2, 1917, pension file of Allen E. Barry, 136.
40. Melvina A. Barry to the Commissioner of Pensions, May 9, 1917, pension file of Allen E. Barry, 167.
41. Rev. Edward Payson Roe, *Barriers Burned Away* (Dodd and Mead, 1872).
42. G. M. Saltzgaber to Melvina A. Barry, May 12, 1917, pension file of Allen E. Barry, 134.

43. On the history of American pension laws from the colonial period into the early twentieth century, see William Henry Glasson, *Federal Military Pensions in the United States* (Oxford University Press, 1918). For a modern assessment, see Olivier Burtin, "The History of Veterans' Policy in the United States—a Comparative Overview," *Historical Social Research* 45, no. 2 (2020): 239–60. Claire Prechtel-Kluskens focuses helpfully on widows' pensions in "For Love and Money: Pension Laws Affecting Widows of Military Veterans," *National Genealogical Society* 42, no. 2 (January–March, 2016): 35–39.
44. I'm influenced here by Brandi Clay Brimmer's "All Her Rights and Privileges: African-American Women and the Politics of Civil War Widows' Pensions" (PhD diss., University of California, 2006), 64.
45. Cohabitation with a woman during widowhood was not a disqualifying factor.
46. The bureau's gender assumptions intersected with racism. Brimmer writes, "When black women—especially the formerly enslaved—claimed the same pension benefits as white women, they directly challenged antebellum legal codes and popular constructions of black women as unworthy dependents devoid of virtue." Brimmer, *Claiming Union Widowhood: Race, Respectability, and Poverty in the Post-Emancipation South* (Duke University Press, 2020), 12.
47. Capehart wrote in a 1905 letter to the Commissioner of Pensions, "I ask that you will please take my case under your consideration and if theire [*sic*] has any injustice been done me in the rejection of my claim I ask that you will have the claim allowed in my favor. . . . I only ask for justice at your hands" (Brimmer, *Claiming Union Widowhood,* 201). On Capehart's petitions, see Brimmer, 150–51 and 201.
48. See especially "Her Claim Is Lawful and Just: Black Women's Petitions for Survivors' Benefits," chapter 3 of Brimmer, *Claiming Union Widowhood,* 77–100.
49. Brimmer, 72 and 95–96.
50. *Sanborn Fire Insurance Map from Joplin, Jasper County, Missouri* (Sanborn Map Company, 1906), https://www.loc.gov/resource/g4164jm.g4164jm_g047181954.
51. Melvina A. Barry to G. M. Saltzgaber, December 17, 1917, pension file of Allen E. Barry, 163–64.
52. "News of Our Own State," *Weekly Pioneer and Democrat* (St. Paul, MN), 3. See also the family tree of Melvina A. Lowell, www.familysearch.org/en/tree/pedigree/landscape/K2YB-1WB.
53. G. M. Saltzgaber to Melvina A. Barry, January 4, 1918, pension of file of Allen E. Barry, 135.

54. Melvina A. Barry to Franklin K. Lane, US Secretary of the Interior, January 9, 1818, pension file of Allen E. Barry, 26.
55. S. G. Stopelius, Assistant Secretary of the Interior, on appeal from the commissioner of pensions, postmarked July 31, 1918, pension file of Allen E. Barry, 189–90.
56. "Provisions of Fuller Pension Bill Now in Force," *Fort Collins Courier,* May 11, 1920, 8, https://www.coloradohistoricnewspapers.org/?a=d&d=FCC19200511.2.88.
57. By premising a divorced woman's eligibility for a pension on her lack of "fault" in ending her marriage, the Fuller Bill persisted in framing pensions as rewards for normative feminine behavior. In the bill's logic, women who committed adultery or lived independently of their husbands (common grounds for at-fault divorce at the time) forfeited their right to compensation.
58. Melvina A. Barry to F. D. Byington, acting commissioner, Bureau of Pensions, Widow Division, October 1, 1920, pension file of Allen E. Barry, 73–74.
59. Allen E. Barry's pension file contains four letters written by Missouri State Representative I. V. McPherson. McPherson sent them to Washington Gardiner on Melvina's behalf on November 8, 1921; December 5, 1921; March 30, 1922; and November 20, 1922. See 94, 130, 146, and 148.
60. S. W. Cuddy to Washington Gardiner, January 6, 1922, pension file of Allen E. Barry, 125. I've inferred the length of Jones's career from the date range of his correspondence with the Bureau of Pensions preserved in the National Archives: "Correspondence with T. Quinn Jones, 1912–1923," in "Correspondence with Special Examiners, 1887–1931" (NAID 7431514, box 40). On the general history of pensions examinations, see Claire Prechtel-Kluskens, "Special Examiners: Records of the Bureau of Pensions' Efforts to Combat Waste, Fraud, and Abuse, 1862–1922," *Federal History* 8 (2016): 109–20.
61. "Half Hours with the Government Departments," *Washington Post,* April 24, 1921, 50.
62. Depositions of certificates of search signed by T. Quinn Jones, April 19 and 21, 1922, pension file of Allen E. Barry, 110.
63. Deposition of Melvina A. Barry, February 13, 1922, pension file of Allen E. Barry, 113.
64. Deposition of Melvina A. Barry, February 13, 1922, 113.
65. Deposition of Melvina A. Barry, February 13, 1922, 115.
66. Deposition of Maude C. Warren, February 13, 1922, pension file of Allen E. Barry, 101.
67. Deposition of Jennie M. Gehrett, April 19, 1922, pension file of Allen E. Barry, 108–9.
68. Deposition of Jennie M. Gehrett, April 19, 1922, 109.

69. Deposition of Jennie M. Gehrett, April 19, 1922, 109.
70. Deposition of John W. Williams, April 19, 1922, pension file of Allen E. Barry, 106–7.
71. "[Belmont] claimed to possess a fortune in England, coming from the house of Maclure, on his mother's side." "In Disguise," *Minneapolis Tribune*, 6.
72. Deposition of Charles. A. Green, April 19, 1922, pension file of Allen E. Barry, 104–5.
73. T. Quinn Jones to the Bureau of Pensions, April 22, 1922, pension file of Allen E. Barry, 124.
74. Melvina and Green were both wrong about Belmont's age. In his deposition, Green estimated that Belmont had been sixty-five in 1902, and in an affidavit, Melina said he had been "about sixty-eight years old" in the same year. Neither of them was close to correct. On the day of his disappearance, Belmont was forty-nine. Deposition of Charles A. Green, April 19, 1922, pension file of Allen E. Barry, 104–5; affidavit of Melvina A. Barry, July 27, 1921, pension file of Allen E. Barry, 39; and birth registration of Addie Liona Walker, Warren, Massachusetts, June 1, 1853, https://www.ancestry.com.
75. This is not true. Belmont was arrested, jailed, and/or detained by police multiple times in the 1870s and 1880, as shown in chapters 3, 4, and 5. Though Melvina may not have known about all of these incidents, she did know about the Belmont sensation of 1880, in which she played a part.
76. Deposition of Melvina A. Barry, April 21, 1922, pension file of Allen E. Barry, 118–21, emphasis added.
77. Deposition of Melvina A. Barry, April 21, 1922, 121 and 99.
78. Melvina would have had little to gain and much to lose from reporting Belmont. Geertje Mak's research into "doubtful sex" in the nineteenth century may apply to Melvina's situation in 1902. *Doubting Sex,* 33.
79. On the case of Nicolai De Raylan, see Skidmore, *True Sex,* 111–16; Jill Austin and Jennifer Brier, eds., *Out in Chicago: LGBT History at the Crossroads* (Chicago History Museum, 2011); and Dennis Rodkin, "The Invention of a Man: The Secret Life and Memorable Death of Nicolai De Raylan," *Chicago* magazine, March 5, 2018.
80. Skidmore, *True Sex,* 115.
81. Manion, *Female Husbands,* 239–40.
82. Skidmore, *True Sex,* 54.
83. De Raylan, Coulton, and Howard affirmed that their husbands were men only under duress, creating room to doubt their sincerity. Manion, *Female Husbands,* 260.
84. On gender fluidity, see Kate Bornstein, *Gender Outlaw: On Men, Women, and the Rest of Us* (Routledge, 1994), 51–52.

85. Greta LaFleur, Masha Raskolnikov, and Anna Kłosowska, eds., *Trans Historical: Gender Plurality Before the Modern* (Cornell University Press, 2021), 1, 373, and 375n4.
86. Manion emphasizes the agentic sides of Sampson's/Shurtliff's gender fluidity by using the language of personal choice. *Female Husbands,* 95 and 97.
87. Belmont to the *Minneapolis Tribune,* "What Is It?" October 31, 1880, 2.
88. Stryker, *Transgender History,* 51–54.
89. Eskridge, *Gaylaw,* 339. See also Jesse Bayker's "Historical Cross-Dressing Laws" map (https://rutgers.maps.arcgis.com/apps/instant/sidebar/index.html?appid=0d662b6809e34eddb552c6fbebac9ca0); and Ulysses Swanson's map titled "City Ordinances Criminalizing People in 'A Dress' or 'Disguise' 'Not Belonging To' or 'Becoming Of' His or Her Sex, 1848–1986" (https://www.google.com/maps/d/viewer?mid=1p99OaGS_nnikYJCY3bKOItYGeJX3Q-s&usp=sharing).
90. Eskridge, *Gaylaw,* 339.
91. Manion, *Female Husbands,* 263.
92. Skidmore, *True Sex,* 52.
93. Skidmore, *True Sex,* 48. Skidmore takes care to show that although the newspaper coverage of George Green was invasive, it was nonetheless positive and nonjudgmental. The *Richmond Times,* for example, chose to reproduce Mary Green's judgment of him as "the noblest soul that ever lived." Quoted in Skidmore, 49.
94. Report of T. Quinn Jones to the US Bureau of Pensions, April 22, 1922, pension file of Allen E. Barry, 122–23.
95. Report of T. Quinn Jones to the US Bureau of Pensions, April 22, 1922, 122–23.
96. I. V. McPherson to Commissioner of Pensions, November 20, 1922, pension file of Allen E. Barry, 95.
97. Death certificate of Maude C. Warren, Missouri State Board of Health, 1922, https://www.ancestry.com.
98. Death certificate of Melvina A. Barry, Missouri State Board of Health, 1931, https://www.ancestry.com.

9. The Mother, 1913–1927

1. Special examination of Jennie M. Gehrett, April 19, 1922, US Bureau of Pensions, pension file of Allen E. Barry, 109.
2. 1910 US census, Springfield (Greene County, MO), https://www.ancestry.com.
3. General affidavit of Melvina Belmont, September 28, 1920, US Bureau of Pensions, pension file of Allen E. Barry, 78.

4. Special examination of Jennie M. Gehrett, April 19, 1922, pension file of Allen E. Barry, 109.
5. On Nova McClure's claim of marriage to Mr. Carr/Karr, see special examination of Jennie M. Gehrett, 26, and report of Special Examiner T. Quinn Jones, April 22, 1922, 6, pension file of Allen E. Barry. I've found no records of Nova McClure marrying a man named K/Carr, or a man with any name, in the 1910s.
6. Gwendolyn Mink, *The Wages of Motherhood: Inequality in the Welfare State, 1917–1942* (Cornell University Press, 1995), 33.
7. I use the phrase "chose her own family" to amplify the echoes of McClure's kinship fashioning that I hear in the lives of self-identified queer people in the twenty-first century. Although the term "chosen family" did not emerge among queer scholars in the United States until the 1990s, Belmont/McClure participated in a tradition of kinship innovation that predates that decade. For a foundational study, see Kath Weston, *Families We Choose: Lesbians, Gays, Kinship* (Columbia University Press, 1991). For a review of literature on queer kinship/solidarity in chosen families between the 1980s and 2022, see Cristina M. Dominguez, "Staying in the Trying: Queer Kinship Solidarity as Liberation Praxis" (PhD diss., University of North Carolina Greensboro, 2022), 24–30.
8. Jodi Vandenberg-Daves, *Modern Motherhood: An American History* (Rutgers University Press, 2014), 3.
9. When Rima A. Apple formulated the concept of scientific motherhood in the 1990s, she defined it as "the insistence that women require expert scientific and medical advice to raise their children healthfully." "Constructing Mothers: Scientific Motherhood in the Nineteenth and Twentieth Centuries," in *Mothers and Motherhood: Readings in American History* (Ohio State University Press, 1997), 90.
10. Vandenberg-Daves, *Modern Motherhood*, 94.
11. Vandenberg-Daves, 102.
12. Vandenberg-Daves, 90 and 102.
13. Linda Gordon, "Single Mothers and Child Neglect, 1800–1920," *American Quarterly* 37, no. 2 (Summer 1985): 174–75.
14. Gordon, "Single Mothers and Child Neglect," 174.
15. Mink, *The Wages of Motherhood*, 33.
16. "Table 62.—Median and Quartile Rates and Earnings in Kansas, 1916–1924, by Industry," in Mildred J. Gordon, *The Development of Minimum-wage Laws in the United States, 1912 to 1927*, Bulletin of the Women's Bureau, no. 61 (US Department of Labor, Women's Bureau, 1928), 343, https://babel.hathitrust.org/cgi/pt?id=msu.31293012197376&seq=1031.

17. “Median Weekly Earnings by Industry,” in Mary N. Winslow, *Women’s Wages in Kansas* (Government Printing Office, 1921), 26, https://babel.hathitrust.org/cgi/pt?id=hvd.hl28l3&seq=36.
18. “Table 3.1, Ratios of Female to Male Full-Time Earnings in Agricultural and Manufacturing Employment and Across All Occupations, 1815–1987,” in Claudia Dale Goldin, *Understanding the Gender Gap: An Economic History of American Women* (Oxford University Press, 1990), 60, https://archive.org/details/understandinggen0000gold/mode/2up.
19. Winslow, *Women’s Wages in Kansas,* 51.
20. Ellen Herman, *Kinship by Design: A History of Adoption in the Modern United States* (University of Chicago Press, 2008), 21–22.
21. Rebecca Wellington, *Who Is a Worthy Mother? An Intimate History of Adoption* (University of Oklahoma Press, 2024), 37–38.
22. Karen Balcom, “The Logic of Exchange: The Child Welfare League of America, the Adoption Resource Exchange Movement and the Indian Adoption Project, 1958–1967,” *Adoption & Culture* 1, no. 1 (2007): 5–67.
23. Newspaper articles from the 1920s refer to Kenneth as Nova’s foster son rather than her adopted son, making room for a financial motive for Nova’s decision to be a parent. On some mothers’ profit-motivated fostering in the 1910s, see Catherine E. Rymph, *Raising Government Children: A History of Foster Care and the American Welfare State* (University of North Carolina Press, 2017), 25–26.
24. An entry for “Mrs. Nova Carr, masseuse,” boarding at 2221 Main Street, appears in the 1916 Parsons city directory, Kansas Historical Society, Topeka.
25. “A Masquerade at Presbyterian Church,” *Parsons Daily Eclipse,* October 30, 1915, 4.
26. “Third Ward Garden Clubs Starting,” *Parsons Daily Sun,* March 9, 1917, 1.
27. Charles Lathrop Pack organized the National War Garden Commission to encourage Americans to grow their own food in March 1917, at about the same time the *Parsons Daily Sun* was fawning over Kenneth McClure’s garden. Charles Lathrop Pack, *The War Garden Victorious* (Applewood Books, 2009), 2.
28. For the Boy Scout picnic, see “Picnic at the Cabin,” *Parsons Daily Eclipse,* May 25, 1917, 3. For the drill work, see “Exhibition and Good Times,” *Parsons Daily Eclipse,* June 23, 1917, 4.
29. “Pig Club Organized,” *Parsons Daily Republican,* July 26, 1918, 5.
30. For the Valentine’s Day party, see “Christian Church Choir,” *Parsons Daily Eclipse,* February 4, 1921, 3. For the Thanksgiving pageant, see “Class to Give Pageant,” *Parsons Daily Sun,* November 25, 1921, 1.
31. “In Society,” *Parsons Daily Republican,* December 24, 1921, 3.
32. “U and I Banquet,” *Parsons Daily Republican,* October 1, 1921, 3.
33. “Obituary—Mrs. A. Nora Carr,” *Parsons Daily Sun,* January 24, 1927, 4.

34. Richard Pankratz and Cornelia Wyma, "Carnegie Library," National Register of Historic Places nomination form, property #76000824, January 30, 1976, https://npgallery.nps.gov/GetAsset/74c78d39-b38d-4c50-bald-0276fb0af579.
35. "Dudley Natitorium [*sic*] to Open Soon," *Parsons Daily Sun,* July 21, 1915, 1, and "Local News Happenings," *Parsons Daily Sun,* July 23, 1915, 3.
36. April 1923 Sanborn fire insurance map (Apr. 1923 MS-1339), Kansas Historical Society, Topeka, and "Orpheum Theatre to Open Monday," *Parsons Daily Republican,* May 20, 1921, 1.
37. [No title], May 24, 1919, *Parsons Daily Eclipse,* 6, and April 1923 Sanborn fire insurance map. The January 25, 1919, issue of the *Parsons Daily Republican* advertises two different movie theaters in town: the New Elks (later renamed the Liberty) and the Best Theatre. See "Great Bill at Best" and "New Elks First Run Pictures" (advertisement), 5.
38. The MKT Railway (Katy), on which the Parsons economy depended as the town's biggest employer, struggled in the 1930s. See Victor V. Masterson, *The Katy Railroad and the Last Frontier* (University of Missouri Press, 1988), vii. For the population of Parsons in 1923, see the April 1923 Sanborn fire insurance map of Parsons.
39. Kansas Department of Labor and Industry, *Thirty-Fifth Annual Report* (Kansas State Printing Plant, 1921), 24, https://www.google.com/books/edition/_/GBNBAQAAMAAJ. The figure of 2,000 Katy workers comes from "100% Strike at Parsons," *Coffeyville Daily Journal,* July 1, 1922, 2; and "Shopmen Out 100PCT," *Parsons Daily Sun,* July 1, 1922, 1. This contradicts the number (1,250) cited in "Looks Like a Cold Winter," *Parsons Daily Sun,* September 25, 1922, 1.
40. April 1923 Sanborn fire insurance map of Parsons and Sanborn fire insurance map, Parsons, Labette County, Kansas, 1911, Library of Congress, https://www.loc.gov/item/sanborn03055_006.
41. April 1923 Sanborn fire insurance map of Parsons.
42. Masterson, *The Katy Railroad and the Last Frontier,* 283.
43. Masterson, 283–85.
44. The federal census of 1920 (Labette County, KS) records Kenneth McClure's profession as "railroad foreman" (https://www.ancestry.com).
45. Parsons city directory, 1918, Kansas Historical Society, Topeka.
46. I've inferred distances and Kenneth McClure's walking route from the 1911 and 1924 Sanborn maps of Parsons cross-referenced with Google maps.
47. "[Mrs. Carr] said the boy was to come into a legacy at the age of 24 provided he had learned a trade." "Had Signed Up with the Katy; Now Missing!" *Parsons Daily Republican,* November 17, 1922, 1.
48. Colin J. Davis, *Power at Odds: The 1922 National Railroad Shopmen's Strike* (University of Illinois Press, 1997), 1.

49. Becoming Modern: American in the 1920s. America in Class, National Humanities Center, https://americainclass.org/sources/becomingmodern/prosperity/text6/text6.htm.
50. Christopher Klein, "Why Labor Unions Declined in the 1920s," History.com, February 18, 2021, https://www.history.com/news/american-labor-unions-decline-1920s.
51. Davis, *Power at Odds,* 11.
52. Davis, Table 1, 13.
53. Davis, 56.
54. Davis, 54.
55. Davis, 63, and Table 7, 67.
56. "Had Signed Up with the Katy."
57. Davis, *Power at Odds,* 88.
58. Davis, 155.
59. "Pair of Bombs Take Place of Alarm Clock," *Parsons Daily Sun,* September 8, 1922, 1 and 8. Strikers detonated bombs and/or dynamite in the same week in Iowa, California, and Ohio. See "Lull in Violence One of Week's Developments," *Railway Age* 73, no. 12 (September 16, 1922): 504, https://archive.org/details/railwayage73newy/page/504.
60. "Decisive Action by General Martin in Strike Situation," *Parsons Daily Sun,* September 9, 1922, 1.
61. "Shop Crafts Condemn Acts of Bombers," *Parsons Daily Sun,* September 9, 1922, 1.
62. Davis, *Power at Odds,* 131.
63. "Had Signed Up with the Katy."
64. "Had Signed Up with the Katy."
65. "Had Signed Up with the Katy."
66. "Troops Stay at Parsons," *Iola Daily Register,* November 20, 1922, 6.
67. The report that Kenneth had set out for Oklahoma City contradicted testimony from Kenneth's coworkers in the shops, who claimed the young man had taken a train in the opposite direction—to Kansas City. "Had Signed Up with the Katy."
68. "Round About Coffeyville," *Coffeyville Daily Journal,* November 18, 1922, 4.
69. "Had Signed Up with the Katy."
70. "Round About Coffeyville."
71. "Martial Law Reimposed in Kansas Rail Towns," *New-York Tribune,* November 20, 1922, 3.
72. "Will Retain Troops for Present," *Dispatch Republican,* November 20, 1922; "Martial Law Reimposed in Kansas Rail Towns"; and "Troops Stay at Parsons."
73. "Had Signed Up with the Katy."
74. "Round About Coffeyville."

75. "McClure Back but Silent as to His Absence," *Parsons Daily Sun,* November 20, 1922, 1.
76. MK&T system maps, 1904 and 1932, Katy Railroad Historical Society, https://katyrailroad.org/map.
77. "McClure Back but Silent as to His Absence."
78. "More Deputies Are Sent Here," *Parsons Daily Republican,* November 21, 1922, 1.
79. "Round About Coffeyville," *Coffeyville Daily Journal,* November 21, 1922, 5, and "More Deputies Are Sent Here."
80. The *Parsons Daily Sun* ("McClure Back but Silent as to His Absence") found a source who said Kenneth had returned to work the morning after his return. The master mechanic at the MK&T shops denied seeing him.
81. Kansas state census, 1925, Parsons (Labette County, KS), https://www.ancestry.com.
82. Kenneth sang a vocal solo in "Let Me Not Wander," by E. H. Heyser, at Central Christian Church during a morning service held on June 20, 1925. "Central Christian Church," *Parsons Daily Sun,* June 20, 1925, 2.
83. "Presbyterians Observing Easter," *Parsons Daily Sun,* April 3, 1926, 5.
84. "Junior Band to Play," *Parsons Daily Sun,* December 8, 1926, 6; and "Sang for Shop Men," *Parsons Daily Sun,* December 16, 1926, 8.
85. "Central Christian Church," *Parsons Daily Sun,* August 20, 1925, 3.
86. "Scouts Camping," *Parsons Daily Sun,* November 4, 1926, 6.
87. [Untitled], *Parsons Daily Sun,* December 17, 1926, 9.
88. "Obituary," *Parsons Daily Sun,* January 24, 1927, 4.
89. Laura Davidow Hirshbein, "The Flapper and the Fogy: Representations of Gender and Age in the 1920s," *Journal of Family History* 26, no. 1 (January 2001): 113–14. Hirshbein draws from Ann Douglas's book *Terrible Honesty: Mongrel Manhattan in the 1920s* (Farrar, Straus and Giroux, 1995).
90. Rachael Alexander, *Imagining Gender and Consumerism in 1920s Magazines* (Cambridge University Press, online version, 2021), 13–14.
91. Hirshbein, "The Flapper and the Fogy," 114. See also Hirshbein's comment that "social commentators articulated a complicated system of oppositions in which definitions of masculinity and femininity depended on age" (117).
92. Deposition of John W. Williams, April 19, 1922, pension file of Allen E. Barry, 106–7.
93. Kansas Board of Health, *Fourteenth Biennial Report of the State Board of Health of the State of Kansas* (B. P. Walker, state printer: 1928), 77, https://kgi.contentdm.oclc.org/digital/collection/p16884coll4/id/2052.
94. "Obituary," January 24, 1927, *Parsons Daily Sun,* 4. Although the obituary does not state how Carr died, organic heart disease was the leading cause of death in Kansas in 1926 and 1927, especially among people in their

seventies. *Fourteenth Biennial Report of the State Board of Health of the State of Kansas,* 229.

95. "Obituary."
96. Oakwood Cemetery office records, Parsons, Kansas.
97. Conversation with Matt Cornett, Oakwood Cemetery's sexton, October 4, 2023.
98. In the cemetery's burial records, Nova Carr appears as "Nova Karr."

Postscript

1. "In Disguise," *Minneapolis Tribune,* October 30, 1880, 6.
2. Deposition of Melvina A. Barry, April 21, 1922, US Bureau of Pensions, US Civil War Widows' Pensions, 1861–1910, pension file of Allen E. Barry (WC38058), 119, https://www.fold3.com.
3. Special examination of Jennie M. Gehrett, April 19, 1922, US Bureau of Pensions, pension file of Allen E. Barry, 109, https://www.fold3.com.
4. "Obituary," January 24, 1927, *Parsons Daily Sun,* 4.
5. Ida F. West in the 1870 US census (Montgomery County, KS), https://www.ancestry.com.
6. Marriage license of O. E. Peters and Adeliza (Ida) F. West (Labette County, KS), 1901, https://www.ancestry.com; and marriage license of William West and Ida Roberts (Cass County, MO), 1968, https://www.ancestry.com.
7. "The Annual Report of the Parsons Home and Hospital for the Year Ending June 1, 1914," *Parsons Daily Sun,* June 17, 1914, 2.
8. "Had Signed Up with the Katy; Now Missing!" *Parsons Daily Republican,* November 17, 1922, 1.
9. "Round About Coffeyville," *Coffeyville Daily Journal,* November 18, 1922, 4.
10. "Pair of Bombs Take Place of Alarm Clock," *Parsons Daily Sun,* September 8, 1922, 1 and 8.
11. "Round About Coffeyville," *Coffeyville Daily Journal,* November 21, 1922, 5.
12. Marriage license of Kenneth P. McClure and Berneatha Baker (Genesee County, MI), 1936, https://www.ancestry.com.
13. 1930 United States Census, Flint City, Genesee County, Michigan, https://www.ancestry.com.
14. Marriage license of Kenneth P. McClure and Berneatha Baker.
15. 1940 United States Census, Flint City, Genesee County, Michigan, https://www.ancestry.com.
16. World War II draft registration card of Kenneth P. McClure, https://www.ancestry.com.
17. Kenneth P. McClure in the Michigan Death Index, 1971–1996, https://www.ancestry.com.

Index

Lizzie Ehrenhalt is an editor and public historian who specializes in the history of gender and sexuality. She is editor of MNopedia, the encyclopedia of Minnesota history produced by the Minnesota Historical Society, and coeditor of *Precious and Adored: The Love Letters of Rose Cleveland and Evangeline Simpson Whipple, 1890–1918.*